USING PARTICIPATORY METHODS TO EXPLORE FREEDOM OF RELIGION AND BELIEF

Whose Reality Counts?

Edited by
Jo Howard and Mariz Tadros

First published in Great Britain in 2023 by

Bristol University Press
University of Bristol
1-9 Old Park Hill
Bristol
BS2 8BB
UK
t: +44 (0)117 374 6645
e: bup-info@bristol.ac.uk

Details of international sales and distribution partners are available at bristoluniversitypress.co.uk

Editorial selection, editorial matter and Chapters 1 and 14 © Jo Howard and Mariz Tadros
Other individual chapters © Bristol University Press 2023

The digital PDF and EPUB versions of this title are available Open Access and distributed under the terms of the Creative Commons Attribution-NonCommercial-NoDerivatives 4.0 International licence (https://creativecommons.org/licenses/by-nc-nd/4.0/) which permits reproduction and distribution for non-commercial use without further permission provided the original work is attributed.

British Library Cataloguing in Publication Data
A catalogue record for this book is available from the British Library

ISBN 978-1-5292-2928-8 paperback
ISBN 978-1-5292-2930-1 ePub
ISBN 978-1-5292-2929-5 OA Pdf

The right of Jo Howard and Mariz Tadros to be identified as editors of this work has been asserted by them in accordance with the Copyright, Designs and Patents Act 1988.

All rights reserved: no part of this publication may be reproduced, stored in a retrieval system, or transmitted in any form or by any means, electronic, mechanical, photocopying, recording, or otherwise without the prior permission of Bristol University Press.

Every reasonable effort has been made to obtain permission to reproduce copyrighted material. If, however, anyone knows of an oversight, please contact the publisher.

The statements and opinions contained within this publication are solely those of the editors and contributors and not of the University of Bristol or Bristol University Press. The University of Bristol and Bristol University Press disclaim responsibility for any injury to persons or property resulting from any material published in this publication.

Bristol University Press works to counter discrimination on grounds of gender,
race, disability, age and sexuality.

Cover design: Hayes Design and Advertising
Front cover image: Artwork by Kathryn Cheeseman

Contents

List of Figures, Tables and Boxes v
Notes on Contributors vi

1 Religious Inequalities: The Blind Spot in Participatory   1
   Methodologies and Understandings of Freedom of Religion
   or Belief
   Jo Howard and Mariz Tadros

India

2 Participatory Methods and the Freedom of Religion or Belief 37
   Rebecca Shah and Timothy Shah
3 The Personal, the Relational and the Community: 54
   Researching with Dalit Christian Women in India during
   COVID-19
   Rebecca Shah with Lata John
4 Faith and Researcher Positionality: Researching with Dalit   64
   Muslim Women in India during COVID-19
   Rebecca Shah with Laila Khan

Nigeria

5 Using Participatory Methodologies in the Context of Fragility 79
   Plangsat Bitrus Dayil
6 Applying Participatory Methodologies in Understanding   99
   the Impact of the COVID-19 Epidemic on Religious
   Communities in Nigeria
   Henry Gyang Mang
7 Working with Survivors of Trauma: Using Participatory   114
   Ranking to Explore the Experiences of Izala Women in
   Northern Nigeria
   Fatima Suleiman

Iraq

8	Facilitating Peer Research for Freedom of Religion or Belief in Iraq *Sofya Shahab*	125
9	Participatory Learning and Action (PLA) and Reflective Practices: Training Teachers to Become Effective Promoters of Freedom of Religion or Belief Principles in Education *Yusra Mahdi*	144
10	Embracing Emotion and Building Confidence: Using Participatory Methods with Yazidi Women in Iraq *Zeri Khairi Gadi*	163

Pakistan

11	Lessons Learned Using Participatory Methodologies in Exploring Intersectional Marginalization of Religious and Sectarian Minorities in Pakistan *Asad Shoaib and Jaffer Abbas Mirza*	173
12	Using Participatory Research Methodology to Understand Daily Experiences of Religiously Marginalized Communities: A Case Study of Christians in Joseph Colony (Lahore) and Rimsha Colony (Islamabad) and Shi'as in Balti Basti (Karachi) *Maryam Kanwer and Jaffer Abbas Mirza*	190
13	Using Participatory Methods with Ahmadis in Exile *M.K.*	202
14	Addressing the Intersection of Religious and Other Inequalities through Participatory Methodologies *Mariz Tadros and Jo Howard*	210

Index — 238

List of Figures, Tables and Boxes

Figures

9.1	Cycle of discrimination against religious minorities in Iraq	146
9.2	Theory of change	146
9.3	Emerging challenges	147
9.4	Emerging challenges and learning	148
9.5	Kolb's Experiential Learning Cycle	149
12.1	Community mapping exercise among Christians of Rimsha Colony and Joseph Colony and Shi'as of Balti Basti	192

Tables

2.1	Participant ranking of factors that enabled Dalit Muslim men to cope with the pandemic in Vyasarpadi slum in Chennai in March 2021	49
6.1	Bassa, Plateau State Nigeria: PRA matrix ranking for Christian men (challenges)	105
6.2	Bassa, Plateau State Nigeria: PRA matrix ranking for Christian men (enablers)	106
7.1	Participatory ranking exercise with Izala women in northern Nigeria	117

Boxes

9.1	Chapter 1 of the new pro-pluralism curriculum	152
9.2	Case studies of Freedom of Religion or Belief application through microteaching methods	153
9.3	Case studies about scenarios from teachers' personal experiences	155

Notes on Contributors

Plangsat B. Dayil is a Lecturer in the Department of Political Science, University of Jos, and currently the Director, Centre for Gender and Women Studies (CGWS), University of Jos. Dr Dayil's research interests and areas of expertise include gender, politics and governance, security sector reform, conflict, peace-building and diversity management, social inclusion and safeguarding issues. She is a fellow of the Institute of Strategic Management of Nigeria (ISMN), a member of the Nigerian National Platform on Security Sector Reform and Governance (SSRG), of the International Political Science Association (IPSA) and of Peace Women Partners' (PWP) World Council of Leaders.

Zeri Khairi Gadi is a Yazidi activist from Bashiqa, Iraq, working with civil society organizations to promote peace, stability and security following the liberation of the region from Daesh in 2016.

Jo Howard is a Research Fellow at the Institute of Development Studies. She leads the Participation, Inclusion and Social Change research cluster. Her work focuses on the contributions of participatory research methodologies for fostering individual and group agency, in contexts of multiple and intersecting forms of marginalization. She works with community-based organizations, INGOs and donors and other development actors in Africa, Asia, Latin America and Europe.

Lata John (pseudonym) is a female Christian researcher in India. Her name has been changed to protect her identity.

Maryam Kanwer is a human rights activist. Her work focuses on the persecution of marginalized groups based on their ethnic or religious backgrounds. She has worked on youth development through community resilience, peace-building messaging, conflict resolution and freedom of religion or belief (FoRB). Maryam has been working extensively in human development for over ten years and is currently affiliated with the Coalition for Religious Equality and Inclusive Development (CREID). She is also an International Visitor Leadership Program (IVLP) Alumnus 2015 on Countering Violent Extremism (CVE) and an executive member of a global campaign called Women against Extremism (WaE).

Laila Khan (pseudonym) is a female Muslim researcher in India. Her name has been changed to protect her identity.

Yusra Mahdi possesses both a depth and a breadth of experience in a wide variety of monitoring, evaluation and learning systems from within the research, NGO and private sectors. Yusra managed the implementation and monitoring, evaluation and learning systems for the CREID programme in Iraq focusing on freedom of religion or belief (FoRB), religious education reform in primary and secondary schools, curriculum development, participatory research methods and training of teachers. With a background in journalism and media production, Yusra has also developed in-depth knowledge about problems on the ground pertaining to ethnic and sectarian conflicts, press freedoms, displacement and poverty. She is a bilingual English- and Arabic-speaker and has an MA in Human Rights and International Relations from Roehampton University.

Henry Gyang Mang teaches Conflict and Military History at the Nigerian Army University, Biu, Borno State, Nigeria. He has a BA in History from the University of Jos, an MSc in African Studies from the University of Oxford, an MA in Military History from the Nigerian Defence Academy Post-Graduate School, Kaduna, and also a PhD in Military History from the same Nigerian Defence Academy Post-Graduate School, Kaduna.

Jaffer Abbas Mirza is a researcher. In 2016 he was awarded a Chevening scholarship to study for a master's in Religion in Global Politics at the School of Oriental and African Studies (SOAS), London. He has been writing and working on countering violent extremism (CVE) and FoRB. He focuses on civil society engagement and violence against religious minorities in Pakistan and Afghanistan. He is currently associated with CREID.

M.K. is a leader from the Ahmadiyya Muslim Community (AMC) who currently works at an international organization. His name has been anonymized for security reasons, due to the persecution Ahmadi Muslims face.

Rebecca Shah is Special Advisor to the President for Global Initiatives at the University of Dallas and Senior Fellow and Principal Investigator for the Religion and Economic Empowerment Project (REEP) led by the Archbridge Institute in Washington, DC. Based in India and Washington, DC,

Professor Shah consults with international organizations and governments on development policy. Shah's key expertise is clarifying and quantifying the economic and social impact of religion, including FoRB, in the lives of vulnerable populations, particularly women, in the Global South. She led the first outcome evaluation of the international religious freedom programme for the US Department of State. In 2019 she was commissioned by the FCO and DFID to draft the 'Guidance Note: Protecting Vulnerable Religious Minorities in Conflict and Crisis Settings'. Initially funded by the FCO, Shah manages the online SMART Survey to provide real-time, policy-relevant data, drawing on in-country expertise, to address individual and institutional restrictions on FoRB across the globe. During COVID-19, Shah conducted research on vulnerability and poverty among religious minorities in India.

Timothy Samuel Shah is based in Bangalore, India, with his wife, Rebecca Shah. Together they pursue a variety of research and action initiatives designed to analyse and advance the fruitful intersection of religion, culture, political progress and economic development, particularly in South Asia and South-East Asia. Dr Shah is a non-residential Distinguished Research Scholar in the Politics Department at the University of Dallas, and Director of Strategic Initiatives for the Center for Shared Civilizational Values, which he co-founded with leaders of the Indonesia-based Nahdlatul Ulama, the world's largest Muslim organization. Among his numerous books *is God's Century: Resurgent Religion and Global Politics* (2011, W.W. Norton).

Sofya Shahab is a Research Officer in Power and Popular Politics at the Institute of Development Studies at the University of Sussex. She holds a PhD in Social Anthropology from Deakin University, Melbourne. Her research employs anthropological approaches to understand the lived experiences of conflict, violence, migration and oppression. Sofya has over ten years' experience working across the humanitarian/development nexus specializing in the project design, monitoring and evaluation of programmes most directly related to livelihoods, psychosocial support and women's empowerment in the Middle East and North Africa region.

Asad Shoaib is an academic and development researcher with more than seven years' experience of working with prominent national and international organizations and think tanks. He has produced numerous reports on social exclusion, electoral reforms, local governance and marginalization. He can be reached at asad.shoaibx@gmail.com

Fatima Suleiman is Executive Director of the Islamic Counselling Initiative of Nigeria (ICIN), a community- and interfaith-based organization promoting intercultural and inter-religious dialogue, especially among poor minority groups. ICIN aims to challenge stereotypes and exclusivity and to promote the inclusion of women in decision-making processes.

Mariz Tadros is a professor of politics and development at the Institute of Development Studies, University of Sussex. She has authored several publications on democratization, Islamist politics, gender and development and religious pluralism in the Middle East. Mariz has led several multi-disciplinary, multi-country research initiatives and currently directs the Coalition for Religious Equality and Inclusive Development (CREID), launched in November 2018.

1

Religious Inequalities: The Blind Spot in Participatory Methodologies and Understandings of Freedom of Religion or Belief

Jo Howard and Mariz Tadros

This book brings together reflections, knowledge and learning about the experiences of religious minorities in countries where religious pluralism is in decline, and about how this learning was enabled through the use of participatory research methods to explore freedom of religion or belief (FoRB). To our knowledge, it is the first book to bring together reflections on using participatory methods to research the experiences of religious minorities and explore what FoRB means to such groups, from their own experiences and lived realities. The book shares learning on how we have used participatory methodologies to research FoRB and religious inequalities, and highlights the important contribution of a participatory research approach to this field. The book includes a range of contributions authored by both academics and practitioners. Some of the practitioner authors are peer researchers, deeply embedded in the realities of the groups they are working with; their contributions are presented in order to maintain the integrity of their voice and narrative, and should be read as extended narratives or vignettes which powerfully evoke their personal experience and embeddedness in the issues we are researching (see India, Chapters 3 and 4; Nigeria, Chapter 7; Iraq, Chapter 10; and Pakistan, Chapter 13).

Participatory research (PR) is a paradigm which comprises a range of methodologies that aim to challenge unequal power hierarchies and are oriented towards social justice. It puts the people whose realities are the subject of inquiry at the centre of the research, and enables them to gain knowledge and understanding of the issues that affect them (Ospina, Burns and Howard, 2021). PR seeks to generate knowledge for social change: this may mean that participants produce outputs for policy influence, or identify local action that is needed. Core characteristics which are common across participatory methodologies are: (1) the importance of group-based co-construction of knowledge, learning and collective understanding; (2) the recognition and sharing of power (leadership, agency, capabilities) within the research process and beyond it; (3) valuing different ways of knowing (experiential, practical and presentational as well as cognitive or conceptual); and (4) enabling these to be expressed through accessible, creative and culturally relevant methods.

The case studies are drawn from work undertaken through the Coalition for Religious Equality and Inclusive Development (CREID). The Pew Research ten-year (2007–17) report revealed that, in 2017, 52 governments imposed 'either "high" or "very high" levels of restrictions on religion, up from 40 in 2007' (Pew Research Center, 2019: 5).[1] However, the language of FoRB and FoRB violation rankings can feel disconnected from those affected, and from their vocabularies and experiences. In this book, researchers in Iraq, India, Pakistan and Nigeria reflect on their experiences of using research methods which create space for participants to reflect on their realities in a group setting. They consider the implications for people's agency when the research methods enable participants to put their own experience and analysis at the centre of the process.

This introduction is structured as follows. We first present the dual lens of the two editors in how participatory methods and understanding FoRB came to inform their own interpretive frameworks, and in turn how these came to shape the approach to this book. In Part I, Jo Howard situates this volume in current participatory research scholarship and, reflecting on her own positionality, describes why academics, practitioners and others committed to participatory methods need to engage epistemologically and ethically with the religious otherization of people on the margins, and what such a journey of accompaniment with those committed to redressing religious inequalities entails. In Part 2, Mariz Tadros, also reflecting on her own positionality, makes the case for how participatory methods can broaden the ways through which we conceptualize FoRB and capture its fluid and dynamic nature. Part 3 describes the rationale for the book as well as its intended readership, followed by a brief overview of the contexts and methods covered in the various case studies. Part 4 highlights how the chapters in this book are organized and clustered.

Part I: Jo – a participatory research perspective

In PR, we are concerned with methods which offer possibilities for those who experience the issues being researched to have their knowledge acknowledged, for them to bring this knowledge into dialogue with others and the learning, knowledge and actions that can emerge from this (Ospina, Burns and Howard, 2021). Participatory researchers often seek to work with people in contexts of marginalization, since participatory research embraces different ways of knowing, its principles are democratic and inclusive and its aim is to transform inequities. These aims and principles have their roots in the emancipatory methodologies and pedagogies of Paolo Freire, Orlando Fals Borda and Agosto Boal in Latin America, Myles Horton in the US, Robert Chambers, Rajesh Tandon and others working in India and Africa and in the democratizing pedagogies of Dewey and Gustavsen. PR has since been challenged and enriched through the critiques and contributions of feminist participatory researchers (Maguire, 1987), of disability inclusive researchers (Wickenden and Franco, 2021), and indigenous research (Cram, 2009; Smith, 2021).

Current PR scholarship is shaped and informed by these influences and critiques and brings an intersectional lens to all stages of the research process in order to analyse, work with and shift power – the principles of feminist PR speak to the broader field as set out by Guy and Arthur (2021): rejection of value-free research; inclusivity; power, voice and empowerment; positionality; and relationships and collaboration. Innovations are taking place in research design: for example, linking participatory methods into processes which explore the system which drives marginalization, identifying critical junctures and entry points for actions for change (Burns and Worsley, 2015). PR is also moving into new spaces: for example, into humanitarian and conflict-affected settings to facilitate dialogue and learning and action in complex and insecure contexts (Hyslop, 2021).

PR has long engaged with creative, embodied and visual methods, and is now advancing how different kinds of knowledge can be expressed through combinations of these methods for greater equity and intercultural justice: for example, '*senti-pensante*' (feeling-thinking) (Rendon, 2012), and participatory theatre (Kaptani et al, 2021). These methods enable participants to express lived experience less easily accessed through cognitive or verbal modes of expression. Methods are combined in a participatory research process which supports participants to move from expression through to group recognition of experience and analysis of underlying factors which drive marginalization. Participatory methods can be mixed with other research methods such as ethnography to explore sites and dimensions of conflict (see Santamaria Chavarro, 2022). A core dimension across all methods is their emphasis on dialogue as the process through which participants move from telling their individual experiences to critical reflection and collective analysis (Esteva, 2022).

While a conceptualization of inequalities as intersectional is central to PR, the particular application of participatory methodologies to researching religious inequalities has been very little discussed in the PR field. In the research discussed in this book, we have been using such methods in contexts of extreme discrimination, persecution and encroachments of rights and freedoms. This book therefore shares learning about the contribution of participatory methods to researching FoRB, reflects on the kind of data that is produced, the learning for FoRB policy recommendations and the quality of experience and potential outcomes for those involved. Importantly, it also explores the ethics and limitations of conducting PR with people in these challenging contexts.

I came to this collaboration with 30 years' experience in participatory research and practice. Throughout my career (in academic and in practice settings), I have focused on methods which enable marginalized people, groups and communities to gather data and analyse their own realities and, where possible, to bring this knowledge into dialogue with duty bearers – service providers, local councillors, parliamentarians and so forth. My reasons for using participatory methods are practical, epistemological and ethical. From a practical perspective, data that is gathered and analysed by people who themselves experience issues of marginalization in their everyday lives is likely to provide a more accurate account of what is happening and why than data that is gathered by external actors. Potential actions and solutions are more likely to be relevant to them, so that policy recommendations can be more carefully shaped to respond to their needs.

From an epistemological perspective, PR offers epistemological pluralism as its methods engage with different ways of knowing. This is important in contexts of marginalization because the knowledge that is held by the people that experience this marginalization may be tacit, that is, held within their bodies and emotions and not expressed in words. This may be because they have not been able to articulate these experiences or have never been offered the space to reflect on them. When creative methods are used which help them to access unspoken, tacit or taboo knowledge, new knowledge can be generated (Higginbottom and Liamputtong, 2015; Lewin and Shaw, 2021).

From an ethical perspective, PR can democratize how knowledge is produced, and the relationship between researcher and research 'subjects', the latter becoming co-researchers as they generate knowledge together. The power relationship between academic researchers and community members has long been ignored, allowing colonial behaviours and attitudes to perpetuate in the academic world, within and between countries. PR principles and methods offer ways to create spaces that counter existing power hierarchies: by recognizing and supporting the capacities and potentials of research participants to analyse their own realities, and by building more collaborative relationships between researchers in the global South and North.

Inequalities are increasing around the world (Chancel et al, 2021) and have been exacerbated by the COVID-19 pandemic (ILO, 2022). At the same time, and linked, there has been an increase in authoritarian polities, with FoRB often eroded within these polarizing ideological projects, along with other rights and freedoms. Research into inequalities has tended to focus on the intersection of economic and social inequalities, and tends not to include religion and faith: and if it does, it does so superficially (Tadros and Sabates-Wheeler, 2020). This suggests an assumption that religion is not a significant driver of inequalities, or not one that 'development' engages with, because development is (tacitly) understood as secular.

My own PR has focused on building understanding of drivers of inequalities, of how people experience the intersection of these in their own lives and for identifying pathways for change. Over many years, my work in collaboration with others has helped to identify power structures and relationships which perpetuate inequalities, especially relating to gender, class and race. However, on reflection, I am aware that I failed to pay attention to the role of religious identity. For example, in work with Denotified and Nomadic Tribes (DNTs) in India, the identity-based inequalities that we focused on were ethnicity and gender, and how these intersected with economic and spatial disadvantage. In Ghana, working with marginalized salt-winner women, we focused on gender-based inequalities and how these intersected with environmental, economic and political marginalization (Shaw, Howard and Franco, 2020).[2]

The process of engaging with the CREID programme to bring participatory methods to the study of FoRB has significantly expanded my understanding of marginalization and revealed to me my blind spot with regard to how religious inequalities are an important part of the picture, and how these intersect with other inequalities to profoundly shape and limit people's opportunities, rights and freedoms. Furthermore, it has highlighted for me the importance of religion and faith as a source of strength and collective identity. An understanding of the FoRB lens enabled us to return to our work with DNTs in India, to retrospectively reflect on experiences of religious inequalities and their intersection (Bharadwaj, Howard and Narayanan, 2021).

PR is very rarely applied in the field of religion and belief. Denning and colleagues (2020) note that participatory approaches to researching geographies of religion are still 'embryonic', and identify just two studies which 'demonstrate their value in this context' (Denning, Scriven and Slatter, 2020: 4, citing Williams, 2017, and Dwyer et al, 2018) The *Routledge Handbook of Research Methods in the Study of Religion* (Engler and Stausberg, 2022) does not feature PR at all. On the other hand, the *SAGE Handbook of Participatory Research and Inquiry* (Burns, Howard and Ospina, 2021) does not include any example of using PR to explore FoRB or religious inequalities.

Why this mutual ignorance, reluctance, conscious or unconscious rejection? Key thinkers in the 1970s and 1980s (Freire, Fals Borda, Chambers, Hall, Tandon) developed participatory epistemologies and methodologies which were informed by worldviews that challenged structures of power and sources of inequality (for example, Marxism and anti- and post-colonialism) – schools of thought that often sat uncomfortably with religious faith (liberation theology being an important exception). The PR community may have perceived faith as less relevant than class, race and gender, and indeed were critiqued by feminist scholars for neglecting analysis of patriarchy (Maguire, 1987), or have simply been uncomfortable with bringing religious views into dialogue, even today when third-wave feminism has introduced an intersectional lens to participatory research (Guy and Arthur, 2021).

Bringing my knowledge of participatory methods to study religious inequalities has challenged me to consider how people's religion and belief are profoundly connected to how they experience the world. PR is a paradigm committed to the flourishing and sustainability of human and planetary life, which has at its heart a belief in people and that meaningful research should be 'with', not 'on', them (Bradbury and Reason, 2003). However, bringing PR to explore FoRB is not a simple task of adding methods to a researcher kitbag. There are serious challenges for working in settings where there is profound mistrust between different communities, or between certain groups and their government, due to discrimination, persecution and even lynching and murder.

A central feature of PR is the opening and sustaining of a 'communicative space' (Reason and Gayá, 2009; Wicks, 2009), in which dialogue between different experiences can be enabled. How is this possible in such contexts of insecurity and risk? Is it possible to enable different perspectives to come into dialogue? Up to what point is participatory research safe, ethical, possible?

One way to ensure good practice in these contexts is to work with extraordinary researchers, who are sensitive to the issues and to the methods, and who can build a rapport with participants in very challenging contexts. The chapters in this book demonstrate that such extraordinary researchers do exist! We know that good facilitation skills are necessary to bring different perspectives into conversation in ways which enable dialogue and understanding (Dick, 2021). PR needs to be understood as a process rooted in the specific context and in people's everyday realities. As such, we have recommended that, where possible, researcher-facilitators are the same religion and sex as the group they are working with, so that participants feel confident to speak, and so that hidden issues are more likely to emerge.

Moreover, effective dialogic PR needs an investment in time to build trust, or to build on pre-existing relationships. In this volume, researchers talk of how trust was built over time to access highly stigmatized groups (see Shoaib and Mirza, Chapter 11; some researchers had to manage within a short time-scale but helped people to overcome their fears by providing a facilitator who shared their faith (see, for example, Mang, Chapter 6); other researchers are activists who are deeply embedded in the communities they are researching (for example, Suleiman, Chapter 7; M.K., Chapter 13).

It is important to highlight that almost all the researchers who have contributed to this research and this book were unaccustomed to using PR methods. We trained them in participatory methods, and we co-constructed participatory principles and ethical guidelines for undertaking the work. This book provides insights into their experiences of the methods, into their fears about stepping out of familiar ways of conducting research (for example, the safety of the semi-structured interview with its list of questions) and allowing space for new perspectives to emerge, and into their reflections, which are generating important learning for participatory researchers as well as on FoRB. They speak of the value of participatory methods and of how they are considering incorporating them into their work in the future, while also reflecting on where they see the limits and challenges.

Part II: Mariz – a FoRB perspective

During my 20 years' experience of researching and writing about encroachments on religious pluralism in the Middle East and the homogenizing ideologies and practices of state and non-state actors, I often turned to participatory methods to understand the experiences of people's day-to-day realities of encroachment and to create the space for community members to reflect on their own experiences and on what they have found helpful on their journeys.[3] Where contexts allowed, individuals and groups with whom participatory methods were undertaken would build on the process, by sharpening their thinking around strategic opportunities for redressing religious inequalities and for weighing the risks of encroachment. Where contexts were too dangerous (from a security point of view), the very process of reflecting and sharing was at the very least cathartic. However, in order to understand national-level power configurations, I used more conventional methods of gathering qualitative and quantitative data (interviews and surveys), all the while combining them with participatory methods implemented with grass-roots communities.

In 2018 I was privileged to assume directorship of the Coalition for Religious Equality and Inclusive Development (CREID). This is a consortium which brings together academic, human rights and development leaders from secular and faith-based backgrounds to make development thinking, policy and practice more aware of and responsive to the realities experienced by socio-economically marginalized people on account of their real or perceived religious affiliation (see www.creid.ac for partners). CREID focuses on a wide array of people's experiences religious otherization:

- people associated with a minority religion in a context where religious majoritarianism is pervasive;
- people who wield norms and beliefs that they hold as sacred but which they do not necessarily speak of as religion (such as indigenous people);
- people who belong to the majority religion but diverge in their interpretations, practices or denominational affiliation;
- none-ists (those who do not profess an affiliation to a particular religion) and atheists living in contexts where religiosity is the expected norm.

Undoubtedly, within and across the groups mentioned above, there are varying degrees of religious otherization, both in scope and scale. By 'religious otherization' we mean more than having a different religion: we mean where this difference in religious affiliation (real or perceived) becomes the basis of identifying someone as 'the other', as not 'one of us'. With reference to the use of the term 'religious otherization' in our context, it is reflective of a relationship of power, rather than a numerical status (Tadros, 2020).

The rationale for establishing CREID in November 2018 was to make visible the intersecting inequalities experienced by people who are religiously marginalized. We engaged with freedom of religion or belief through the prism of religious equality. Freedom of religion or belief is a deeply contested term, and there is no consensus around one particular definition (Fox, 2016; Gatti et al, 2019; Marshall, 2021). We use the terms 'freedom of religion or belief' and 'religious equality' interchangeably. Religious equality, in particular when it intersects with equality on other axes such as class, gender, location, ethnicity, political orientation and so forth, allows us to understand the dynamics of power through an inter- and intra-group perspective as well as at an individual level (see Tadros, 2022 for further discussion of the concept).

CREID had a two-tier system of implementation: first were 'core' countries in which we implemented projects and undertook research. These included the following: Egypt, Myanmar, Iraq, Nigeria, Pakistan and (later) India. The second tier of countries were ones in which we commissioned research but did not implement projects (about 13 other countries: see creid.ac for details). The selection of the first-tier countries was informed by a number of criteria (they were high on the UK government's 2008 list of FoRB violators) and they had varying levels and sources of fragility (rule of law, security, quality of governance, nature of threat from inter- and intra-state non-state actors). They had different levels of religious inequality: Myanmar and Iraq were the most extreme as countries having experienced genocides; Nigeria was in the middle with high levels of violence; Pakistan and India had strong political projects of religious homogenization and frequent incidents of violence; and Egypt showed evidence of systemic religious otherization and some cases of violence.

The countries also represented different majoritarian ideologies: Buddhist in Myanmar, Hindu in India, Islamist in Pakistan and Egypt, and various ideologies in Nigeria, according to region. Finally, and of equal importance, was the fact that these were countries in which our partners had legitimacy and a strong standing. The selection of case studies presented in this book represents to a very large extent the geographical focus of the consortium. We are aware that there aren't examples from all continents covered here: Latin America and Europe are absent even though a number of countries are led by power holders whose discourse and policies encroach on religious equality. We hope to encourage others to understand the overlapping forces of exclusion experienced by targeted religious minorities, and present these case studies in this book, to provide practical examples of ways in which others have experimented with participatory methods.

Our understanding of religious equalities is informed by the idea of situated minoritiness.[4] This refers to the fact that power inequalities experienced by a numerical minority are very much informed by how power holders are engaging with members of a group according to very specific contextual factors. Thus, 'situated' refers to both geographic location and how power holders in any given moment of time perceive and treat them. This situatedness may shift with time, with location, with changes in leadership (both of power holders as well as within the group) and in response to a myriad of other factors. Reference to the changing context of majority–minority relations is to recognize that a group that may be a minority in one part of a country may be a majority in the other. Moreover, the experience of power inequalities is across different shades of intensity and scales of discrimination and targeting. Recognizing the dynamic nature of power hierarchies as they shape religious inequalities is useful in showing how:

- the same minority in the same country may have very different experiences of religious inequalities; for example, the Muslims of Myanmar, depending on whether they are from the Rohingya or not;
- the experience of different religious minorities in a given territory of a country may vary greatly: for example, the Yazidis as distinct from the Sabaens in Iraq; and

- the country may not be homogeneous in terms of its majority–minority demographics: for example, variations between northern Nigeria, the middle belt and Nigeria's southern states.

The idea of understanding religious inequalities as being dynamic and so significantly shaped by their context sheds light on differentiated experiences, and therefore enables a deeper and more nuanced understanding of power dynamics. Despite some common patterns underpinning the different case studies presented in this collection, our comparative approach in this stream of work recognizes the differentiation in experiences within and across religious minorities. Hence, there is no single study undertaken by a single author on all of the religious minorities in any given context. A nuanced approach is needed to understand how geographic locality, caste, class, gender and the doctrinal position of the mainstream religion lead to differentiated realities on the ground. This allows us not to assume that the realities of all individuals who belong to religious minorities within a given context are shaped by the same dynamics or the same set of inequalities. Participatory methods allow for the uncovering of such nuances. Religious hostilities, as Birdsall and Beaman (2020) note, are never uniform across a country.

Part III: Rationale and intended readership

In CREID, we wanted to speak to those with a commitment to poverty reduction, social justice and inclusive development, and those whose vision entailed redressing inequalities experienced on the basis of class, ethnicity, gender, geographic location and political orientation but for whom inequalities created or exacerbated on the basis of religious affiliation was a blind spot (see Tadros, 2022 for what accounts for this blind spot and Tadros and Sabates-Wheeler, 2020 for its manifestations).

The use of indicators of religious freedom and violations in most international development and humanitarian institutions at present is quite limited. Integrating ways in which religious indicators, including of FoRB, treatment and welfare of religious minorities, and FoRB and other human rights violations into the many measures of development progress and challenges is a topic that deserves reflection and priority action. This applies especially for governance and fragile state situations but has implications for human development and humanitarian work in all its many dimensions. This book contributes to addressing this gap in international development and humanitarian actors' understanding of religious equalities and issues of freedom of religion or belief. We hope that familiarity among international development and humanitarian actors with participatory methodologies over many decades may also contribute to breaking the taboo around engaging with anything that is 'religious'.

FoRB as an idea has its genealogy in human rights. The most widely used definition of FoRB in much of the literature is informed by article 18 of the Universal Declaration of Human Rights, which stipulates that 'everyone has the right to freedom of thought, conscience and religion, this right includes freedom to change, either alone or in community with others and in public or private, to manifest his religion or belief in teaching, practice, worship and observance'. The uptake of freedom of religion or belief among international human rights actors, however, has been sporadic. Petersen and Marshall (2019: 15) have noted that: 'Among secular human rights organizations, conversely, this misperception of FoRB as a right that primarily concerns religious communities and individuals is – in part – to blame for their lack of engagement with FoRB.' FoRB promotion may be perceived as defending religion, and this would be problematic on several grounds, including that human rights organizations would be perceived as privileging one religion over another or that some religious doctrine may be incongruent with other rights (most notably women's rights or rights of those who do not profess the same faith) (Petersen and Marshall, 2019).

Conceptual clarity here is key for unpacking whose freedom is considered: in the words of Heiner Bielefeldt, a former UN rapporteur for FoRB, at the centre of FoRB are 'believers rather than beliefs' (Bielefeldt and Schirrmacher, 2017: 168). In a similar vein, Shah notes that FoRB 'constitutes a claim on behalf of persons. It is not a claim that all religions are equally true or that all religion is good for society' (Shah, Franck and Farr, 2012: 18) The implications are that the state has a duty to protect the individual, and not the religion:

> If the state protects the doctrinal and normative contents of one particular religion as such, this will almost inevitably lead to discrimination against adherents of other religions or beliefs, which would be unacceptable from a human rights perspective. It is not least for this reason that human rights epitomize a shift of focus from beliefs to believers, in order to appreciate existing religious or belief diversity on the basis of non-discrimination or equality. Accordingly, the human right to freedom of religion or belief does not protect religious traditions per se, but instead facilitates the free search and development of faith-related identities of human beings, as individuals and in community with others. (Bielefeldt, and Schirrmacher, 2017: 169)

This conceptual framing of FoRB being the right of individuals as opposed to religions also informs the framing of our inquiry here and in CREID more broadly. There is a recognition that sometimes the lines between persons and what they believe is blurred; however, operationally, in all four countries, we have focused on working with individuals who face multiple intersecting inequalities on the basis of socio-economic exclusion intertwining with other factors. In other words, the focus has not been their belief system or the doctrines they hold but their experiences as individuals and members of communities.

With the focus on the person, rather than the belief system, we can interrogate conceptually and empirically how FoRB features in the day-to-day lives of the marginalized. Conceptually, this is made possible through an intersecting inequalities lens. In the human rights scholarship, there is a recognition that FoRB as a human right is interconnected with other rights (Petersen and Marshall, 2019). However, in our inquiry, our point of reference is not the framing of how different human rights speak to each other, but rather how individuals living on the margins of society experience power and powerlessness in their daily lives, from which we can gauge how the intersections of inequalities play out along various axes. Development scholarship on the intersections of inequalities can be found, for example, in David Mosse's (2018) exploration on how the intersection between caste, religious affiliation and discrimination impacts on people's access to development in India. Such work also includes Frances Stewart's (2005, 2008) important work on horizontal inequalities relating to religious and ethnic drivers. On the level of development policy framings, the exploration of experiences of religious and other intersecting inequalities has been virtually absent, most conspicuously in the FoRB-blind nature of the Sustainable Development Goals (Shaheed, 2020; Petersen, 2022) The Sustainable Development Goals' indicators allow for an exploration of how poverty intersects with gender, geography, profession, age and other factors, yet there is hardly any mention of religious marginality as an axis of inequality.

Empirically, we believe that participatory methodologies enable a grounded theory approach to the exploration of intersecting inequalities as experienced by religiously and socio-economically marginalized individuals. Academics, practitioners and activists are using participatory methodologies to engage in the praxis of understanding the experiences of power inequalities by people who are marginalized (see, for example, Shaw, Howard and Franco, 2020). We hope that the use of these methods paves the way for a recognition, and a more nuanced understanding, of the experiences of religious otherization and exclusion. In other words, we hope that the book will encourage the adoption of participatory methods to generate new understandings of the role of religious discrimination in the lives of people living on the margins. By providing practical examples of how evidence can be gathered through participatory tools – which are highly popular among many development and community practitioners – we hope that development and humanitarian actors can integrate a religious inequalities-sensitive lens in their work with communities and ultimately, in future global development policy frameworks. However, the focus of this book on the nexus of freedom of religion or belief and participatory methods also speaks to a broader audience beyond those who are working in international development/humanitarianism. As is evident from the studies presented here, the authors range from human rights activists to (lay) community leaders, faith leaders, academics from social science and humanities, and development professionals.

Opportunities and pitfalls in global approaches to FoRB assessment

Methods of understanding and monitoring the status of freedom of religion or belief in different contexts are fraught with danger. Jonathan Fox (2016) notes that variations in understandings and measurements of FoRB have implications for whose experiences of violations are at the centre, the kind of normative judgements that inform assessing the scale of violations and the kind of policy recommendations emanating from the methodology applied. The most popular methods of FoRB measurement have been those using quantitative methods to generate data on the scale of FoRB violations and to generate lists of countries that are the worst violators (see Marshall, 2021 for the most prominent actors and a discussion of their approaches).

There is growing consensus (Fox, 2016; Gatti et al, 2019; Birdsall and Beaman, 2020; Marshall, 2021) that the most prevalent forms of measuring FoRB through quantitative data are flawed. For example, in their review of the Pew Survey, the most influential and most widely cited of instruments for the measurement of FoRB, Birdsall and Beaman (2020) raise a number of concerns with the Pew Survey's much quoted number with reference to FoRB violations (Pew's finding that 83 per cent of the world's population lives in countries with 'high' or 'very high' levels of restrictions on religion). They note that the numbers widely in circulation, and which users assume to be objective, need to be scrutinized in terms of the finer details of approach, methodology and the process of the human element of weighing evidence to arrive at judgements.

Ultimately, they note that

> Numbers are not neutral. Behind any quantification of religion or FoRB, there are a range of qualitative assumptions and decisions as to what constitutes religion, religiosity, a restriction on religious belief or practice, or a social hostility involving religion. It's both an art and a science. (Birdsall and Beaman, 2020: 66)

The figures are quoted as if the process of aggregating the data is pure science, devoid of any 'human' intervention or role. However, the 'art' of developing the architecture, the criteria and the weighting ultimately reflects human choices which are in turn informed by normative standpoints and assumptions. However, it is understandable that the Pew Survey is considered authoritative, given the very high level of transparency in sharing its methodology and its calculations, and in view of the absence of alternative methods of comparing and contrasting the situation of freedom of religion or belief globally.

Nevertheless, for an understanding of the drivers and different levels of religious otherization, there is no alternative to qualitative data collection. Birdsall and Beaman note that

> There is no replacement for qualitative data. To be sure, there are numerous benefits to quantitative data. But narrative accounts and analysis are needed to more fully capture the gradations, nuances, tensions, debates, regional variations, and the complex ways religion is embedded within a range of other socio-cultural dynamics. Just as single-story narratives do not give the big picture, numbers without narrative lack nuance. (Birdsall and Beaman, 2020: 67)

The need for caution and nuance as noted by Birdsall and Beaman in the above quote may apply to many complex social, political and economic phenomena globally, but it is particularly pertinent to the study of FoRB or religious equality on several counts.

First, in many contexts in which religious homogenization is acute, it is highly risky for people to share their opinions openly and honestly or to talk about their experiences with strangers in surveys, for example, without fear of reprisals. Conversely, even in contexts celebrating religious pluralism, participants in a survey may also not disclose their real opinions out of political correctness. They may not wish to disclose how they honestly feel about the 'religious other' or disclose experiences out of fear of being called intolerant.

Second, on account of access and sensitivities, it may be difficult for those doing research via surveys (including online or telephone) to ensure that they have outreach to those on the very margins, economically, socially and politically, among the religious minorities. The process of selecting participants may be skewed in favour of those with whom connections or access is secured. This is not to suggest that the generation of numbers is not important for understanding freedom of religion or belief violations: without numbers, the process of ranking encroachments and forms of discrimination may be impossible.

However, the key issue is to recognize that it is impossible to arrive at an instrument for measuring FoRB that is neutral. All forms of data generation on freedom of religion or belief/religious equality are necessarily partial. Consider this statement by Gatti et al:

> Much of the reporting, especially by certain governments and think tanks, is exceptionally good. But some of the activist literature on persecution presents a partial, biased, or even erroneous picture. Some reports are generalised and imprecise and thus portray a situation of systemic persecution in a given country whereas actual cases of discrimination of violence based on religion or belief may be episodic and localised. There's also the challenge of what to make of first-hand accounts. It is important to hear the voices of the persecuted, but we must remember that their accounts are limited and perspectival. (Gatti et al, 2019: 93)

There are a number of postulations here that need careful unpacking. Undoubtedly, interest groups may at times engage with the process of gathering, interpreting and presenting data in such a manner that it advances the policy recommendations they wish to put forward. However, what is concerning is to assume that the other sources of data, those emanating from governments or think tanks, are necessarily impartial, objective and neutral.

Governments may be driven by a political agenda of under-reporting the overall number of persons belonging to religious minorities in their national surveys (see Tadros, 2013 for the dispute between the government, the church and human rights activists on the number of Copts in the national surveys in Egypt). Religious minorities may not self-identify out of fear of reprisals and may hide their religious identities (for example, the Kakais in Iraq and the Ahmadiyya in Pakistan). These government surveys, considered by many to be authoritative, are then reproduced in international think tank reports without interrogation.

Moreover, think tanks' FoRB measurements may rely on elite interviews among representatives from religious minorities whose experiences of day-to-day religious targeting and encroachment may be very different from those living in poverty or away from the city centres. In both cases, the data collection process is heavily influenced by the positionality of the data collectors themselves, and yet in most cases, researchers are not required to disclose their positionality. In participatory methods, a key element of the approach is to interrogate and recognize both researchers' own normative standpoints on the issues and how they are perceived by the participants.

Gatti et al's (2019) concerns about primary data in the form of first-hand accounts being 'limited and perspectival' are valid. Individual narratives of persecution, for example, are likely to be informed by the person's own experience and interpretive lens, both of which are important but may not offer insights into the drivers of their targeting that are not apparent to them. However, as will be discussed below, participatory methods allow for addressing the limitations of individual narratives and acquiring multiple perspectives to address concerns for engaging with first-hand empirical data, although participatory methods also have their limitations and are by no means 'neutral' (see below). The key to making any FoRB measurement useful for policy engagement is to begin with an acknowledgement of ways in which each approach is limited in its neutrality by being transparent about all the inherent biases in the design, process and interpretation of data. This does not make attempts at FoRB measurement necessarily invalid. The acknowledgement of internal biases only makes an assessment stronger and more credible, since it allows for an informed use of the data.

CREID's approach to participatory methods

While fully aware that there is no perfect FoRB measurement approach, the choice of participatory methodologies was informed by our desire to address some of the problematics of current approaches to FoRB by demonstrating the strengths of participatory approaches, while also acknowledging their limitations. Our engagement with participatory methods, without excluding their combination with other methods as needed, was informed by capitalizing on the strength of participatory methods as well as addressing the gaps in other approaches. The research inquiry was co-constructed between external actors presiding over the CREID programme as well as local researchers and participants. Scholarship has suggested that co-production of research offers more control to participants over the inquiry, leading to a more empowering experience of using participatory methodologies (Facer and Enright, 2016). In our inquiries, we tried to establish a balance between the need to formulate the parameters of our inquiry around understanding how FoRB issues feature in the lives of the marginalized and the importance of ensuring that the terms of engagement around this issue correspond to what participants identify as meaningful for them.

We engaged with participatory methods in the following way. We embraced the principles and epistemology of PR and, with our partners, developed adapted participatory research processes in context. The PR process and the 'action' element therein, varied according to the local partners' existing work, relationships and capacities. Some partners had long-standing relationships and work with the target communities; some partners provided services as well as conducting research; other partners were more experienced in bringing research findings to influence state-level or national policy.

Given our focus on FoRB, our entry point across all of the research was about understanding the day-to-day experiences of intersecting inequalities.

Questions revolved, for example, around how gender and religious marginality affect women and their communities in Pakistan, Nigeria and Iraq. In two settings, for example (Nigeria and India), we focused the inquiry to understand the experiences and amplify the voices of religiously targeted groups during the pandemic. This meant that broad areas of interest were identified with the local facilitators and researchers. However, it was up to them and the participants to decide on the weight of different issues and to analyse the significance (or lack thereof) of different research questions for their lives. Undoubtedly, religious discrimination is not the only issue that features as a site of inequality in participants' narratives. In Iraq, education, employment and religious discrimination comprised the three issues most identified by members of different religiously marginalized groups (Tadros, Shahab and Quinn-Graham, 2022: 30). The challenges of accessing good-quality education and employment are grievances that women and men from religious minority backgrounds would share with all Iraqis, independently of their religious/ethnic affiliation (Tadros, Shahab and Quinn-Graham, 2022). However, the participatory methodologies reveal how, for example, in the realm of education, experiences are mediated by religious marginality in terms of access, recognition and treatment. Participants also shared how prospects of decent employment are circumscribed by whether one belongs to the majority or minority backgrounds (for example, Toma and Zaya, 2022; Yousef and Butti, 2022).

Relevance and usefulness

The strengths of participatory methods for researching FoRB relate to the practical, epistemological and ethical criteria emphasized earlier in this introduction: they can produce more accurate and relevant data, drawing on more diverse and inclusive ways of knowing, and on ways which reduce extractivism and maximize participants' ownership of the data.

Local partners were very open to learning about participatory methods, on account of a strong consensus among the majority that the undertaking of national surveys would not generate reliable data or be viable. A key incentive was that the data collection process and its outputs would be useful and of practical significance to the communities with whom they are working (see section below). In other words, who this data was being collected for and how it will be used greatly influenced the choice of methodology.

CREID offered an opportunity to explore the links between research and practice, since the programme both implements projects on the ground and generates data on religious inequalities and FoRB. We therefore chose to engage through a participatory and action-oriented approach from the outset. By 'action-oriented', we refer to the regular reflection and action taking place during the implementation of projects via frequent 'pulse checks' on the course of the work, through which researchers and local partners were able to reflect on the highly dynamic power configurations on the ground and adjust the activities.

In some cases, where the time and context permitted, action-learning cycles involving participants and local researchers identified new actions (see, for example, Mahdi's account of using participatory methods to advance inclusive religious education in Iraq (Chapter 9); or Maryam Kanwer and Jaffer Mirza's description of how participatory methods helped gradually build trust among religious minorities mistrustful of outsiders in Pakistan (Chapter 12). It also meant that research necessarily needed to be both robust and rigorous from an academic perspective, and also meaningful and relevant for our local partners and all those involved in community change.

Positionality and partnerships

Participatory researchers and practitioners are often working in contexts of injustice and marginalization, and deeply aware of the need to manage power relationships – between local actors, but also between research participants and researchers themselves. For this reason, our approach to using participatory methods in CREID has paid careful attention to the positionality of the researchers and the quality of relationships between them and research participants, at all stages of engagement: the design, process, validation, interpretation and policy recommendations. In the first year of CREID we undertook, with our local partners, a series of scoping studies intended to understand how socio-economically marginalized people experience religious otherization.

One of the essential criteria for choosing partners was that they are locally well embedded and enjoy substantial legitimacy in their communities. Undoubtedly, legitimacy is in the eye of the beholder, who has multiple identities (religious, ethnic, class, gender, profession and so forth). In the majority of cases, we engaged with partners both lay and faith-based who have trust and credibility in the religiously marginalized community (by and large, since there are intra-group differences within any given group). What gives individuals or groups legitimacy in the eyes of those whom they engage with is informed by a myriad of factors both agential and structural. However, central to legitimacy is the concept of positionality: how a person's multiple identities affect not only their own perceptions and disposition towards the group but also how the members of the group themselves perceive and relate to the researcher/facilitator.

The two may not necessarily be the same; for example, a human rights activist who is from a Hindu majority and an upper class may be sympathetic as an individual to the plight of a Muslim Dalit, keen to gain trust and advocate on their behalf to secure their rights as a religious minority in

India. However, on account of a cumulative experience of oppression, the Muslim Dalit may not have the same perception and may be deeply mistrustful of the intent of those not from the same community. Positionality is two-way and relational. Hence, our selection of partners was informed by how their positionality influences their ability to secure the trust and willingness to collaborate among religiously marginalized groups, as well as to empathetically convey the pulse on the ground as it is experienced by those groups.

Peer research

To strengthen the studies' connections with the ground and to build in potential for community action and change, we also engaged peer researchers. These are researchers who themselves experience the issues being researched, and may also live in the same communities. A CREID workshop which took place fortuitously in early 2020, before the COVID-19 pandemic shut us off from one another, brought together participants from Egypt, Iraq, Myanmar, Nigeria and Pakistan who had either experience of the women's movement in their country or experience of living as a member of a religious minority group (Tadros, 2020). The workshop sought to deepen our collective understanding of the intersection of inequalities, specifically of being a woman and a member of a marginalized religious group in these contexts. It also helped to illuminate the implications of this intersection for women's positions and roles in relation to the state, social justice and development policy and practice more broadly. An example of peer research in Iraq is provided by Sofya Shahab (Chapter 8), who offers a detailed account and some beautiful insights into how peer researchers can be trained and supported effectively in a challenging context.

Researchers are highly attuned to the issues and the context, and have special access and legitimacy when conducting research in the community. Researchers who share the same religious identity as the group they are researching are likely to achieve greater rapport and have better access, especially in contexts where people fear reprisals. In Chapters 3 and 4, Muslim and Christian practitioner-researchers in India share their reflections on the participatory exercise. Their reflections were gathered through interviews held by Dr Shah, who wrote up their accounts and added her own reflection on the profound importance of these researchers' religious identities and practitioner experiences, without which, she feels, the research would not have been possible.

Our partners and the peer researchers also informed our research ethics. The research addressed difficult topics, and facilitators needed to be able to support people when they were revisiting traumatic experiences. Facilitators mainly came from the same religious communities as the participants, which meant that they were trusted and people felt able to open up. Issues around dealing with trauma and not causing harm were discussed in the training and capacity-building phases of each research project. Many facilitators were also practitioners and had developed skills in engaging with people who have experienced trauma. Some facilitators from academic backgrounds were experiencing this kind of personal storytelling and group discussion for the first time. Their reflections afterwards were of surprise and appreciation at the way people drew, shared and reflected so readily, and all facilitators noted how the participatory research process – the exercises, the group discussion – was itself a source of comfort and support to the participants (see Chapter 14). Furthermore, the researchers were not working alone – we worked with local community organizations to select participants and organize the research meetings in communities which have their own mechanisms for support which we could connect participants to where needed.

Corroboration and triangulation

However, there is also a need to which we are very sensitive, which is to address bias. In participatory research, we start from people's lived experience and their knowledge. Individual narratives are necessarily subjective and partial, and an important way by which participatory methods recognize and allow for this is through mixing methods and enabling group dialogue and analysis. In such a process, an individual perspective can shift as it comes into dialogue with others' knowledge. Individuals can open up further, and the group can begin to identify commonalities as well as differences in their experiences. This process enables participants to identify factors common across their individual experiences which are drivers of inequalities, and factors which are supportive of their well-being.

Yet because perspectives shared in a group may reflect a particular set of contextual factors that have shaped their perspectives, it is important, if possible, to gather a multitude of perspectives from other groups as well. Triangulation of this knowledge with other sources of data is important, and especially so in contexts of fear, polarization, suspicion and 'othering'. Triangulation refers to 'a process of studying a problem using different methods to gain a more complete picture' (O'Cathain, Murphy and Nicholl, 2010: section 2). In the case of the application of the principle of triangulation of participatory methods to understand the realities of religious marginalization, group inquiries were complemented with participatory ranking and the results from the different methods were compared. This is crucial as it enabled a validation of the perspectives gathered through the method of group discussions, together with the numbers generated from the participatory ranking exercise in which individuals shared their views. Corroboration of research allows us to use different kinds of data to enhance the validity of the findings. This is particularly important when participants are sharing data that can be cross-corroborated: that is, dates of particular happenings that can be fact-checked against historical accounts.

Part IV: What to expect in this book

In this book, we have aimed to include a range of voices and perspectives, recognizing the diverse positionalities of the researchers and the richness that this diversity brings to the volume. Some are academic researchers; others are experienced practitioners and activists. Some shared their stories through interviews which were written up; others wrote academic or reflective pieces. All were experienced in engaging with individuals and groups who are religiously marginalized, but the majority had little experience of participatory research methods. We reflect on our collective learning in the concluding chapter to this book.

The methods employed were a mix of largely participatory methods with some semi-structured interviews. The participatory methods included and linked qualitative story-gathering/storytelling with prioritizing and quantitative ranking exercises. Individual interviews were conducted either with people identified in the group inquiry sessions whose stories the researcher felt needed to be heard in more detail or with people who were unable to come to the group inquiry sessions because of logistical or security reasons. In this way, different perspectives were sought and opportunities created for individuals whose stories might not otherwise be heard. What is important is that this data is drawn from people's own accounts of their lived realities and their direct experience of encroachments, challenges and enablers in their daily lives. Much of the research was conducted during the COVID-19 pandemic and provides insights into the particular impacts of lockdown on religious minority groups and a nuanced understanding of the intra-group dynamics. Particular insights on the experiences of women belonging to religious minorities and the possibilities of engaging isolated women and building their confidence through participatory research methods is discussed in the context of Nigeria in Chapter 7 (Suleiman) and in Iraq in Chapter 10 (Zeri).

How the participatory methods were approached and implemented varied considerably across the sites. In some cases, where researchers had sufficient time to develop and accompany a more extended process, a participatory action research process unfolded (see Chapters 11 and 12). In most other settings, the research team was entirely new to participatory methods, and received training from the CREID team. Among these, two core participatory research methods feature: storytelling facilitated through the 'Rivers of Life' method and participatory matrix ranking. The participatory activities were sometimes conducted by academic researchers, sometimes by experienced practitioners and activists. The river (or road – see Nigeria, Chapters 5 and 6) of life method was used to elicit stories of lived experience, which were analysed by the group to identify factors, challenges and enablers. These were then ranked through a participatory ranking process.

A Yazidi woman activist-practitioner in Iraq used only the participatory ranking method, and generated fascinating rich data through an extended stage of identifying the issues, before the group discussed and ranked them. How these methods were adapted and used in the context of Nigeria during the pandemic and the particular intersections of insecurity, lockdown restrictions and religious inequalities are described in Chapters 5 (Dayil) and 6 (Mang). How these methods were adopted and adapted in the context of India is described in Chapters 1–3. Reading across the academic chapter (2) and the two practitioner-led interview/reflection pieces (3 and 4) provides deep insights about FoRB restrictions and other intersecting inequalities, how they were experienced in different settings in two Indian states (Karnataka and Tamil Nadu) and with different groups (Muslim, Christian and Hindu Dalits) and also the limitations of the methods. Storytelling and matrix ranking were also used to produce knowledge with Ahmadiyya Muslims (see Chapter 13), methods which were new to the researcher, who reflects on the power of creative methods to enable participation and rich data generation.

Participatory methods for researching FoRB are extended, innovated and reflected on in Chapters 9, 11 and 12. In Chapter 9, Mahdi discusses using participatory learning and action and reflective practice as aspects of participatory action research, to bring FoRB principles into teacher training and practice in Iraq. In the context of Pakistan (Chapters 11 and 12) Kanwer and Mirza discuss using a combination of community-driven participatory methodologies to engage with religiously marginalized communities. They designed a rich participatory process which began with a community mapping exercise, followed by storytelling, community consultations and matrix ranking. The process culminated with an action-planning stage, which they reflect on as a critical way of strengthening and extending the participatory approach and its relevance and usefulness to the participants.

Countries where the research was conducted

The research was conducted in four countries, and within these countries specific regions, states and local sites were selected.

India is a religiously diverse country. Hindus make up 79.8 per cent of the population while Muslims comprise the second largest religious group and 14.2 per cent of India's population (approximately 172 million people, the second largest Muslim population in the world, after Indonesia). Christians are the next largest grouping, at 2.3 per cent, with Christian populations found across the country, but with greater concentrations in the northeast and in the southern states of Kerala, Tamil Nadu and Goa. Other religious minorities include Sikhs, Buddhists and Jains, which have millions of followers in India but constitute a very small percentage of the total population. (Pew Research Center, 2021). More than 250 million people, or 24 per cent of India's population, belong to Scheduled Castes (SC, also known as Dalits) and Scheduled Tribes. Historically, members of SC communities have been converts from Hinduism to other religions, especially Christianity and Islam, possibly motivated in part to escape caste discrimination. Many continue to face discrimination and other impediments to social advancement. The 2019 amendment to the Citizenship Act, 1955 (Citizenship Amendment Act (CAA)), introduced by the Bharatiya Janata Party (BJP), provides a pathway to citizenship for persecuted religious minorities but excludes Muslims, which led to widespread protests in 2019/20.

Karnataka and Tamil Nadu states: In Karnataka, there are few restrictions on religious minorities; in fact, the main restrictions apply to its majority Hindus. In Tamil Nadu, however, there has been a rise in anti-Christian intimidation, harassment and violence across the state, with 322 anti-Christian incidents between 2011 and mid-2020. Three Muslim-led protests in Tamil Nadu in early 2020 (in response to the CAA) led to arrests by police of a large group from Al Jamaat (a Muslim missionary organization) and 15 other Muslim organizations in Coimbatore city. Some of the Muslims living in Chennai who participated in the research claimed to have been wrongfully arrested on charges of assaulting Hindus under the Unlawful Activities Prevention Act. In the state of Karnataka, consistent with the state–region pattern of religious violence and religious restriction in BJP-controlled states, right-wing Hindu nationalist activists have prompted communal clashes and religion-related violent attacks. On 11 August 2020 violent clashes took place in a Muslim-majority slum in Bangalore, triggered by an inflammatory Facebook post about the Prophet Muhammad, said to have been posted by the nephew of a state legislator of the Indian National Congress.

The selected research sites were slums in north Chennai and north Bangalore, both capital cities of their respective states, to facilitate a deeper understanding of the multi-factor dynamics of urban poverty and well-being in the context of the current COVID-19 pandemic. In Chennai, most slum residents are Dalits, particularly Dalit Muslims who have lived there for decades. They are mostly daily wage labourers who formerly worked in the harbour, at the railway station and as domestic labourers and lost their jobs during the pandemic. North Bangalore has one of the largest concentrations of low-income Muslims and Christians in Karnataka state and is managed by the Indian National Congress Party (the opposition party) municipal council members – relevant for an understanding of political party impact on religious minority experiences.

Nigeria returned to democratic rule in 1999 after 29 years of military rule (1966–99, with a four-year period of civilian rule between 1979 and 1983), followed by an upsurge in sectarian conflicts around boundary and resource control, and ethno-religious divisions. Twelve states in northern Nigeria declared the institution of Sharia Law in 2000, perceived as a protest reaction of the northern elite to the election of the first Christian president and the first president from the south of Nigeria in 20 years. In 2009 Boko Haram, an Islamist fundamentalist sect, launched a series of attacks on government agents and installations as well as on churches and Christian minorities in the northeast. This was the beginning of Boko Haram's violent insurgency against the Nigerian state. Boko Haram terrorists have since extended their attacks to Muslim moderates in opposition to their interpretation of Islam. Following this, both the 2015 and 2019 elections were infused with intense public rhetoric around ethno-religious contestations. These contestations are complicated further by conflicting geopolitical competition for resource control, the presence of an Islamic state, calls for restructuring and secession as well as rising crime, particularly kidnapping, cultism, ritual killings and banditry.

Climate change, increased desertification, and the fallout from intrastate civil strife in the Maghreb region have impacted on the livelihoods of pastoralists. Muslim Fulani cattle herders are moving southwards towards Nigeria's Middle Belt in search of pasture for their herds. Their practice of open grazing has resulted in frequent clashes with Christian farming communities, who accuse them of damaging their crops, while the Fulani themselves claim to have been attacked by gangs from these communities trying to steal their cattle. The situation is aggravated by the proliferation of small arms and light weapons which a presidential committee in 2016 linked to the infiltration of militants and mercenaries across Nigeria's northern borders after regime collapse in Libya and Mali. Beyond these clashes over resources, many Fulani pastoralists have joined Islamist militant groups (for myriad reasons) and, as a result, Fulani-attributed attacks have become more violent – for example, rape, abduction and murder – and more sectarian in nature – for example, targeting Christian religious days and sites. The situation is exacerbated by a lack of prosecution of perpetrators of violence and little or no protection from the federal or state governments. Additionally, President Muhammadu Buhari, who is himself Fulani, is sometimes perceived as being 'soft' on the herders, which deepens political and ethnic divisions.

Plateau and Kaduna states: Plateau state is predominantly Christian, consisting of mainly non-Hausa/non-Fulani indigenous ethnic groups. In

Kaduna, Christian peoples populate the southern part of the state, while Muslims constitute a numeric majority in its central and northern zones. They are also politically dominant in the state. Within the larger context of a predominantly Muslim northern Nigeria, Christians in Plateau and Kaduna states feel victimized by centuries of Islamic domination. Conversely, Muslims who have long settled in Plateau state and southern Kaduna often feel marginalized by Nigeria's indigene/settler polarization engineered by constitutional fault lines. The nation's inability to manage its diversity, the competing quests for political power and the struggle by various ethnic nationalities to protect and maintain cultural/religious distance continue to complicate efforts towards democratic consolidation. In both states, Muslims and Christians lay claim to marginalization and minority status for diverse reasons (Howard et al, 2021). Violence against farming communities has escalated, with Christians particularly badly affected by both Fulani herder and Islamist militant attacks on their villages. According to the Humanitarian Aid Relief Trust, more than a thousand Christians were killed in such attacks between January and November 2019.

Research sites: Ancha and Hukke villages in Miango district of Bassa Local Government Area (LGA) of Plateau state were attacked in April 2020 and, subsequently, the villagers were displaced by Fulani militia. An attack was carried out on 15 April 2020 in Bassa LGA in which suspected herdsmen killed about nine people and razed over 200 houses. In southern Kaduna state, herdsmen militia attacked a community on 11 May 2020, killing many and displacing others. A day after this attack, militants – who often pose as herdsmen – killed 17 people in Gonan Rogo village in Kajuru LGA, Kaduna state.

Iraq is home to a myriad of ethnic, religious and linguistic groups, some of them with an existence that stretches back thousands of years. Governance approaches to management of pluralism has varied over the years from genocidal to tolerance, according to which group is in question. Since 2003, the year of the US-led invasion of the country, the situation has been highly volatile and turbulent, with sectarian politics infusing division and deep faultiness in the polity. Minorites have been particularly vulnerable on account of their numerical disadvantage and many, most notably the Yazidis but also Christians and others, were the target of a genocidal plan on the part of ISIS in 2014. Iraq is a mosaic of ethnic, religious, linguistic and cultural components, the effects of which are still very much felt today. Ninety-nine per cent of Iraqis are Muslim, of whom 60 to 65 per cent are Shia and 32 to 37 per cent are Sunni (Minority Rights Group Country Report, undated). The remaining 1 per cent of the population comprise the following religious minorities: an estimated 350,000 Christians in Iraq, 500,000 Yazidis, 200,000 Kakai, fewer than 5,000 Sabean-Mandaeans and a small number of Bahai (Minority Rights Group Country Report, undated).

Our research was undertaken in two main parts of Iraq where the greatest concentration of religious minorities preside: Baghdad, the capital city, and the area around Ninewa governorate and Erbil, which historically had a large concentration of minorities, a situation that was aggravated by the arrival of hundreds of thousands of displaced persons after the onslaught of ISIS. The sites of research are under two administrations, the Baghdad administration and the Kurdish jurisdiction, which have meant variations in governance of minority affairs as well as in some of the policies and regulations affecting everyday life. For engaging with the realities of the Yazidi minority, research was undertaken in Bashiqa and Behzane – two neighbouring towns which were occupied by ISIS but to which families have begun to return following rehabilitation. The other site was within internally displaced person (IDP) camps in Iraqi Kurdistan (the displaced Essian camp and the Shariya camp in Dohuk). Among those in the camps were survivors, Yazidi women who had been kidnapped and enslaved by ISIS. The research in the latter was undertaken by a peer researcher who is herself a survivor. In terms of the rationale for undertaking two research processes among the Christians, this was done in recognition of the plurality of denominational affiliation and of how, when intertwined with location, this produces slightly differentiated readings of the drivers and outcomes of power configurations on the ground. A significant part of the research was undertaken in the area around the Ninevah valleh (for the Shabak), while for the Sabean-Mandean research was conducted in Baghdad and Erbil, where the few remaining families reside. As the Christian communities vary denominationally, research was undertaken with the Assyrians, many of whom had been displaced from Mosul by ISIS, and research was undertaken with the Chaldean Catholic and Orthodox at Hamdaniyah and Bartella and Ankawa and Erbil. Among all minorities, the lack of safety was a major concern, since they did not have the numbers to protect them in a context where non-state militias are very active.

The top-ranked causes of grievances are interconnected and point to a vicious circle, the lack of personal and communal safety, education and job opportunities, all amplified by religious discrimination, making it more likely that families will try to leave the country. The more families emigrate, the more vulnerable those left behind feel, thereby increasing their desire to leave the country as well.

Pakistan's religious demography is 96.28 per cent Muslims and 3.72 per cent religious minorities, including Christians, Hindus, Ahmadis, Scheduled Castes and others (Sikhs, Parsis, Bhais). A large part of the population of Hindus and Christians in Pakistan reside in Sindh and Punjab, where the great majority of women who belong to these minorities work in both the formal and informal labour sectors, such as in agriculture, sanitation, the brick-kiln industry and as domestic workers. Research among the

Pakistani Christian Dalits was undertaken in Yuhannabad, Lahore, said to be the largest Christian community settlement in Pakistan. Women predominantly worked as domestic servant, factory and sanitation workers. Ninety per cent of Pakistan's Hindu population is poor and marginalized, living across communities of approximately 40 different 'Scheduled [lower] Castes'. The majority of marginalized Hindus live in rural Sindh, where girls and women in households bear a disproportionate share of the work of, and responsibility for, feeding and caring for family members through unpaid household work, alongside collecting firewood, water and fodder and caring for the livestock. Research was undertaken in Karachi, Pakistan's largest city, where women were almost always engaged in working indoors, alongside outside jobs such as being domestic workers (housekeeping), labourers, sanitary workers, sweepers and selling dried fruits and bangles.

Shia account for approximately 10–15 per cent of the Muslim population in Pakistan, which has a largely Sunni Muslim population. Anti-Shia violence, led by extremist militant groups, dates to 1979 and has resulted in thousands being killed and injured in terrorist attacks over the years. Hazara Shia, who are both an ethnic and a religious minority, make an easy target for extremist groups as they are physically distinctive. The majority live in Quetta, the provincial capital of Balochistan in central Pakistan, where the research was undertaken among the largely ghettoized areas.

As for the research on the situation of Ahmediyyas, this presented the most challenges with respect to access on account of duty of care towards members of the community in view of the high risks of putting them in danger. It is a criminal offence in Pakistan for Ahmadi Muslims to express their views and to talk about their religious beliefs in public. Therefore, this research took place outside of Pakistan with a group of Ahmadi Muslims who have fled Pakistan and registered as refugees with the United Nations High Commissioner for Refugees in Thailand, in order to escape the extreme persecution facing them in their home country. The research was carried out through focus group discussions with economically excluded Ahmadi women and men using open-ended questions and participatory ranking by a leading member of the Ahmadiyya community.

Structure of the book

The book is organized into country sections. For each country context, we have assembled three chapters: one academic piece, which provides a more detailed account of the research setting and process and reflects on the benefits of using participatory methodologies to research FoRB in the particular context, with reference to wider literature; and two practitioner pieces, which provide more in-depth, personal accounts of the experience of using these methods in their context with a particular group experiencing religious and other inequalities. These accounts are personal, emotional, sometimes lyrical and consistently powerful. The combination of these pieces provides deep, nuanced, situated insights into the intersectional impact of religious inequalities with other inequalities, in the lives of different groups, but also into the participants' courage and faith. The pieces also provide a fascinating account of how participatory methods can be applied, and how they are experienced by researchers, in contexts of encroachments on religious freedoms.

Our rationale for this structure is that we wanted to show the relevance and usefulness of these methods in their application to FoRB for readers across a broad range of perspectives and positions — such as academics, activists, practitioners, policy makers and so forth — while also recognizing that many of the contributors are scholar–practitioners, and that this distinction between 'academic' and 'practitioner' is a construct which does not always apply. To clarify, we wanted the 'practitioner' pieces to provide insights into practical ways in which the methods were used and adapted in highly challenging contexts, to describe the steps in sufficient clarity for the reader to understand how the methods are applied and the contextual adaptations and challenges that were navigated. The 'academic' pieces show the conceptual contribution to FoRB that the methods have enabled, as well as discussing how the application of participatory methods to FoRB contributes to our knowledge about the dynamic application of participatory methods.

What informed our conception of the book in terms of engaging with participatory methods for understanding religious otherization through this combination of academic and practitioner-oriented pieces was thus ontological as much as practical. Ontologically, we wanted to show that the application of participatory methods to understand religious inequalities generates knowledge from among the practitioners themselves about the nature of FoRB. In other words, we wanted to show how a grounded approach to theorization can reveal insights about the phenomenon of FoRB itself. On a practical level, we wanted to show the relevance and usefulness of these methods in their application to FoRB, when they are adapted and tailored to different contexts. The authors' descriptions of how they engaged with participatory methods in these highly volatile contexts are not intended to be prescriptive or present a blueprint for action. However, it is hoped that some of the tips and insights the authors offer in their chapters prove to be useful for readers designing their own participatory inquiries into religious otherization in their own contexts.

Notes

[1] It is acknowledged later in this introduction that these figures are contested.

2. Salt winning is a small-scale artisanal activity through which salt is collected as sea water evaporates from small pools around the shore of the lagoon.
3. In particular, 'rivers of life', group inquiry, participatory ranking and action research (all described in Part IV of this chapter).
4. I am grateful to Dr Elizabeth Monier, who coined the term 'minoritiness'.

References

Bharadwaj, S., Howard, J. and Narayanan, P. (2021) Using Participatory Action Research Methodologies for Engaging and Researching with Religious Minorities in Contexts of Intersecting Inequalities, CREID Working Paper 5, Coalition for Religious Equality and Inclusive Development, Brighton: Institute of Development Studies.

Bielefeldt, H., and Schirrmacher, T. (2017) Freedom of Religion or Belief Thematic Reports of the UN Special Rapporteur 2010–2016, Bonn: Verlag für Kultur und Wissenschaft.

Birdsall, J., and Beaman, L. (2020) 'Faith in numbers: can we trust quantitative data on religious affiliation and religious freedom?', *The Review of Faith and International Affairs*, 18(3): 60–68, DOI: 10.1080/15570274.2020.1795401.

Bradbury, H., and Reason, P. (2003) 'Action research: an opportunity for revitalizing research purpose and practices', *Qualitative Social Work*, 2(2): 155–75.

Burns, D., and Worsley, S. (2015) *Navigating Complexity in International Development: Facilitating Sustainable Change at Scale*, Rugby: Practical Action Publishing.

Burns, D., Howard, J. and Ospina, S.M. (eds) (2021) *The SAGE Handbook of Participatory Research and Inquiry*, vol. 1, London: SAGE.

Chancel, L., Piketty, T., Saez, E. and Zucman, G. (2021) *World Inequality Report 2022*, World Inequality Lab, Paris: Paris School of Economics.

Cram, F. (2009) 'Maintaining indigenous voices', in D.M. Mertens and P.E. Ginsberg (eds) *The Handbook of Social Research Ethics*, Thousand Oaks, CA/London: SAGE, pp 308–22.

Denning, S., Scriven, R. and Slatter, R. (2020) 'Three participatory geographers: reflections on positionality and working with participants in researching religions, spiritualities, and faith', *Social and Cultural Geography*, DOI: 10.1080/14649365.2020.1815826.

Dick, B. (2021) 'Facilitating participatory research', in D. Burns, J. Howard and S.M. Ospina (eds) *The SAGE Handbook of Participatory Research and Inquiry*, vol. 1, London: SAGE, pp 207–19.

Dwyer, C., Beinart, K., and Ahmed, N. (2018) 'My life is but a weaving: embroidering geographies of faith and place', *Cultural Geographies*, 26: 113–40.

Engler, S., and Stausberg, M. (eds) (2022) *The Routledge Handbook of Research Methods in the Study of Religion*, London: Routledge.

Esteva, G. (2022) 'The path towards the dialogue of vivires (lived experiences)', in *Gustavo Esteva*, G. Esteva, *A Critique of Development and Other Essays*, New York/Abingdon: Routledge, pp 132–54.

Facer, K., and Enright, B. (2016) *Creating Living Knowledge: The Connected Communities Programme, Community-University Partnerships and the Participatory Turn in the Production of Knowledge*, Bristol: University of Bristol/AHRC/Connected Communities.

Fox, J. (2016) *The Unfree Exercise of Religion: A World Survey of Discrimination against Religious Minorities*, Cambridge: Cambridge University Press.

Gatti, M., Annicchino, P., Birdsall, J., Fabretti, V. and Ventura, M. (2019) 'Quantifying persecution: developing an international law-based measurement of freedom of religion or belief', *The Review of Faith and International Affairs*, 17(2): 87–96.

Guy, B., and Arthur, B. (2021) 'Feminism and participatory research: exploring intersectionality, relationships, and voice in participatory research from a feminist perspective', in D. Burns, J. Howard and S.M. Ospina (eds) *The SAGE Handbook of Participatory Research and Inquiry*, vol. 1, London: SAGE, pp 93–107.

Higginbottom, G., and Liamputtong, P. (eds) (2015) *Participatory Qualitative Research Methodologies in Health*, London: SAGE.

Howard, J., Para-Mallam, O., Dayil, P.B., Best, K., Mang, G., Abubakar, D., Muazu, R., Sabo, A., Joshua, S., Saeel, S., Hayap, P., Danfulani-Tsilpi, C., Samuel, C., Katung, K., Saulawa, H., Yakassai, M., Babangida, K. and Galla, A. (2021) Understanding Intersecting Vulnerabilities Experienced by Religious Minorities Living in Poverty in the Shadows of COVID-19, CREID Intersections Series; Religious Inequalities and COVID-19, Coalition for Religious Equality and Inclusive Development, Brighton: Institute of Development Studies, DOI: 10.19088/CREID.2021.012

Hyslop, D. (2021) 'Interpeace's experience with participatory action research in conflict and post-conflict contexts', in D. Burns, J. Howard and S.M. Ospina (eds) *The SAGE Handbook of Participatory Research and Inquiry*, vol. 1, London: SAGE, pp 339–52.

ILO (2022) *World Employment and Social Outlook: Trends 2022*, Geneva: International Labour Organization.

Kaptani, E., Erel, U., O'Neill, M. and Reynolds, T. (2021) 'Methodological innovation in research: participatory theater with migrant families on conflicts and transformations over the politics of belonging', *Journal of Immigrant and Refugee Studies*, 19(1): 68–81.

Lewin, T., and Shaw, J. (2021) 'Collective becoming: visual and performative methodologies for participatory research', in D. Burns, J. Howard and S.M. Ospina (eds), The SAGE Handbook of Participatory Research and Inquiry, vol. 2, London: SAGE, pp 711–22.

Maguire, P. (1987) *Doing Participatory Research: A Feminist Approach*, Amherst, MA: Center for International Education, School of Education, University of Massachusetts.

Marshall, K. (2021) Towards Enriching Understandings and Assessments of Freedom of Religion or Belief: Politics, Debates, Methodologies, and Practices, CREID Working Paper 6, Coalition for Religious Equality and Inclusive Development, Brighton: Institute of Development Studies, 10.19088/CREID.2021.001.

Minority Rights Group Country Report, https://minorityrights.org/country/iraq/ [accessed 1 December 2022]

Mosse, D. (2018) 'Caste and development: contemporary perspectives on a structure of discrimination and advantage', *World Development*, 110: 422–36.

O'Cathain, A., Murphy, E. and Nicholl, J. (2010) 'Three techniques for integrating data in mixed methods studies', *British Medical Journal*, 341: c4587.

Ospina, S., Burns, D. and Howard, J. (2021) 'Navigating the complex and dynamic landscape of participatory research and inquiry', in D. Burns, J. Howard and S.M. Ospina (eds), *The SAGE Handbook of Participatory Research and Inquiry*, vol. 1, London: SAGE, pp 3–16.

Petersen, J. (2022) *Leave No One Behind: Briefing Paper Number 11: Freedom of Religion or Belief and the Sustainable Development Goals*, Copenhagen: Freedom of Religion or Belief Leadership Network and the Danish Institute for Human Rights.

Petersen, P., and Marshall, K. (2019) *The International Promotion of Freedom of Religion or Belief: Sketching the Contours of a Common Framework*, Copenhagen: The Danish Institute for Human Rights. Available at: https://www.humanrights.dk/sites/humanrights.dk/files/media/dokumenter/udgivelser/research/2019/rapport_internationalpromotion_12.pdf

Pew Research Center (2019) *A Closer Look at How Religious Restrictions Have Risen around the World*, Washington, DC: Pew Research Center.

Pew Research Center (2021) 'Religious Composition of India', Washington, DC: Pew Research Center, https://www.pewresearch.org/religion/2021/09/21/religious-composition-of-india/

Reason, P., and Gayá Wicks, P. (2009) 'Initiating action research', *Action Research*, 7(3): 243–62.

Rendón, L.I. (2012) *Sentipensante (Sensing/Thinking) Pedagogy: Educating for Wholeness, Social Justice and Liberation*. Sterling, VA: Stylus.

Santamaria Chavarro, A. (2022) *De sabedoras y sakus en el posacuerdo: educación intercultural para la paz con mujeres indígenas en la Sierra Nevada de Santa Marta y la Amazonia colombiana*. Bogotá: Universidad del Rosario.

Shah, T., Franck, M., and Farr, T. (2012) *Religious Freedom, Why Now? Defending an Embattled Human Right: The Witherspoon Institute Task Force on International Religious Freedom*. Princeton, NJ: Witherspoon Institute.

Shaheed, A. (2020) Interim report of the Special Rapporteur on freedom of religion or belief: elimination of all forms of religious intolerance. Presented at 75th session of the UN General Assembly, Available at: https://www.ohchr.org/en/documents/thematic-reports/a75385-interim-report-special-rapporteur-freedom-religion-or-belief

Shaw, J., Howard, J. and Franco, E.L. (2020) 'Building inclusive community activism and accountable relations through an intersecting inequalities approach', *Community Development Journal*, 55(1): 7–25.

Shah, T., Franck, M., and Farr, T. (2012) *Religious Freedom, Why Now? Defending an Embattled Human Right: The Witherspoon Institute Task Force on International Religious Freedom*. Princeton, NJ: Witherspoon Institute.

Smith, L.T. (2021) *Decolonizing Methodologies: Research and Indigenous Peoples*, London: Bloomsbury.

Stewart, F. (2005) 'Horizontal inequalities: a neglected dimension of development', in *Wider Perspectives on Global Development*, London: Palgrave Macmillan, pp 101–35.

Stewart, F. (2008) 'Horizontal inequalities and conflict: an introduction and some hypotheses', in *Horizontal Inequalities and Conflict*, London: Palgrave Macmillan, pp 3–24.

Tadros, M. (2013) Promoting and Protecting Religious Diversity in the Middle East, IDS Rapid Response Briefing 5, Brighton: Institute of Development Studies.

Tadros, M. (2020) Invisible Targets of Hatred: Socioeconomically Excluded Women from Religious Minority Backgrounds, CREID Working Paper 2, Coalition for Religious Equality and Inclusive Development, Brighton: Institute of Development Studies.

Tadros, M. (ed.) (2022) *What about Us? Global Perspectives on Redressing Religious Inequalities*, Brighton: Institute of Development Studies.

Tadros, M., and Sabates-Wheeler, R. (2020) Inclusive Development: Beyond Need not Creed, CREID Working Paper 1, Brighton: Coalition for Religious Equality and Inclusive Development, Institute of Development Studies.

Tadros, M., Shahab, S. and Quinn-Graham, A. (2022) Violence and Discrimination against Women of Religious Minority Backgrounds in Iraq, Intersections Series, Brighton: Institute of Development Studies, Available at: https://opendocs.ids.ac.uk/opendocs/bitstream/handle/20.500.12413/17780/CREID_Intersections_Iraq.pdf?sequence=1&isAllowed=y

Toma, S., and Zaya, O. (2022) Violence and Discrimination against the Assyrian People in the Kurdistan Region of Iraq, Brighton: CREID, Institute of Development Studies.

Wickenden, M., and Franco, E.L. (2021) 'Don't leave us out: disability inclusive participatory research – why and how?', in D. Burns, J. Howard and S.M. Ospina (eds) *The SAGE Handbook of Participatory Research and Inquiry*, vol. 1, London: SAGE, pp 321–38.

Williams, A. (2017) 'Residential ethnography, mixed loyalties, and religious power: ethical dilemmas in faith-based addiction treatment', *Social & Cultural Geography*, 18: 1016–38.

Yousef, Y., and Butti, N. (2022) The Lived Experiences of Marginalised Christian Chaldean Catholic and Orthodox Women and Their Families in Iraq, Brighton: CREID, Institute of Development Studies.

India

2

Participatory Methods and the Freedom of Religion or Belief

Rebecca Shah and Timothy Shah

For scholars, activists and practitioners, particularly those who have adopted a 'decolonial' turn in their work and practice, participatory methods are useful, portable and accessible tools of representation and analysis. For example, participatory methodology is congruent with Audra Simpson's (2007) concern that scholars pay attention to 'what people say', instead of 'writing away from and to dominant forms of knowing' (Simpson, 2007: 68). It is what the marginalized and restricted themselves believe, think and feel, in other words, rather than dominant discourses or prevailing centres of knowledge production, that should set the terms of the discussion. Participatory methods are a highly effective way to serve this simultaneously epistemic and ethical aspiration. Yet very little (Bharadwaj, Howard and Narayanan, 2020) has been written on the application of participatory methodologies to freedom of religion or belief (FoRB), and, specifically, on their relevance to the task of clarifying how the protection of FoRB might promote the overall flourishing and well-being of the poorest and most marginalized members of the human family.

This chapter explores the value and suitability of participatory action research methods for protecting and promoting FoRB. Funded by the Coalition for Religious Equality and Inclusive Development (CREID) at the University of Sussex, our research is based on our experiences working with religious minority communities in India during the current COVID-19 pandemic.

In this chapter, we will first introduce how and why we employed participatory methods in our research in the Indian context. We will then provide a broad evaluation of participatory methods and the role they played in our research in India. Our analysis and evaluation will focus on the potential contributions of participatory methods to understanding and safeguarding the dignity of marginalized individuals, and to protecting and enhancing that fundamental spiritual freedom – the freedom of religion or belief – that is an indispensable foundation and component of their human dignity and all-around flourishing.

The location

The River of Life participant methodology was combined with a participant ranking method and employed among 12 groups of Dalit men and women in two urban-poor slums in Bangalore and Chennai in South India.[1] In each city, the inquiry groups were segregated based on gender and religion. Facilitators were of the same gender and were mostly drawn from the same religious tradition. In Chennai, while a majority of the Dalit Christian women (90 per cent) were converted to independent forms of Pentecostalism, the facilitator, Lata John, was a Catholic Christian who had extensive experience working with these women in the slum.[2] The Chennai-based groups met in a low-income neighbourhood of Korukkupet in northern Chennai.

The Chennai Sample

The city of Chennai (formerly Madras) is divided into four zones: south, north, central and southeast. The northern part of the sprawling city has significantly more slums than any of the other zones. In 2016, the Tamil Nadu Slum Clearance Board (TNSCB) conducted a survey as part of its slum-free city plan and it was found that north Chennai has 470 out of the 1,131 slums in the city. While this is still a significant undercount, it gives us a picture of the level of poverty and deprivation in this part of the city. Most of the residents of the slums in Korukkupet live on land that is unhealthy and environmentally unsafe. Open sewers run beside their dwellings, and there is limited access to clean running water. While some of the single-room houses are made of brick and cement, most of them do not have a *patta* (legal title), which leaves residents vulnerable to eviction and land-grabbing by politicians and local gangs. As part of its ongoing election promise, the current state government has expressed concerns about the condition of the homes and sanitation in the slum and has planned to 'resettle' the residents within the next six to eight months.

The Muslim inquiry groups drew their participants from another north Chennai slum, called Vyasarpadi. The Vyasarpadi slum is one of the oldest slums in the city. Most of the residents of the slum are Dalits, including large numbers of Dalit Muslims who have lived there for decades. The slum is in a low-lying area of the city and suffers from frequent flooding during the monsoons. Most of the homes do not have electricity connections, safe water or sanitation. A scarcity of primary health clinics means that residents are forced to go outside the slum for decent healthcare. As is the case with the residents of the Korukkupet slum, government officials have ordered Vyasarpadi slum-dwellers to vacate their current three-storey tenements while the government constructs 13-storey housing blocks. Most residents have resisted the government order and fear forced eviction.

The Bangalore sample

All the Inquiry Groups (IGs), including comparator groups and semi-structured interviews, were conducted in a collection of slums in north Bangalore. Nestled beneath a high-speed flyover that links the downtown business district and the Kempegowda Bangalore International airport are a collection of three low-income urban neighbourhoods. They are Lingarajapuram, Sait Palya and New Lingarajapuram. Our study respondents were drawn from these three neighbourhoods. A majority of the inhabitants belong to Dalit (or 'untouchable') backgrounds and speak Tamil, Kannada, Urdu and English.

Following the initiation of India's economic liberalization policies in 1991, Bangalore saw the creation of special economic zones whereby government incentives were used to attract information technology (IT) and electronic companies to the city. In the early 1990s, Bangalore opened its first 'Electronic City', located on some 330 acres of prime land along the highway linking the state of Karnataka with the neighbouring state of Tamil Nadu. Electronic City became a hub for over 200 IT companies, including international firms such as Bosch and General Electric. Bangalore thus developed a reputation as the 'Silicon Valley of South Asia', drawing thousands of software engineers and IT specialists.

Spurred on by a booming global IT-driven economy, Bangalore has seen a dramatic rise in land prices as well as housing prices and, consequently, an acute lack of affordable housing. Lower- and middle-income wage earners were asked to leave their homes so large-scale apartment complexes could be erected to house the growing numbers of workers arriving in the city from across India. Since 2001, the population living in tenement housing in Bangalore has tripled, with at least two to three hundred large slums dotted across the city. This rapid increase in the slum population in Bangalore is also a result of increased rural–urban migration from northern Karnataka. A study conducted by Duke University in 2018 found that Bangalore had over 2,000 slums, while the government only recognized 597 (Rains,

Krishna and Wibbels, 2019, cited in Rains, Krishna and Wibbels, 2019). Most of the slums exist on prime real estate in the centre of the city and face the risk of being demolished, should the government decide to sell the land to developers.

Our examination of the three large slums in our sample area reveals that the majority of dwellings are a mix of informal shelters, in which families live under blue plastic tarpaulin roofs, and one-room dwellings with mud floors and asbestos roofs. Most families in Bangalore's slums spend their entire lives living under tarpaulin roofs, mainly because of the extraordinarily high cost of housing in those areas of the city where jobs are available and where the slums are now established.

How and why we used participatory methodology in our investigation

Scholars and development practitioners in the Global South wish to understand and engage with issues of freedom and flourishing in a proactive manner, drawing on the authentic perspectives and experiences of their own contexts, and not simply on the terms set by Western agencies, discourses and agendas. After all, authentic human freedom and authentic human flourishing, by definition, require that individuals and communities enjoy dignity, agency and freedom from undue domination, coercion and manipulation. Furthermore, religious leaders and communities in Asia, Africa and Latin America wish to be involved in leading and guiding a genuine conversation about FoRB, which – if it is to be a true conversation and dialogue – cannot be dominated or dictated by organizations and governments from more economically and politically powerful regions of the world. At the same time, we need to acknowledge that actors in the Global South can also wield power over the vulnerable in unhelpful ways, yielding their own forms of subjugation and subordination. This can of course characterize the exercise of power by religious leaders in the Global South as well.

To support and inform a genuine conversation about authentic human freedom and flourishing, we believe that it is imperative to employ methodologies that are designed to respect the integrity and dignity of marginalized individuals and communities and, ultimately, to empower them to shape and even lead a global conversation about FoRB. Such a truly global conversation, including voices from South Asia as central contributors, is all the more important and urgent in light of rising restrictions on FoRB across the globe in general and on the Indian subcontinent in particular. Furthermore, participatory methods became particularly relevant and appropriate in the last two years, as many marginalized communities became subject to yet more acute governmental and social restrictions and pressures during the COVID-19 pandemic – restrictions and pressures that caused many of these communities to experience even greater levels of marginalization, voicelessness and helplessness than they do in 'normal' times.

In other words, our interest in adopting the participatory methodologies to gather information on the impact of COVID-19 on religious minorities in India did not grow out of an isolated interest in matters of research methodology. Rather, we started with a strong conviction, enhanced by an accumulation of first-hand experiences, that participatory methods (such as the River of Life exercise) could highlight the lived experiences of marginalized communities, including religious minorities and Dalit Hindus, and that such methods could empower them to find their own voice, speak up and challenge the power structures and dynamics that constrained their ability to thrive before and after the pandemic.

The participatory methods we employed were drawn from a cluster of methods available to social scientists and practitioners. In incorporating these methods into our research, we combined genuine participant inquiry with an awareness of an ethical responsibility to cast a critical spotlight on prevailing social, political, and discursive patterns that contribute to the marginalization of low-income minority communities. Among these social, political and discursive patterns, we included established and privileged discourses around FoRB in India, which we did not take for granted and about which we invited critical attention and scrutiny instead. To that extent, we deliberately employed available participatory methods to enlarge both our ethical imagination and our epistemic understanding concerning what it means to be human. This required asking what it means to be a human being who is socially, politically and economically disrespected and diminished, especially amid the upheaval and distress brought about by COVID-19, and yet *simultaneously* deeply religious and drawn to the transcendent and to ultimate sources of dignity, freedom and flourishing.

As such, with the guidance of the leaders and scholars associated with the Coalition for Religious Equality and Inclusive Development (CREID), we employed and adapted certain participatory methods to empower Dalit women and men of diverse religious backgrounds – Muslim, Christian and Hindu – to shine their own critical spotlight on their own social reality. We consciously undertook a wholeheartedly participatory approach, to increase our own understanding of the context and intersecting challenges of the religiously, socially and economically marginalized in India. At the same time, because we invited our participants to serve as intellectual collaborators and leaders of our inquiry group discussions, we pursued an equally important objective: namely, to invite and encourage our interlocutors to view themselves as agents capable of assessing, challenging and changing at least some features of their social, religious and cultural context.

Unlike the regimented and bounded reach of traditional methods, such as structured and semi-structured interviews, the participatory methodological approach of using a reasonably flexible and open method of inquiry such as the River of Life drawing exercise was designed to encourage local voices to be expressed, with as little external direction as possible. Inquiry group participants were gathered and asked to draw their lives as rivers flowing through the period before COVID-19 and continuing through the pandemic period. Participants were then asked to pictorially depict whatever 'enablers' and 'challenges' they may have faced along their River of Life, in whatever way they wished. After the drawing exercise was over, the participants were asked to rank various factors that either helped or hindered them over the past couple of years during the pandemic. The facilitator then summarized the factors the group identified as having 'enabled' or 'constrained' their lives before and during the COVID-19 pandemic. In two other chapters in this book, which include detailed interviews with Lata John and Laila Khan, we explore in detail the reasons why we found the participatory methods we employed – particularly participatory drawing – to be highly effective, inclusive and appropriate for the marginalized and often illiterate minorities in our sample area.

What is the value and suitability of the methodology for protecting and promoting FoRB?

Drawing on our experience working with minority communities in India, including Dalits, during the COVID-19 pandemic, this section will highlight the potential effectiveness and suitability of participatory methods in general and the River of Life methodology in particular. Specifically, we will unpack and explore their fitness relative to the purpose of acquiring insight into the role of FoRB in the lives of the poor during the pandemic.

Moving backward to moving forward: can participatory methods help the poor navigate their way out of poverty?

Launched at a time of significant economic, social and spiritual upheaval, the research was deliberately forward-looking and aimed at identifying and addressing the problems and issues our participants perceived as significant. Consequently, our facilitators had to be patient and wait for key issues to emerge from the focus group discussions. For many participants, the focus group gatherings were the first time in months that they had met other people in the neighbourhood. Therefore, the very act of gathering and recreating an in-person community was restorative and empowering, and, in and of itself, demonstrated the utility and credibility of our interactive approach, both to our facilitators and to our participants. This reflected the broader lesson that our use of participatory methods helped to give our participants some basic tools – and added confidence – for developing their strategies for negotiating the severe constraints they confronted during the pandemic. The community itself, it became clear, was one of our participants' most important tools and strategies for responding to COVID-19 as well as other challenges.

During the River of Life exercise, individuals from deeply marginalized communities living in some of the most crowded slums in Chennai and Bangalore were asked to draw their life shortly before and during the pandemic. None of the participants had ever been a part of such an exercise, and few, if any of them, had held a pencil for years. Yet here they were, ready to begin to draw their 'River of Life' – or, in the case of one of the men in Chennai, a 'road of life'. The following is an excerpt from this man's 'road of life' description:

David: I drew myself as a vehicle. Since I drew myself as a vehicle, I have coloured it green just to show that 2019 is happy, to be green, right? My start in 2019 was good. It was going smoothly without any problems. But looking back at that curfew in 2020, things were still going a little better at the time. But a bit of unemployment started in the month of May. I am a daily wager. I did not work at all during the heavy curfew. Then, see these two ditches that come across my way as my vehicle goes on the road. One ditch is unemployment, the other is the house rent problem. Both are major problems in my life.

Facilitator: What is this black line that you have drawn on the road?

David: The black line indicates sadness. Life has become so frustrating. When I look at why this has happened, I have lost something in my life. One thing I was looking for was God and my church. My car, which is my life, did not run, just stopped. But then I got to go to church. That's what red is for. I put it in front of me like a cart pulling mine. My vehicle started to run which had stopped because my God and my prayer and even my church were there. God was with me.[3]

The excerpt illustrates the sudden and disastrous impact of the pandemic on the lives of daily wage labourers such as David. Yet David used a stark, dramatic black line to depict what he described as his darkest sadness: the loss of his freedom to go to church and, for him, the irreplaceable access church attendance gave him to the Transcendent. When religious institutions were shut down during the lockdown for more than six months, David writes, 'My car, which is my life, did not run.' David's experience is not an isolated one. Dalit Muslim men who could not go to the mosque during Ramzan, spoke of being 'depressed', because the mosque was the only place they felt at peace. Such findings are of utmost significance, for they reveal that the FoRB in the experience of our participants is not an isolated 'right' or 'liberty' in some catalogue of human rights. Instead, FoRB is a multi-dimensional resource or stock of fungible capital – spiritual, moral, psychological and emotional capital – without which their overall resilience and ability to cope with COVID-19 and its panoply of consequences was drastically diminished. Restrictions on FoRB, therefore, were not an isolated harm, but helped drive an interactive vicious cycle in which a lack of access to the Transcendent and religious community rendered our poor and marginalized participants less able to bear their new suffering and respond creatively to it.

As the transcript above indicates, the role of the facilitator in all the focus group discussions was to wait on the participants to share their own experiences and insights, in their own words. But the facilitator's role was also to offer questions and interventions at the right moment to encourage participants to identify what factors might help them to go forward rather than backward along their river of life. The visual tool of the River of Life, with its river (or road) running across the years, invites participants to look backward and forward along the flow of their lives, and dramatizes that their lives are not static, fixed or imprisoned within a single episode. This helped them to see that no single episode – even one as difficult as the pandemic – permanently defines or constrains their lives, but that every episode is a passage to navigate.

That the participatory methodology compelled the researcher and the focus group to review the past few traumatic months, which then forced them back in time to relive the sometimes traumatic difficulties of being locked down and isolated, underscores the broader fact that the method compelled the 'data-gathering' facilitators to do more than collect data or extract information from de-personalized 'subjects'. The methodology encouraged and enabled the facilitators not simply to intervene by asking questions and seeking responses of their own, but rather in a sense to be immersed in the research process 'not [just] attentionally but intentionally' (Ingold, 2013).

To truly examine the ravages of the pandemic in the lives of the poor, particularly those who belonged to Dalit and minority religious communities, required that the facilitator trade places with the participants, inviting the participants to lead and drive their conversation. Our research objectives and methods required, as Tim Ingold states, to 'observe from inside' (Ingold, 2013: 389). This meant that the facilitator had to come to grips with the nature and level of restrictions on freedom of religion or belief in the lives of the participants. But the facilitator also had to feel and attend to their frustration and pain. The imperative to ensure that the data we collected was reliable and credible was one we embraced wholeheartedly, partly because we were conscious that what we found did, and does, have the potential to shape policy. Indeed, we collected important information about indebtedness, financial insecurity, hunger, depression and the many problems facing vulnerable groups during the COVID-19 pandemic. Yet, even as we collected and quantified reliable data using the rating matrix and other tools, the researchers and facilitators of the focus groups were encouraged to empathize with the overall subjective experiences of the participants as complete human beings.[4] The facilitators belonged to the same gender and the same religious community as the participants in the slums, which made it less difficult for them to identify with the perspectives and experiences of participants.

Decolonizing data: are participatory methods a way to inclusive and community-driven change after COVID?

Broad progress on development requires policies that will help the poor identify and overcome internal and external constraints on their ability to lift themselves out of poverty. So too with FoRB. The methods of data-gathering that are so important for policy making, however, should be shaped by an intimate understanding of the dynamics of the groups in ways that recognize potential sources of conflict that limit and constrain FoRB, particularly for the very poor and marginalized. For example, during the participant ranking exercise, Dalit Hindu men ranked 'police violence' and 'goondaism' ('goonda' is the Tamil word for thug or criminal), as key challenges inhibiting progress in the slum. At first glance, one would expect police violence to be directed primarily at religious minority communities such as Dalit Muslims and Dalit Christians. Indeed, our data from Bangalore suggests that fear of the police is a significant concern for Dalit Muslims in the city. Yet in Chennai neither Dalit Muslims nor Dalit Christians identified police violence or 'goondaism' as a troubling factor during the pandemic.

The responsibility to protect vulnerable communities such as Dalit Hindus and Dalit Muslims demands that we pay close attention to the context in order to properly shape interventions globally, nationally and, most importantly, locally. Our participatory ranking exercise paid deliberate attention to nitty-gritty, ground-level details, incorporating close attention to the local context and employing facilitators in Chennai and Bangalore belonging to the same neighbourhood, religion and gender as the participants.

Our approach was qualitatively different in both spirit and method from some traditional data-gathering exercises undertaken during the pandemic to gather information on religion and COVID-19. While the aims of some of these data-gathering schemes are to provide data to practitioners and scholars across the globe to develop context-appropriate and timely interventions, including policies, which help the poor and marginalized, much of the data is extracted from communities, including vulnerable communities, in a purely impersonal process involving neither interaction with nor the consent of the populations from whom data is collected. Furthermore, the knowledge that is 'curated' by Western scholars and development practitioners, ostensibly to aid vulnerable communities during the COVID-19 pandemic, is generated and utilized from the extracted data without any involvement or input from the rightful owners. The irony here is that although development agencies, scholars and practitioners are making concerted efforts to decolonize aid, they often ignore this aspiration when it comes to gathering data from the Global South. This extraction of data over the past few decades in general, and during COVID-19 in particular, recreates a different kind of power imbalance between the data collectors, often in the West or part of Western institutions, and the rightful data owners in the South.

Over the course of our research, the participatory methods that were used to collect data in India sought to empower rather than disempower the poor, even as the main aim of the participant ranking exercise was to describe and document their experiences with a view to converting the key results of our conversations into data-gathering exercises destined to yield results and create quantifiable matrices that would inform policy documents and briefings. And this brings us to the core difference between the suite of data-gathering participatory methods and the traditional data collection methods that occur in isolation from the rightful data owners in the countries and communities in the South. In most cases, data collectors who employ traditional extractive data gathering methods create systems and promote ideologies that justify their appropriation of data in the name of rigour and data quality that, it is claimed, are needed for proper project management and evaluation. However, from our experience, good-quality, quantifiable data on the challenges and enablers that most affected vulnerable populations at the height of the pandemic was achievable with deliberate effort and patience on the part of the trained facilitators who spent time explaining how the ranking exercise works and the ways in which the community could benefit from the data that was gathered.

Consider the following discussion between the facilitator and the Dalit Muslim men in Chennai, who discussed how they might quantify the various factors that helped or enabled them during the pandemic:

Facilitator (looking at Ijaz):	How much do you want me to put beside help from the Jamaad (Mosque/religious community)?
Hassan:	In Jammad, they helped me, sir. You can put 3.[5]
Facilitator (looking around the room):	Your group has identified 'friends' as supports during COVID, what should I put here?
Ijaz:	3! Because they always gave me things in my time of need.
Facilitator:	OK, I have the government down here, what do I put down?
Ijaz:	They gave me 2,000 rupees, so you can put down 1 or 0 – only because they gave us our own money back (laughing).

The discussion between the facilitator and Ijaz during the ranking exercise, which was part of our mixed-method approach to gathering data during the pandemic, illustrates the way in which the Dalit Muslim participants (Hassan and Ijaz, in this case) were deeply involved in the quantification and evaluation of factors and categories that supported his community members during the pandemic. The participative ranking methodology employed in Chennai and Bangalore was an important tool that can enable policy makers to determine how and where vulnerable communities were assisted and supported during the pandemic, based on what members of these communities actually saw and experienced.

Meanwhile, it is likely that the data being gathered and analysed via the traditional methods employed by Western universities and think tanks will be used to inform the policies of governments and international aid agencies, public and private, and, in the process, that it will be used to determine how and where aid money flows. In this way, traditional research extracts data *from* communities, without their consent or involvement, but then shapes policies and decisions concerning how money and other resources flow *to* these communities. This being the case, if 'no taxation without representation' is a foundational principle of democratic politics, perhaps 'no data collection without representation' should be a foundational principle of responsible research, especially since how data is collected, analysed and utilized can significantly affect the well-being and governance of vulnerable communities.

Traditional research methods that extract data with a minimum of personal interaction or dialogue with research 'subjects' are problematic for the additional reason that they are particularly vulnerable to what

Talal Asad has described as the inherent problems of 'translation' across discourses. Participatory methods place a premium on what participants say and how they say it. On the other hand, as Asad has noted in his seminal work, traditional Western social-scientific methods tend to extract isolated 'data points' from 'foreign discourses' and place them in a Western academic or social discourse in order to make them intelligible and useful in Western terms (Asad, 1986; Asad and Stanford University Press, 2018). This process of translation has the effect of reducing and constraining the lived cultural experiences of 'foreign people', fragmenting, co-opting and assimilating their distinct perspectives and experiences into Western discourses.[6] While this is a risk even in participatory research, participatory methods turn research 'subjects' into active research participants and dialogue partners, forcing the process of research into a higher level of attention and accountability to the lived perspectives and discourses of the individuals and communities being studied.

During the 12 participant ranking exercises conducted in Chennai and Bangalore among male and female participants from Dalit Hindu, Dalit Muslim and Dalit Christian communities, the members of the groups worked collaboratively to prioritize factors that helped or hindered their ability to cope during the pandemic. It was during this exercise that Dalit Muslim men in north Chennai's Vyasarpadi slum identified the indispensable role of religious institutions for poor Dalit Muslims at a time when both societal and governmental restrictions on Muslims were high due to a variety of issues, including the Tablighi Jamaat controversy in Delhi and because Dalit Muslims, despite being lower caste or Dalit, do not qualify for government affirmative action benefits.[7]

The following table shows that help from mosques or Jamaad (religious institutions) ranks far above the help received from secular not-for-profit organizations or from the government. In fact, Dalit Muslim men rank assistance from the government as the lowest level (3) compared to assistance from religious institutions (14) (see Table 2.1). In addition, the collection, analysis and interpretation of the data were owned and driven by the rightful owners – the community of Dalit Muslim men.

The freedom to believe or not to believe: can participatory methods help us understand vulnerable populations on their own terms?

It is crucial to stress, however, that precisely because our participatory methods invited our participants to articulate their own authentic and often critical voices, they did not necessarily encourage or privilege the presentation of perspectives that were culturally or religiously traditional, conventional, popular or pious. For example, the participatory methods that

Table 2.1: Participant ranking of factors that enabled Dalit Muslim men to cope with the pandemic in Vyasarpadi slum in Chennai in March 2021

Serial number	Name	Help from Jamaad/ mosque	Help from friends	Help from relatives	Help from NGOs	Help from the government
1.	Shafi	2	3	0	2	0
2.	Muhammad	1	3	2	0	0
3.	Shyed Farried	2	2	0	0	0
4.	Hassan	0	0	0	0	0
5.	Basha	3	3	0	0	0
6.	Abdul	0	0	0	0	1
7.	Karim	3	0	1	3	1
8.	Khader	3	0	1	3	1
Total		14	11	4	8	3

Note: All names are anonymised.

were employed in our research enabled the Dalit Hindu men in the sample to express the freedom to talk about their religion, and religious experience, in a way that reflected their agency and authenticity.

To illustrate this issue, consider the discussion between the facilitator and a group of Dalit Hindu men who talked about their faith at a time when they were struggling to find food to feed their families:

Facilitator: Tell me about your life, your family, your faith. What have you drawn in your river of life?

Thamodaran: My river here is fresh and broad, but it become dark and narrow after COVID. Religion? Faith? There was only hunger. Hunger, more hunger. When we are in hunger, we forget those philosophies. But food was our basic need at the time, we could only think of finding food. When I have not eaten lunch, whatever was said would not go into my head because I was hungry.

While many of our participants reported that religion was an important and even central reality and source of power and solace during the most difficult periods of the COVID-19 pandemic, some were like Thamodaran. For them, religion was an airy 'philosophy', a luxury, which had little relevance amid the urgent demands of survival.

In another instance, the same group of men mocked the way Hindu temples were locked down during the pandemic:

Facilitator: So, did you go to the temple?
Kumar: The temple was closed, so how could we go? At least we saved our gods from Coronavirus (laughing). Because if lots of people went there and formed a crowd, the god would get COVID. Right?

FoRB includes the freedom to adhere to a religion, but of course it also includes the freedom to critique one's religion and its institutions. However, while it might appear that they were mocking the practices and policies of 'Hinduism' during COVID-19, their statement reflects more disappointment than hostility or impiety. As other moments in the conversation described below underscore, the men were disappointed and even angry that the temples were closed *during a period when they felt they needed their gods most*. The reason that Hindu temples were closed, however, was not because of the decisions of autonomous Hindu leaders or denominations but because of the state-imposed closures of Hindu temples across the country, which in some cases lasted longer than the closures of mosques and churches.

Indeed, the nearly wholesale nationalization and state control of Hindu religious institutions seriously complicated the access of Dalit Hindus to their religious institutions during the pandemic. The following short exchange between the group facilitator and one Dalit Hindu man in Bangalore illustrates this pattern:

Facilitator: What help did you get from your religious community? You said you went to the Mariamma temple on the main road.
Anand: I didn't get any help from the temple.
Facilitator: What do you mean?
Anand: Listen, all the temples were closed, no? The gates were shut. There was a lock on the gate, sir. It was our festival, so I just removed my footwear and bowed down before the God before the closed gates and left … Even when we were bowing before God, the police came and beat us. The police came and warned us that if we stood before the temple, they will arrest us. So, we left.

While many Christian and Muslim participants in our sample reported that they received some form of assistance from their respective religious communities and institutions, Hindus were faced with locked doors and even turned away by police when they approached their temples. The revelation that Hindus faced religious restrictions that were in some respects more serious than the restrictions experienced by Muslims and Christians was but one example of a finding made possible by our use of participatory methods, and an empirical reality in India that has generally been ignored by prevailing Western discourses and traditional research approaches, imprisoned as they tend to be in a discourse framed by the assumption that only religious 'minorities' in India are or can be the victims of serious religious restrictions inimical to human flourishing and development.

Conclusion

To what extent do participatory methods contribute to understanding FoRB and redressing religious inequities among minority and other marginalized communities? Furthermore, to what extent can participatory methods illuminate the role of FoRB in development efforts among the poor and marginalized – for the benefit of the participants being researched, most importantly, but also the benefit of the academic community?

Our use of participatory methods illuminated the reality that, from within the perspectives and priorities of our participants, FoRB tends to be conceptualized and prioritized less as a negative freedom from constraint (tethered to the higher purpose of maximizing personal autonomy, say) and more as a positive freedom or opportunity for intimacy and harmony with Something – or Someone – higher and better. The preservation and promotion of FoRB among the poor and marginalized in India assume meaning and importance in the context of deeply held religious beliefs, practices and the indispensable role of religious institutions in the lives of the poorest and most vulnerable members of the human family. Unlike some conceptions of FoRB that lay particular stress on FoRB as including and requiring a freedom *from* religion, FoRB in the context of the communities we have studied in India is more often understood and sought as the freedom to enjoy access to the Transcendent, in whatever way this transcendent reality might be understood. For our participants, in this context, this freedom *for* religion is the primary reason for protecting FoRB. Furthermore, we found that protecting and promoting FoRB among the poor, marginalized and vulnerable is not merely a matter of protecting an isolated civil liberty or human right but investing in a fungible form of capital, a fund of moral and spiritual resources whereby the poor can, at least potentially, more effectively negotiate and seek to overcome their multi-dimensional deprivations and challenges.

In addition, our participatory methods were able to gather data and document the role of FoRB in the lives of the poor in a manner where the individuals who were being 'evaluated' were not regarded as subjects or objects but as active and engaged participants who were a part of their own data accumulation, analysis and interpretation. One of the greatest advantages of participatory methods in general and the River of Life and ranking exercises we adopted in our work during the current COVID-19 pandemic was how the method harnessed the contextual advantage of working with hard-to-reach populations, including Dalit Muslim women, in very poor slum communities at the height of the pandemic. In short, the use of participatory methods to understand, examine and assess religious restrictions and constraints on freedom of religion or belief (FoRB) holds great promise, both for religious individuals and communities and for the wider conversation about religious freedom across the globe. Applied to the context of FoRB, participatory methodology has the potential to empower and equip religious groups and particularly marginalized religious minorities, so that they might develop and enhance native freedoms and capabilities, including the effective capacity to understand, protect and promote their own deeply held religious beliefs and practices, even amid religious restrictions and opposition.

Notes

[1] You can read more about the facilitators of the focus groups in Chennai by accessing Chapters 3 and 4 in this volume.
[2] Lata John was the facilitator of the Dalit Christian Women's groups in Chennai.
[3] Name changed to protect the identity of respondents.
[4] To discover more about the participant methodology, please see: https://www.alnap.org/system/files/content/resource/files/main/prmmanual-v1-1.pdf.
[5] A ranking of 3 is the highest rank a person could give as part of the participatory ranking exercise.
[6] For an excellent discussion on Talal Asad's understanding of cultural translation, see Fadil (2020).
[7] https://www.aljazeera.com/news/2021/3/25/tablighi-jamaat-members-held-for-spreading-covid-stuck-in-india; https://scroll.in/article/970613/for-70-years-dalits-have-been-denied-freedom-of-religion-through-a-presidential-order.

References

Asad, T. (1986) 'The concept of cultural translation in British social anthropology', in J. Clifford and G.E. Marcus (eds) *Writing Culture: the Poetics and Politics of Ethnography*, Berkeley: University of California Press.

Asad, T. and (2018) *Formations of the Secular: Christianity, Islam, Modernity*, Stanford, CA: Stanford University Press.

Bharadwaj, S., Howard, J. and Narayanan, P. (2020) Using Participatory Action Research Methodologies for Engaging and Researching with Religious Minorities in Contexts of Intersecting Inequalities, *CREID Working Paper 5*, Coalition for Religious Equality and Inclusive Development, Brighton: Institute of Development Studies. Available at: https://opendocs.ids.ac.uk/opendocs/handle/20.500.12413/15896

Fadil, N. (2020) 'On anthropology as translation', *Religion and Society, 11*.

Ingold, T. (2013) 'That's enough about ethnography!' *HAU: Journal of Ethnographic Theory*, 4(1): 383–95.

Lembani, M., de, Pinho, H., Delobelle, P., Zarowsky, C., Mathole, T. and Ager, A. (2020) *A Guide for Participatory Systems Analysis Using a Group Model Building Approach*, London: SAGE.

Rains, E., Krishna, A., and Wibbels, E. (2019) 'Combining satellite and survey data to study Indian slums: evidence on the range of conditions and implications for urban policy', *Environment and Urbanization*, 31(1): 267–92, https://doi.org/10.1177/0956247818798744

Simpson, A. (2007) 'On Ethnographic Refusal: Indigeneity, "Voice", and Colonial Citizenship', *Junctures*, 9: 67–80.

3

The Personal, the Relational and the Community: Researching with Dalit Christian Women in India during COVID-19

Rebecca Shah with Lata John

Introduction

> 'The river is like our lives; we are happy when the river is full and flowing. But then, when our lives are going badly, the river stops. When it rains, the river fills up and then again when the rain stops, the river runs dry.' (River of Life participant in Korukkupet slum, Chennai, southern India)

Situated beside the sewage-laden River Cooum in central Chennai, the Korukkupet slum was the site of a study to assess the impact of the COVID-19 pandemic on marginalized populations in southern India.[1]

In early March 2021, eight women from the Dalit Christian community in Korukkupet gathered in a local community building to share their experiences of living as marginalized minorities during what the *New York Times* newspaper called 'the world's largest Coronavirus lockdown'.[2] On 24 March 2020, with no more than four hours' warning, more than 1.3 billion Indians, including daily-wage labourers like the women seated in the community centre in Korukkupet slum, were informed by Prime Minister Narendra Modi that 'every state, every district, every lane, every village will be under lockdown'.[3]

The nationwide lockdown saw thousands of migrant workers and hundreds of men and women who were dependent on daily wages stream out of major cities and closed bus and railway stations heading on foot towards their villages, many of which were hundreds of miles away from the now desolate urban centres. The Dalit Christian women who assembled at the centre a year after the nationwide lockdown arrived to discuss the ways in which their Christian religious identity influenced their ability to care for themselves and their families. In addition to their religious identity as part of a minority community, the women who participated in the meeting also belonged to Dalit or Scheduled Caste communities. Despite the overall reduction in poverty rates across India in the past ten years, five out of six multidimensionally poor individuals are from lower castes or tribes.[4] People are counted as multidimensionally poor if they are deprived in one-third or more of ten indicators, where each indicator is equally weighted with its dimension.[5]

In Korukkupet, slum residents live near open sewers and with limited access to clean and running water. While some of the single-roomed houses have cement floors and solid brick walls, most residents do not have legal documents to indicate that they own their home, which leaves them vulnerable to eviction by local gangs and land-grabbing politicians. According to the 2011 census, almost one of every five people in Chennai, which is the capital city of the state of Tamil Nadu in southern India, belongs to a Scheduled Caste community. The official data does not consider Scheduled Castes or Dalits who belong to Christian or Muslim religious communities. In other words, close to 25 to 30 per cent of the population of Chennai are Dalits or members of Scheduled Castes. Most of the Dalits in Chennai live in slums like Korukkupet in the northern part of the city.

Purpose of this chapter

This chapter shares the experience of employing participatory methodology by a female Christian researcher working with Dalit Christian women in the Indian city of Chennai. The research sought to highlight the impact of religious identity, particularly the restrictions on the freedom of religion or belief of religious minority communities during the COVID-19 pandemic. While religious minority groups of men and women were the primary focus of the study, the participatory methodology was also used among Dalit Hindu men and women from the same slum communities in order to isolate the impact of religion, including the influence of majority religious traditions, on existing vulnerabilities. The following discussion on the methodology draws on the experiences of eight Dalit Christian women who met in a local community centre in Korukkupet slum in early 2021.

In March 2021 India had just emerged from the first wave of the COVID-19 pandemic. However, there was increasing concern about a second wave that could affect thousands of people, particularly the poor and individuals from marginalized communities who had limited access to vaccination centres. The second wave of the pandemic arrived a month later, in April 2021, and carried the dreadful 'Delta variant', which killed thousands of people due to lack of access to oxygen and suitable medical care.

To clarify the impact of COVID-19 on poor religious minority communities, a group of five local researchers assembled in Chennai. They gathered in order to learn how to conduct two participatory research exercises – the 'River of Life' and 'Participatory Ranking' exercises – with men and women from one of the poorest slums in Chennai. Led by researcher Lata John,[6] the Dalit Christian women's group engaged in these exercises in order to surface, discuss and quantify the challenges and enablers that the group faced during the pandemic. All the women who joined the group belong to Scheduled Caste or Dalit communities. Most of the women were married, and almost all of them identified as 'converts' from Hinduism to Christianity. Like hundreds of other Dalit women who lived in the slum, the participants were either daily wage labourers, housemaids or homemakers.

Description of the methodology used among Dalit Christian women in Chennai, India

The meeting began with introductions. Then Lata started to talk about the River of Life methodology. Participants were given a two-year time frame to examine their lives before and after the COVID-19 pandemic. Describing their lives as a river, Lata asked the women to draw 'the good things' in their lives as well as the 'bad things'. She explained to the participants that they could use colours and symbols to illustrate the challenges and opportunities they faced before the current COVID-19 pandemic and up until they met in March 2021:

> 'So, in this river of life we are going to draw the good things in our life and bad things too. You can draw the flowers, or show how nicely the river flows, or something you feel indicates the good things in your life. Or you can draw whatever you want to describe. Or else you can use such colours that will indicate things in your life.'

Once the women drew their pictures, they were asked to explain what they drew in their own words:

> 'Ok, we have drawn our own river of life. Let's talk about the things that we drew, and why we drew these things. Why is a crane there? Why is a snake there? We are going to explain it all. why did we draw all those things? That's all. What is the reason? Why did we draw a net, fish, use this colour? Everything has a reason, right?'

The purpose of this part of the participatory exercise was to enable the women to use their visual depictions to begin to share about their experiences during the pandemic. The prompt for the River of Life drawing exercise was: 'Draw your life as a river over the past two years since before COVID-19 and up until the present day.' In response to this prompt, the women drew various objects in their river, denoting the challenges, obstacles, joys and opportunities they faced during the previous two years. Presented in the visual form of a drawing, the women's experiences took shape and revealed their powerful personal perspectives on the pandemic and how it affected their own everyday lives. Some of the women included details such as a crane catching a fish to depict good things in their experience. Likewise, they used stones and snakes to symbolize how the coronavirus destroyed their happiness. Lata explained that it was striking that most of the women drew flowers or fish to depict the role of faith or their faith community during the pandemic.

Following the discussion, Lata asked the women to identify five or six key obstacles that hindered them during the pandemic, as well as the same number of enablers that helped them. The women were given an opportunity to rank the challenges and enablers using the following method:

> 'So, now we spoke about our river of life, right? We are going to put the score from 0 to 3 marks. If there are no problems, you can put 0. For every problem, there will be different levels. If the problem was at its peak, you can put 3. Or if it is a little problem, you can put 1 or 2. If you couldn't handle the problem, you can give it a score of 3, or if you were able to cope up with it, you can give it a 2. First, let us score the issue of financial crisis.'

According to Lata, the ranking 'pinned people down and gave them a chance to look at their lives on a chart'. Unlike traditional methods of data collection, such as semi-structured interviews and questionnaire-based surveys, the participatory methods gave respondents an opportunity to identify why they struggled during the pandemic and what factors gave them the confidence to weather the lockdown and the problems associated with being without food or employment.

However, Lata felt that the women needed the freedom to set the upper and lower limits for themselves. Giving the participants a chance to rank their problems by using their own numerical limits would give them a chance to own the process and express their concerns and experiences within the bounds of the methodology.

> 'I wanted to say, "You give me a number. What should be the number?" Probably we should have done that. I don't think that I should have

limited them to 0–3. I could have asked them to say what number should be given. ... They can discuss and they come up with the number instead of us giving them a number. They can say, "We will have 1 to 5."'

Is a river enough?

Lata also suggested that the methodology might be limited insofar as it did not allow participants to depict the vital and indispensable role of 'community' in their lives. While the participants were encouraged to provide a visual depiction of the impact of the pandemic on their lives, *the tool restricted each participant to framing their own perceptions and their own lived realities as isolated individuals*. As described above, the exercise invited them to create images that pertained primarily to their own individual lives and personal experiences. By drawing just one river, an individual was constrained to drawing or illustrating what happened in the course of her own particular life experience. At least within the parameters of this particular visual method, she could not readily depict what happened to her community, or how her community shaped her, for better and for worse, in the course of the pandemic.

Among Dalits in Korukkupet slum, however, the lives and experiences of the poorest and most marginalized individuals are inseparable from the lives and experiences of their neighbours and family members and, likewise, are profoundly enmeshed with the life of their faith community and their neighbourhood as a whole. Therefore, participatory methodologies that seek to quantify and clarify the impact of a phenomenon such as COVID-19 on the lives of marginalized individuals in a richer and more contextualized manner than may be possible within the framework of traditional methods might nonetheless have their own limitations and problems. The River of Life methodology, at least as it is typically structured and presented, may be constrained by the predominantly Western notion that individuals experience and negotiate challenges largely on their own and not in an integrated relational context of family and community. Drawing a single river, representing one's 'own life experience', may make it difficult to depict how one's experiences and decisions are interpenetrated with – and, in profound ways, inseparable from – one's communities of family, neighbourhood and faith.

Indeed, Lata found that surviving the pandemic was far more a 'community' than a 'personal' experience:

'It is like so many things, isn't it? ... I felt they really ranked coming together as important. COVID-19 gave them the opportunity to hold on to each other. ... I found that more than you know. Dealing with COVID-19 was more of a community experience than a personal experience. This was particularly so for the Christian minority.'

Religious identity

In seeing the participants as religious minorities, it was particularly difficult for Lata to single out this inequity in a sea of competing inequities such as caste, gender, employment and lack of education. The reason for this is not hard to understand. Important as religious identity is, it is inextricably tied up with the many different deprivations the women face in their slum community. The inequities faced by the women because they belong to a Dalit Christian faith community were tied up with the numerous intersecting challenges and inequities.

Against this background of multiple and intersecting restrictions and inequities, the lead researchers in India and the UK informed Lata that, while deprivations of gender and caste are distinct and important, she should endeavour to clarify and isolate the particular role of FoRB. In particular, she should attempt to clarify how the freedom of religion or belief – and restrictions on this freedom – might inform and influence the ways participants experienced and navigated the challenges posed by the pandemic.

> 'I know I had to focus on Christian women. This was unique for me. Particularly for us in India and in our Dalit slum communities, although religion has a strong hold in the lives of people, we don't talk to people about their religion. We don't talk to people about their religion as a particular feature.'

Furthermore, Lata did not want the Dalit Christian women to think that the study was merely interested in their religious identity. At the outset of the meeting, she became deeply concerned that the women might feel that the facilitator was only interested in the restrictions they faced because of their faith and not because of the other factors that adversely affected their everyday lives, both before and during the COVID-19 pandemic.

> 'So I wouldn't want them to feel that I am interviewing [them] only as Christians with a single intention. The reason is the women shared common identities, and the community in which they live is an economically disadvantaged community. These women also belong to a particular caste group, and they also belong to a particular community of people who are deprived of certain privileges. Now I need them to focus on another disadvantage. I had to make them think [about] one more problem, and that is their religion.'

In a slum community like Korukkupet, suspicions abound about the number of women who now self-identify as 'converted Christians'.

The sample of Dalit Christian women who met to discuss the impact of COVID-19 were mostly those who had switched religions from Hinduism to Christianity. Lata was acutely aware of the dangers of drawing attention to converts in the slum because people may wonder why the women were being singled out to meet with an 'outsider' and a 'researcher'.

> 'There was a ... very conscious and alert role I have to play while I am collecting data. ... [U]sually Christians are also seen in communities, particularly in slum communities, as a people who [are] bringing conversion. So, I want to be conscious about that when I was collecting data with them. I do not want them to have that kind of feeling. Because certain questions are [like]: What kind of support [did] you receive from your religious supporters?'

Drawing as empowerment

It was clear that Dalit and 'uneducated' women experienced the invitation to draw pictures about their life as both empowering and terrifying at the same time. By asking the women to visually articulate their pandemic experiences – and, furthermore, to do so from their perspectives as women, Dalits, and members of a religious minority – the methodology compelled them to express the realities of their situation in an intensely personal and painful manner. Experiences such as the sudden death of a loved one or the deliberate disappearance of a spouse were now displayed in black and white, or even colour, on a page in front of them.

Another consequence of the drawing exercise was the fear that many of the participants felt about handling pencils and paper. Most of the women were barely educated and had hardly touched a pencil after what little formal schooling they may have had. When they were asked to draw, the women laughed and asked if they could call their children or grandchildren to draw the pictures. The following is an excerpt from the participatory group gathering with the women in the slum:

Facilitator:	We are going to draw this.
Participant 1:	How to draw?
Facilitator:	I will teach you. You can easily draw. I can help you.
Participant 2:	She's wanting to bring her granddaughter.
Facilitator:	How many years has it been since you have drawn something? Take a pencil or a colour pencil.
Participant 2:	My hand is hurting ....
Facilitator:	Is this because you are drawing? (*Laughing*)

The participants seemed quite content to *talk* about the difficulties they faced during the pandemic and the dangers of raising their families in the slum. The group spent the first 20 minutes talking among themselves and sharing stories about each other. In the quote below, Lata talks about how the women talked to a young woman participant who had eloped from the slum and got married:

> 'Because they knew each other, they talked. One of them was telling [us] that she got married at the age of 15. But he went off when they were dating. So, the other people present knew this story … and they say "Yes, yes". And then she had the other two children. They knew that too. All of us, we were talking, and they were talking.'

However, when Lata asked them to *draw* their experience using the River of Life methodology, the women seemed visibly perturbed. Lata felt that asking participants to conceptualize their problems, graphically and visually, gave expression to months and even years of repressed sadness and fears. In the quotation below, Lata talks about one of the participants who broke down during the drawing exercise:

> 'They were giving data, and they were giving their experiences also. No doubt, no doubt. But when I made her draw, there were meaningful things … coming out, which she was also not aware, and other participants [were] also not aware, about her life.'

The drawing exercise seemed to uncover unrealized feelings about their current conditions, which were difficult to process and handle within a group setting. In the quote below, Lata John explains why she felt that women's reluctance to draw reflected that the exercise created 'more than a physical challenge' but also 'a mental barrier'.

> 'At first they were saying, "No we are not artists we cannot draw." They were trying to push away the pencils. That was the biggest challenge. Some said, "I will call my daughter, she will draw, or my son. We cannot draw, because it's been years since we held a pen. So we cannot draw.. But I thought that it is more than a physical challenge. [There] is a mental barrier. They didn't want to come out with things in their life because they knew what they were going to draw.'

Reflections and evaluation of the methods

To increase the credibility and utility of the river of life and participant ranking methodology, particularly when working on freedom of religion or belief issues and with either minority or majority religious communities, it was appropriate in India in general, and in the Chennai slum in particular, to use facilitators that know the context and, more importantly, that come from a similar faith background. The advantage of using faith-sensitive individuals from similar or the same religious communities is that the participants were easily able to establish trust and confidence with respondents:

> 'Yes, I was able to talk openly with the women because of my Christian faith. Because of my involvement in the community, as well, I [was] able to probe and get certain responses. I was able to [go] deeper.'

To ensure the participatory research was not limited to a one-off exercise, the results of the participant groups were given to the local NGOs working in the community as a basis for follow-up efforts to meet their particular needs.

When discussing sensitive issues such as religious restrictions, Lata felt that it was 'unfair' to give participants a limited time to share their experiences. Lata talked about this when she was asked about possible changes that could be made to the process of conducting the participatory methodology among marginalized religious minorities such as the women she interviewed in Chennai's Korukkupet slum:

> 'It was hard to limit the different parts of the exercise to 15 or 20 minutes, like that. ... Because we called the women, and they were doing a favour by giving their time. But even so, it felt rushed because they had to go back to their families. ... The participants were not prepared for this. This was the first time they were sitting down to draw. It was not so much the drawing, but that fact that they were opening up. I felt that I did not do justice to them. I enabled them to open up, and then I didn't have time for them to talk about it. I didn't talk individually.'

Conclusion

One of the distinguishing features of the CREID participatory research was that it enabled investigators to understand the intersecting vulnerabilities experienced by individuals from marginalized religious minority communities during the COVID-19 pandemic. Although the study sought to clarify and quantify the nature and extent of such vulnerabilities and deprivations, it was structured to focus exclusively – or nearly exclusively – on how they experienced and responded to these vulnerabilities *as individuals*. This conception of vulnerability and need was limited in its ability to fully appreciate that the Dalit Christian women living through COVID-19, in one of poorest urban slums in Chennai, experienced and negotiated the pandemic and its associated challenges in the context of multiple communities, including their faith communities. These communities framed and determined how they received and experienced the pandemic as well as how they experienced their ongoing endemic vulnerabilities and inequities. Their communities also played an indispensable role in helping them develop creative and effective responses to their ongoing challenges and new trials.

Lata summed up her interview by saying:

'That one thing I could see in this community, because I am a Christian. So when they come together as a community, they pray and they put forward their needs. That is how the need was transformed into charity and action. I saw that for sure.'

Notes

[1] This chapter is based on an interview with Lata John (pseudonym), a female Christian researcher in India. Her name has been changed to protect her identity. The interview and the writing were carried out by Dr R. Shah.
[2] https://www.nytimes.com/2020/03/25/world/asia/india-lockdown-coronavirus.html
[3] https://www.nytimes.com/2020/03/24/world/asia/india-coronavirus-lockdown.html
[4] https://www.hdr.undp.org/sites/default/files/2021_mpi_report_en.pdf
[5] To know more about the Multidimensional Poverty Index see page 6 in https://www.hdr.undp.org/sites/default/files/2021_mpi_report_en.pdf
[6] The name of the researcher has been changed to protect her identity. The names of all the participants in India have been changed to protect their identities.

4

Faith and Researcher Positionality: Researching with Dalit Muslim Women in India during COVID-19

Rebecca Shah with Laila Khan[1]

Introduction

In the early hours of the morning of 11 August 2020, as ambulances rushed through the streets carrying people to hospital during the COVID-19 outbreak in Bangalore, a large fight broke out in a densely populated slum in the heart of the city. The slum, DJ Halli, is situated in the east of Bangalore city and is home to mostly Dalit Muslims who work in menial jobs or as day labourers. The fight began as a protest against a social media post written by the nephew of a local politician. But it rapidly metastasized into a violent confrontation between Muslim and Hindu youth, killing four people and injuring 30 residents. More than 140 vehicles, including taxi cabs and autorickshaws, were burned by the angry rioters.

After the riots, a couple of Hindu local politicians registered a case against local Muslim residents under the Unlawful Activities Prevention Act. In the weeks that followed, police arrested 480 individuals who were considered 'suspects' in relation to the disturbances. Those arrested were mostly Dalit Muslim men, and many are still in jail awaiting trial.

The following excerpt from the participatory data collection exercise is drawn from a conversation between our researcher (Laila) and one of the Dalit Muslim women participants during an inquiry group gathering in March 2021:

Participant: Yes, they came, and they were hunting for us. Even now, a few people who were taken after the riots have yet to be returned. We are still very frightened.

Laila:	So, Muslims in your area are facing these problems. ...
Participant:	Yes, the police came.
Participant #2:	It is a bad area. But we are all in danger. They took so many boys away. Muslim boys.
Laila:	Why?
Participant #2:	Simply because they were Muslim.
Laila:	You have faced too many problems.
Participant:	Yes. We are frightened because they have not released these boys.

Against this backdrop of simmering religious tensions between Muslims and Hindus in the state of Karnataka, a group of five Dalit women participated in an inquiry group gathering in Bangalore in March 2021 to share their experiences of living as part of a marginalized minority during the COVID-19 pandemic. The participants in the inquiry groups were Muslim women who lived in Sait Palya, an urban poor slum in northeast Bangalore. The group met in a local school and were interviewed by two Muslim teachers. All the women were married and had children. Only two of the women had been to school.

Situated within a context of increasing religious restrictions imposed on Muslim minorities by national and state-level government agencies and local communities, the Muslim women who joined the group were, at first, reluctant to discuss the recent riots in Bangalore. However, the following chapter illustrates that these women did not appear to experience as threatening or even unwelcome the participatory methodology we deployed in order to understand their vulnerabilities. On the contrary, they appear to have experienced this methodology as empowering insofar as it invited and encouraged them to share remarkably intimate details of their personal histories and narratives with the group as well as with two practitioners who might be regarded as 'outsiders'.

While most of the women came from the southern state of Tamil Nadu and spoke fluent Tamil, all of them chose to speak in Urdu. This was in direct contrast to a similar group of Dalit Muslim women whom we gathered in a slum in north Chennai; they chose to speak in Tamil rather than in Urdu. In some cases, Tamil-speaking or Kannada-speaking Muslims are not seen as 'proper' Muslims by their co-religionists, but are regarded instead as an inferior sub-community among the wider Indian Muslim community. Again, unlike their counterparts in Tamil Nadu who wore saris and no head coverings, the Muslim women in the Bangalore group in Karnataka state all wore traditional black 'burqas' with their heads covered.

This chapter shares the experience of employing participatory methods with a group of Dalit Muslim women in Bangalore, from the perspective of the facilitator, Laila Khan, and reflects on how these methods might contribute to the generation of knowledge about the intersecting vulnerabilities of minorities. Such vulnerabilities include restrictions on the freedom of religion or belief (FoRB) imposed on the poor in the context of the COVID-19 pandemic. Laila Khan and Fatima Qureshi, two Muslim teachers from the local school, served as facilitators for two participatory research exercises: the 'River of Life' drawing exercise and the 'participant ranking' exercise. Five Dalit Muslim women were invited to talk about living through the pandemic. In the River of Life exercise, they were invited to depict various life experiences, both positive and negative, by drawing a river in a way that illustrated the course or 'flow' of their lives. After this drawing exercise, the facilitator asked the women to identify the main enablers and challenges they experienced before and during the pandemic. The women ranked the enablers and challenges between zero (0) and three (3) in ascending order of importance.

The methodology

Eager to share experiences

In contrast to other religious minority inquiry groups, the Dalit Muslim group in Bangalore were eager to discuss the impact of the COVID-19 pandemic on their lives – both as Muslims and as women. In the quotation below, for example, Laila explains that after just ten minutes of conversation, the women were eager to discuss the role of religion during the pandemic:

> 'Initially after 10 minutes of meeting, we spoke to them and just explained the method. Then slowly they were able to discuss about their religion ... about the COVID impact and how they faced all the problems. Then the religious matters came up, and how they were able to get the support from the religious bodies and from the non-religious bodies also.'

Although the inquiry with the women's group began with pre-set questions designed to break the ice, it soon became clear that the participants were keen to talk openly with the investigators about the impact of COVID-19 as well as other difficult issues. Perhaps their candour and freedom reflected the fact that many of these Muslim women were relatively socially isolated from mainstream life, both before the pandemic and even more during the pandemic, and struggled deeply with the effects of persistent isolation. With little recourse to meeting other women from their own neighbourhood and religious community, particularly once the COVID-19 pandemic was in full swing, they seemed to experience the invitation to discuss the recent course of their lives as a welcome and even refreshing opportunity rather than a burden or intrusion.

In late March 2020, at the height of current COVID-19 pandemic, the Indian prime minister, Narendra Modi, imposed a strict nationwide lockdown. The lockdown forced millions of Indians to remain indoors for more than two months. Even after the stringent rules of complete isolation across the nation were lifted, the state of Karnataka continued to monitor the movements of individuals and vehicles.

Furthermore, a couple of days before the nationwide lockdown, the Indian government shut down the headquarters of the Tablighi Jamaat, a Muslim missionary movement, whose members had gathered at their New Delhi meeting house. The government claimed that in early March 2020 over eight thousand members, including foreigners, had visited the headquarters and acted as wanton 'super-spreaders', responsible for circulating the virus across the country. Muslims across India felt stigmatized and became fearful about reprisal attacks.

Our research revealed just how profoundly the Muslims we interviewed experienced various forms and dimensions of stigma, restriction and marginalization in this fraught and fearful atmosphere. It also revealed how these forms and dimensions intersected with, and reinforced, their other vulnerabilities related to gender, caste and socio-economic status.

The poorest and most vulnerable Muslims, like the Dalit men and women in the Sait Palya slum in Bangalore, talked about being targets of suspicion. Some were even stopped from selling vegetables or food; others were accused of being members of the Tablighi Jamaat and spreading the virus. Moreover, when these women often lacked access to opportunities for interaction with outsiders – an isolation compounded by the COVID-19 pandemic – what made it possible for them to share their feelings with others outside their immediate family was our introduction of participatory group discussions.

Interviewer:	So do you think, Laila, that in the Muslim community, which is a closed community for the most part, the methodology gave women a chance open up?
Laila:	It is a very good thing because, most of the time in their life, they are bound within the four walls of their houses. They are not allowed to come out of their houses, they are not allowed to speak and they are not allowed to share their thoughts.

Bangalore was one of the Indian cities worst hit by COVID-19. For example, the state government sent out police patrols to ensure that individuals in densely populated neighbourhoods such as the Sait Palya slum were wearing masks and staying indoors. The Muslim women who joined the inquiry group said they could not leave their homes even to go to the doctor's office because they were worried about the police.

> 'I had health issues during the lockdown and I have an ulcer and I needed to go to the doctor but I had no money. I have been suffering from this ulcer problem for the last six years and I have migraine issues. I went to Jafar Sir in Kalyan Nagar, [and] he helped me. But I am really struggling. I feel so sick.' (participant in the Dalit Muslim women's group)

Drawing as liberation

One of the main advantages of using the participatory drawing method is its inclusive and affirming nature. This is particularly so in a setting where the participants might be reluctant to interact, or if there are particular reasons for individuals to be ashamed or afraid to share the difficult details of their lives.

Muslim women in general, and poor Dalit Muslim women in particular, are frequently cautious and reticent about sharing personal details about their families and their religious community with outsiders. However, because of the methodology's horizontal structure, whereby Laila and her co-facilitator enabled the women to take charge of framing their own experiences during the pandemic by freely and creatively drawing their own realities rather than by responding to pre-set questions, the women were able to develop a certain self-assurance. They experienced, and exhibited, a growing confidence in their own abilities to explain and understand what took place during the harrowing months of lockdown and isolation.

In the following excerpt, Laila talks about the experience of a young Dalit Muslim woman. She was able to harness the non-textual and highly accessible tool of participatory drawing to relate how she coped when her depressed husband abandoned her for a period of months during the nationwide lockdown.

> 'Initially, when she started to speak, she was reluctant to tell us details about her husband going off, as there were other women present, and also ... she was not feeling comfortable. But when it came to her chance to discuss her story in the pictorial form and drawing, by herself she started telling her whole story – about how husband went out for some time and nobody was there to help her, and how she faced many health issues. How her children were abandoned and nobody was there to look after them. So, the pictorial form brought out her emotions very well. Like she took little time initially, a little time, and later she started drawing and showing out her emotions in the pictorial form very well.'

As a trained schoolteacher, Laila immediately recognized that women assembled in the community hall were afraid to talk about their experiences.

It was as if the very formal setting, which was much like a classroom, prompted them to see themselves as uneducated and therefore unfit to contribute to a 'discussion'. The use of the non-textual method, using colours and images, became an accessible and versatile tool whereby she could gradually lead the women into a process of self-disclosure.

> 'OK, many a times as a teacher myself, when we tell some things like pictures, drawing and all – it is naturally embedded in our selves. We did not learn to draw. We learn to write or read but not how to draw. It comes out naturally as human beings. So, when we ask them to draw themselves, and when we give simple examples such as fish, grass, green leaves – all these are simple. And if these simple things are given in the form of colours and crayons, it gave life to their thoughts, and it was very easy.'

Identifying the problems

A distinguishing feature of participatory research is to focus on the subjective experience of the vulnerable and marginalized participants of the study. To explore, examine and assess whether and how religious inequalities exacerbate existing intersecting vulnerabilities, Laila had to facilitate the inquiry group to identify their own problems and challenges as members of a religious minority, as women, as Dalits and sometimes as single mothers and wives abandoned by their husbands.

Given the sensitive nature of the situation and issues involved in the study, the use of pictures and drawings were an invaluable device to channel and voice their hidden and complex feelings about the problems and challenges they faced during the pandemic. Furthermore, in contrast to traditional interview methods, where language can pose a significant barrier to participation, the River of Life methodology relies on tools such as images and colours that are available and accessible to individuals across the literacy spectrum.

In the following excerpt, Laila talks about how the drawn images in the River of Life methodology enabled the women to identify and discuss their problems:

> 'Before COVID the women had drawn fishes, money and green colour things. Then the problems were shown in the form of stones and in the form of snakes, which was very heart-touching to see. To see all those drawings, I mean. After COVID, the stones came down the river and the snakes came down the river. It was the problems coming out … And we could see the pictures and we could relate to the problems with those pictures.'

While the drawings were not a substitute for the discussion and 'voice' of the participants, it was a very effective tool for bringing deep-seated feelings about their predicament to the surface. Indeed, the very practice of generating the images and using different colours, such as green or black, to illustrate the depth of feelings about the issues, helped the women uncover and express a flood of unrealized and subconscious feelings about their predicament.

In the following excerpt, Laila talks about the fact that the participatory research meeting presented possibly the one and only opportunity the Dalit Muslim women had to share their problems:

> 'If not for this meeting, nobody will go and ask these women about their situation. And nobody will talk about the problems they are facing. So, this exercise was a very good thing. Because they opened up at least to share their problems.'

Finding solutions

Ultimately, the objective of participatory research is to solve problems. Indeed, the challenges and inequities facing Dalits in general and Dalit Muslim women in particular are so complex and seemingly insurmountable that policy makers may be compelled to reach for solutions that are technically rigorous and prescriptive. However, ownership and participation are indispensable to lifting people out of their poverty and hopelessness. Solutions that are imposed from the outside might be reluctantly accepted or tolerated but will rarely be adopted or implemented. Ownership and participation are essential for transformative change.

By involving the women in participatory methods, the researchers encouraged participants to acquire the capacity to identify solutions to their problems and find the confidence to implement them. This point is brought home in the following excerpts from the River of Life exercise conducted by Laila and her co-facilitator. Laila asked the women to explain the 'good' things that happened to them during the lockdown. Rather than encouraging the participants to dwell on the challenges and problems they faced, the methodology leads the women in a process of discussing change, thereby altering their ways of thinking about their predicament.

The following excerpts from the River of Life discussion with the women illustrates the crucial role of encouraging the women to find their own solutions:

Laila: So, please tell me about your river? What is this? Is it a stone or is it a flower?

Participant:	After lockdown I had lots of problems. Too many problems. I had ulcers, as I told you. But my husband was working so I could manage.
Laila:	That's good to know. What do your flowers represent?
Participant:	Well, the children were at home, they were with me. That is a joy. I knew Allah was watching over us. We all stayed together. It was good. I liked having my children me. But we all did 'namaz' together.[2] That was good.
Participant:	Yes, I was very afraid to be home alone all the time. Very afraid.
Laila:	Tell me. …
Participant:	My husband would not be with me. I was alone. I was afraid. We were also hungry. But the Christian community around us helped us. We had too much trouble. Allah knows. … We don't know how we managed but Allah knows.

Much of life in the slums of northern Bangalore centres around communities and religious institutions, particularly places of worship. As the excerpts above illustrate, the women found solace and comfort in their communities, their faith and their families. As remarkable as the methodology was in enabling the women to identify solutions to problems, it was limited to the extent that it assumed that people could and should find creative and innovative solutions to their own problems in ways that can be tracked and measured by policy makers. However, for most of the women in the group, the solution to their problems was already there. The women reached deeper. They clung more tightly to their faith and very often the faithful charity of their neighbours. In many ways, the women in the study had already found a kind of solution to their problems, though, again, this kind of solution was very different from the sort that policy makers and development experts and practitioners might recommend or even recognize as a 'solution'.

At the heart of development is a change in ways of thinking. But individuals cannot be forced or cajoled to change the way they think. Deeply marginalized religious minorities such as the Dalit Muslim community may be urged or forced to adopt certain actions. But they cannot be forced to change what drives and gives meaning to their lives. Amid their darkest moments at the height of the pandemic, the Muslim women in an urban-poor slum in north Bangalore found faith in Allah as the solution to their problems.

The positionality and role of the facilitator

A major determinant of success of the participatory methodology was the role of the facilitator and guide. In Bangalore, the primary facilitator was Laila. Over the years of teaching and living in the community as a Muslim woman, Laila had developed a tacit knowledge of the problems and struggles facing the Dalit women sitting before her in the inquiry group in March 2021. Although Laila might be regarded as an 'insider' whose roots were in the local community, she was still in many respects an 'outsider' because of her education and her job as a schoolteacher. As you may recall, all the women in the group were illiterate or semi-literate and were mostly unemployed. To collaborate better with the women and gain their confidence, Laila needed to reduce their perception of her as both an outsider and an expert who knows more and is better able to speak on their behalf. In the following excerpt, Laila began the River of Life exercise by talking about her own fears and worries during the COVID-19 nationwide lockdown:

> 'My friend has talked. Now I will tell you about my river. … See before lockdown, all was good. My husband runs a hotel. But after lockdown things changed. We had no business. Money was less. Think of your life. That was my life.'

As a person of deep religious convictions, a woman, a schoolteacher, a wife and a resident of the local community, Laila occupied multiple positions that intersect. An educated Muslim woman who has the freedom to seek employment outside the home, Laila might be regarded as an 'outsider' who was able to transcend some of the challenges faced by women in her community.[3] Yet Laila was also very clearly an 'insider' who shared the vulnerability and concerns of the women by virtue of her gender, religious tradition and geographic proximity to the slum in which the participants live.

Some difficult questions

A series of difficult questions, however, confront the participatory research we conducted among Dalit Muslim women in Bangalore. For example, did Laila's own worldview or perspective on Islam, and the challenges faced by women in her religious tradition, enter the conversation with the Dalit Muslim women who met to discuss their intersecting vulnerabilities? Did her status as an insider, who was raised and resides within the Islamic tradition, skew or bias the process? Does Laila's commitment and participation in her Muslim faith take certain aspects of the context for granted, leading them, therefore, to be downplayed and ignored? Furthermore, if these limitations obtain, to what extent are we prevented from saying anything with certainty about the extent to which restrictions and limitations on FoRB are responsible for compounding the inequities facing Dalit Muslim women in Bangalore?

To all these questions the best answer we can give is: possibly.

Consider the following excerpt from the interview where Laila talks about her position as both an insider and an outsider:

> 'And being a Muslim woman, I can understand that a lot of them have not studied beyond a certain level. They may have gone through primary school, and they were married very early in their lives. Then they were not allowed to move out very frequently because husbands are there who will be earning. So, I can understand all of these issues. Being a Muslim woman, I know all of these. Even if I am not so like them in every way, I mean, like, I can come out for our work. But even today, like, we don't have that much of freedom to move about. So I could relate to them very easily.'

One way to overcome the multiple positions facilitators such as Laila occupy in contexts of intense religious experience and practices is to make explicit her multiple positions so that we can be wary of blind spots or tensions that arise with hidden assumption and beliefs.

At the same time, if one wishes to engage in mutual dialogue and true conversation with religious minorities about matters related to their deeply held religious beliefs, traditions and practices in the Global South in general and in India in particular, it may be important to understand that engaging a facilitator who is simultaneously an 'insider' as well as an 'outsider' is of vital significance as we deal with very sensitive and context-bound topics of identity and marginality. Indeed, the dichotomy of 'insider' versus 'outsider' in a study on religious identity and religious marginality during the COVID-19 pandemic may reflect what is itself a limited and typically secular Western academic concern – a luxury of contexts and institutions that are somewhat peculiar and, in any case, spiritually, socially and economically detached from the lives and lifestyles of the participants in our study.

It is true that a 'secular' facilitator might limit her own contributions to the conversation and achieve a certain kind of 'distance' and 'neutrality' throughout the research process. Otherwise, it is argued, the facilitator may introduce elements that risk 'contaminating' the dynamics of objective research and the data-gathering exercise. However, one may question whether avoiding all identification with participants is possible or even ethical.

Indeed, it quickly becomes evident that any so-called 'scientific' interrogation of Laila's role in the research process betrays a host of unscientific and usually unexamined assumptions. The status of being an 'insider' implies being someone who is 'other than' or different from an 'outsider' facilitator, while the essence of an 'outsider' is to stay in some sense outside and above the participatory process. But in what sense can any research be genuinely participatory if those conducting or facilitating it remain somehow entirely distant, aloof and 'objective' – that is, totally outside the research process and its participants?

Additionally, can any facilitator be a pure 'insider' or a pure 'outsider'? Would it be even desirable or ethical to employ as a facilitator an 'outsider' so 'objective' and therefore distant from the participants in the research exercise that she is literally incapable of identifying or empathizing with those she is studying? By this strained logic, it would be better to deploy non-human robots – animated perhaps by the new capabilities of 'Artificial Intelligence' – to serve as the ultimate and objective 'outsiders' than to employ human researchers of any kind. For *any human researcher*, is, after all, capable of empathetically feeling, sharing and identifying with the human experiences of those he is trying to understand, and is, in that sense, doomed to be an 'insider' at least to some extent. Here, however, the emptiness of the very aspiration to 'pure' objectivity, distance or neutrality becomes apparent. For genuine human understanding – in which one group of human beings comes to know and understand another group at least to some degree – is probably at some level inseparable from emotional identification. Which is to say that some degree of entry into the world of one's subjects precisely as an 'insider' rather than an 'outsider' is more a prerequisite than a barrier to truly fruitful research and genuine knowledge.

In this situation, powerful Western and often secular academics may be inclined to discredit facilitators such as Laila because she does not withhold her views and may actively contribute to the discussion on religious beliefs and practices. Taking this a stage further, however, one may argue that the very idea that individuals like Laila might be seen by secular academics and policy makers as ineffective and subjective reflects not only unscientific assumptions but also perhaps a power dynamic. A facilitator who is drawn from the same tradition as the research participants or subjects, and who holds similar deeply held religious beliefs, may be expected to meekly accept her assigned status as the quintessential 'insider' and, therefore, as enjoying less intellectual 'authority'.

Conclusion

Research methodology that seeks to study and analyse FoRB among vulnerable populations, such as Dalit Muslim women in Bangalore, simply cannot productively proceed without the invaluable expertise and guidance of facilitators like Laila – that is, facilitators who are devout and unapologetic members of a religious community. Furthermore, Laila is a Muslim woman before she is a facilitator. Thus, her reflections on the group in general, and her theological or spiritually inspired reflections in particular, cannot be disentangled from her identity. Laila's personal and spiritual biography is a significant source of knowledge for understanding the impact of shocks such a COVID-19 on religious minorities and brings a richness and depth of true knowing and understanding into the relatively uncharted area of participatory research on freedom of religion or belief among vulnerable minorities.

Notes

[1] This chapter is based on an interview with Laila Khan (pseudonym), a Muslim researcher in India. The interview was conducted by Dr R. Shah.

[2] T'Namaz' is the word used for prayers performed by Muslims. It is a Persian world adopted by Urdu speakers in India.

[3] The discussion on positionality of the researcher including the use of terms 'insider' and 'outsider' draws on the work of Rosalind Eyben (2009). An extensive discussion of the various role of a researcher/facilitator vis-à-vis her insider or outsider status is not possible due to the limitation of length and scope of this chapter. For a more detailed description of researcher roles in participatory research, please see Brydon-Miller, Aragón and Friedman (2021).

References

Brydon-Miller, M., Aragón, A.O. and Friedman, V.J. (2021) 'The fine art of getting lost: ethics as a guide to transformative learning in participatory research', in D. Burns, J. Howard and S. Ospina (eds) *The SAGE Handbook of Participatory Research and Inquiry*, London: SAGE, pp 248–62.

Eyben, R. (2009) 'Hovering on the threshold: challenges and opportunities for critical and reflexive ethnographic research in support of international aid practice', in C. Widmark and S. Hagberg (eds) *Ethnographic Practice and Public Aid: Methods and Meanings in Development Cooperation*, Studies in Cultural Anthropology 45, Uppsala: University of Uppsala Press, pp 73–100.

Nigeria

5

Using Participatory Methodologies in the Context of Fragility

Plangsat Bitrus Dayil

Introduction

The COVID-19 pandemic had devastating impacts on the world's economy (Pak et al, 2020) and has increased the vulnerability of communities already experiencing marginalization. Religiously marginalized communities and groups in Plateau State came under varying degrees of hardships because of already existing insecurity, poverty, religious targeting and lack of government access. For instance, during the pandemic period lockdown and lockdown restrictions, churches were closed and religious activities were halted. Because churches were closed, Christians were unable to celebrate Easter, while Muslims were permitted to celebrate Ramadan, which fell a few weeks later. Many residents of Jos were furious, fearing that the government's irresponsibility was putting many people's lives in danger and exhibiting recklessness. Despite the stricter measures especially the lockdown put in place by the government to prevent the spread of the COVID-19 virus, reports of movements of herders and herdsmen even within the metropolis did not result in any punitive action. More worrisome are the unprovoked attacks and destruction of farm crops, livestock and killings across the state (Shobayo, 2020). Farm crops were destroyed, homes were demolished and innocent people were killed while sleeping during the pandemic lockdown. The experiences of communities in Jos and Bassa Local Government Area (LGA) particularly in Miango, who have been subjected to unjustified attacks are detailed in this chapter. Using the participatory research methodology and my more than a decade of experience collecting data in fragile contexts, and with religious minorities, the research approach allows respondents to tell their experiences freely, without the pressure of typical question and answer interviews, resulting in fantastic results.

The chapter discusses the use of participatory methods that were combined to encourage people's participation and ability to express themselves through Rivers of Life and then rank their responses. The River of Life methodology allowed respondents to express sensitive emotions consciously and visually, with careful empathetic moderation to support them when recalling painful memories (Dayil, 2016). Further, an overview of religious minorities in Nigeria is followed by a discussion of the use of participatory methodology (PM) in research with selected communities in Plateau State. A special emphasis is placed on community access and respondent recruitment, which necessitated a thorough understanding of local forms of behaviour and social interaction (Dayil, 2016). The River of Life, matrix ranking and other data collection challenges are discussed. Furthermore, the methodology's uniqueness in comparison to other methods is discussed. The chapter concludes with some conclusions and findings.

Background

The situation for religious minorities in Nigeria

The 'larger proportion of conflicts has occurred in the Middle Belt region of Nigeria, with Plateau State as its typical example' (Best, 2007: 3–4 Gwamna, 2010: 7; Dayil, 2015: 42). These conflicts are rooted in religious minority groups' attempts to free themselves from the Hausa-Fulani establishment (Turaki, 1993; Dayil, 2005). Due to protracted hostilities and the operations of militants, bandits and Boko Haram, religious freedom in Nigeria has deteriorated (Pérouse de Montclos, 2014; Kukah, 2021). Plateau State's population, like that of most of Nigeria's central states known as the Middle Belt, is ethnically and religiously diverse. While Christians are the majority, Muslims make up a significant portion of the population. In recent years, Christians have dominated prominent positions in the Plateau State administration and many local governments, leading to feelings of animosity and marginalization among some Muslims. Christians, on the other side, have argued that Muslims control or even monopolize economic activities in some localities (HRW, 2005). For decades, some of these factions have struggled for control of land, economic resources and lucrative government positions.

Though the Nigerian Constitution protects citizens' rights to freedom of religion or belief, political and social tensions have, at times, exacerbated sectarian divides and led to the targeting of individuals and communities based on religious identity (Vellturo, 2020). The foundation for the present-day ethnic, regional and religious conflict in northern Nigeria is still largely due to the structural imbalances reified by or created under British colonial rule (Nnoli, 1980; Turaki, 1993; Kastfelt, 1994; Falola, 1998; Logams, 2004, cited in Dayil, 2015: 11).

In the colonial state, the Northern Minority Groups (NMGs) were subordinated systematically to Hausa-Fulani political control.[1] This system established or perpetuated the differential treatment and uneven socio-political development of ethnic groups, which often included their exclusion from political participation, and stratified group inequality (Turaki, 1993). There are also states that house millions of minority ethnic nationalities, most of whom are Christians, who have been bundled in with large hegemonic groups that wield political and economic power over them.[2] Southern Kaduna, Southern Borno and sections of Gombe Bauchi, Niger, Kwara and Kebbi States are among them. These Christian groups, along with those from Plateau, Benue, Taraba, Adamawa, Kogi and Kwara, have been consistent in their demands for protection from violations and for Christians' fundamental human rights to be upheld, but unjust political structures, institutions and values continue to perpetuate injustice against these large ethnic Christian nationality groups in the current dispensation. Within the Nigerian democracy, such structural differences – today, many would call them injustices – have continued to be preserved and reproduced (Dayil, 2015: 12).

Since the return of Nigeria to civilian rule in 1999, the struggles over economic resources and political power in Jos, as in many parts of the country, have continued along ethnic and religious lines (HRW, 2011). Since the return of democracy in May 1999, fierce and unregulated political competition characterized by ethnic mobilization and violence, coupled with poor governance, economic deregulation and rampant corruption, has severely exacerbated ethnic, religious and regional fault lines (ICG, 2012). According to Tanko (2021), Nigeria is faced with an unprecedented wave of different but overlapping security crises, from kidnapping to extremist insurgencies – almost every corner of the country has been hit by violence and crime. The European Asylum Support Office (2021) reports that

> While all of Nigeria is affected by the farmers–herders crisis, Plateau is one of the states that 'stand out for the sheer regularity, intensity and carnage of the incidents. … Plateau was one of the states where grazing space constituted a crucial cause of clashes between Fulani herdsmen and farming communities. … Nigeria Watch reported that, in 2020, Plateau was the state with the second-highest number of fatalities (106) due to herders-farmers clashes in the country. (European Asylum Support Office 2021: 177–8)

Many religious minority groups, notably in northern Nigeria, are still subjected to long-standing tensions and assaults at the slightest provocation.

In the northern cities of Kano and Kaduna, the implementation of Sharia and the perceived Islamization of public life, as well as discrimination against Christian minorities, led to deadly inter-religious conflict. As a result of this situation, a large number of Christians fled to Plateau State from northern states such as Kano and Bauchi. They carried with them stories of discrimination and massacres, escalating tensions in Jos between religious communities (Krause, 2011: 31). As a result, the conflicts in Jos have remained intertwined with regional and national politics. Furthermore, the way 'high-level religious leaders, academics, and journalists ... invoke the terms "jihad" and "terrorists" to express their positions' to explain the current situation allows the hostilities in Jos to be easily labelled as a direct extension of the nineteenth-century dan Fodio jihad (Krause, 2011: 31).

Jihadist expansion led to the appointment of Hausa-Fulani chiefs to rule over other ethnic nationalities who make up the vast majority of the state's population in many parts of the country, and areas where the British imposed culturally different numerically minority groups to rule over indigenous populations have become hotbeds of conflict between indigenous and immigrant communities. These hostilities increased during the COVID-19 pandemic lockdown, in addition to continuous Boko Haram activity and attacks on rural communities. Christian minorities are frequently vulnerable to unjustifiable violence in these rural places. Many of these villages' farmlands and properties were destroyed, and family members were hacked to death, as a result of the government ordering a total lockdown throughout the state, with no security presence to confront the assailants. According to the *Nigerian Tribune*, between 1 January and 1 April 2020, no fewer than 40 people were killed and eight were injured in 19 separate attacks on 15 communities in Plateau State's Irigwe Chiefdom of Bassa Local Government Area (Shobayo, 2020). A resident lamented in the report that

> 'the situation is really hard to understand. Our people are on lockdown as directed by the state government and some other people who feel they can do anything and get away with it came and attacked them, killing nine of our people and setting their houses on fire. How do you explain this?'

In the same report, one Mr Mathew Danjuma laments the attack in Hurra village (Miango). To him,

> 'It is like they had their target, certain families were deliberately singled out in the operation which lasted for about two hours. In a family, a pregnant woman and her daughter were killed at a close range and their bodies were decimated beyond recognition. ... While all these were

going on, we called on the security agencies especially the police and Operation Safe Haven[3] in charge of security in the Plateau to come to our rescue but there was no immediate response. It was only the police that eventually came when the gunmen had left.'

Further, a participant shared her current lived experience: 'I and my family are experiencing no peace', she claims. 'I'm afraid because sometimes when I'm sleeping, it feels like a dream that some people are coming to the house; I'll immediately wake up, as will my husband and children, and we'll pray; and sometimes it feels like someone has just entered my room' (Female participant, Miango, 2021).

Above is just one scenario of the many untold hardships and agony experienced by the religious minorities in Plateau State. A recent study of affected communities in Miango using PM, revealed that the government is not proactive in ensuring the protection of the citizens against attacks and there is no immediate distribution of relief materials to religious minority groups in need, thereby increasing the suffering of these groups (Howard et al, 2021) in the state. The lived experiences of these minority communities are best understood using a methodological approach that enables religious minority groups in this study to express themselves and rank their experiences in an atmosphere that is devoid of tension but which gives room to visualize collectively what issues affect them the most. This is because PM promotes people's participation and ability to talk about their problems and present them the way they choose and understand them. Similarly, the venue and environment for the exercise were chosen by the respondents, and thus convenient for them. This enabled them to be comfortable and relaxed and thus more open during the process (Dayil, 2016).

Training

The training in Nigeria's Plateau State and Kaduna took place via Zoom. This is because there were still travel restrictions, and also the new normal that came with the pandemic encouraged the use of information and communications technology. The researchers in both sites made an arrangement for all to meet in one place to minimize distraction, support each other and discuss after the sessions. In Plateau State, the team met at the Centre for Gender and Women Studies, University of Jos, while the Kaduna team met at the Federal College of Education Kafanchan. During the training, participants were introduced to the research and the data collection approach. Some of the researchers were coming into contact with PM for the first time. It was exciting, and at the same time researchers were sceptical about how that would work in the field in practical terms. This is because most of the researchers were using the River of Life and matrix ranking for the first time, but was also due to the language for data collection. This was discussed during the training which led to the translation of the data collection instrument to Hausa and uniformity in terms of textual interpretations.

The majority of the data collection was done in Hausa. Interviews were transcribed and translated to English. The advantage of the carefully selected research team was that all could speak, read and write in English, as well as having an excellent understanding of the Hausa language, which is a lingua franca in both Plateau and Kaduna. The research team made contacts with the local community in Miango to arrange for the venue, dates of interviews and recruitment of research participants. The same arrangement was made for Jos North. The venue for Jos North was a Human Rights Office on Bauchi Road – a neutral and enclosed place which would not attract the attention of passers-by. The venue in Miango was a community town hall arranged by the vigilante group who also offered to guard the place throughout the research exercise. During the data collection phase, the vigilante group had to be deployed because the crisis was still ongoing in several sections of the state and Bassa LGA in particular. The presence of the vigilante group reassured the respondents about the researchers' safety and sincerity. Because the battles were still continuing, any gathering might readily draw attention.

By supporting the work of security agencies, vigilante organizations are formed by communities to put an end to the rising tide of criminal activity. Their presence reassured respondents who were initially hesitant to talk about their experiences, but because I spoke the local language with them and sang with them, I encouraged them to loosen up and talk about their experiences in the local language, which greatly aided in the smooth running of the exercise in Miango. Participants felt better able to relate their experiences while they listened to one another, rather than feeling burdened by the interactive approach. It got more involved, prompting an explanation of how they all experience pain and how they deal with it.

The rationale for using PM

PM is an approach that enables respondents to play an active role in the data collection process. It includes using participatory data collection techniques. The methods are easy and fun to use and are culturally adaptable. It allows the researcher to engage easily with vulnerable groups. During the data collection and presentation, respondents from the communities in Bassa LGA and Jos North LGA used their preferred means of describing lived experiences – through a River of Life or Road of Life. The respondents were able to dialogue among themselves while giving details of their turbulent times and moments in which they found comfort. Collectively, the researcher was able to direct the process to enable each respondent to present and conceptualize their lived experience, thereby generating knowledge. This open participation allows for a deeper understanding and analysis (Ager, Stark and Potts, 2010) of the situation of religious minorities living in poverty in the shadows of COVID-19.

Methodology and process

The PM used in this study involved a combination of 'traditional qualitative research methods (semi-structured interviews) with participatory group-based discussions, using visual methods to access and communicate experiences, and facilitating group dialogue around the issues that the groups themselves identify' (Howard et al, 2021: 22). The PM process started with the researcher demonstrating and explaining the entire process to the group. A few of the respondents preferred to use the road of life because they travel almost daily. And since the roads were rough with shorter smooth paths, they agreed it described their situation better since the rivers are drying up and thus difficult to visualize for some. This enabled respondents to use familiar roads to express the obstacles, how they were able to navigate and the success associated with getting safely to the destination. In the inquiry group in Miango, one of the respondents said:

> 'my own is road – I always enjoy the road because you can learn a lot from it. We all use it and walk on it ... now I remember the time we will be walking freely on the road then corona came along. We were happy that time [before corona], eating whatever we feel like eating, I cultivate pepper and tomatoes and even cucumber. When this thing [corona] came I was not happy.'

The PM's flexibility in allowing participants to express themselves in the best way possible is evident, recalling moments of freedom and joy when they moved freely and used the roads prior to the COVID-19 lockdown, which prevented them from experiencing the joy of going out and using the roads to their farms. Using the participants' choice of road of life allowed them to connect with their actual reality of going out to work and returning home, the thrill of using the road to travel and bring back harvest for the family.

The PM process was iterative, in that the researcher worked with respondents to negotiate the objects to use in presenting hurtful moments and how they navigate through them. The River/Road of Life enabled respondents to share their lived experiences before and during the COVID-19 pandemic. Respondents used markers on pieces of cardboard to draw either a river or road of life and placed objects they picked from the environment to tell their stories. It was agreed that leaves and green grass will represent stories of well-being and harmony in their lives, and pebbles/tiny stones would represent difficult periods. Experiences were shared with the wider group afterwards. Other respondents nodded in agreement and empathized while the presentation went on. There were instances when they reminded the respondents and chorused how difficult they felt situations were for the other. I recall one of the respondents drew a pond, and during her presentation some of the participants added emphasis to what she said. Key issues from the shared stories were then summarized on two pieces of cardboard with one summarizing challenges and the other enablers. The group collectively ranked the experiences to establish the extent to which the major themes were common and the coping mechanisms.

As mentioned above, the process is adaptive and interactive. The participant who drew a pond instead of a river or road of life said she drew a pond because she has been living in hardship all her life. According to her:

> 'my problems have been concentrated in one place for as long as I could remember. I have been living with them and none have been resolved. I feel I am drowning.' (Female respondent, Miango)

Similarly, a respondent in the inquiry group in Miango revealed why she had a few green leaves at the end of her road of life. She claimed that:

> 'Why I said I was not happy is because when they started lockdown the things we use to get like fertiliser increased in price and there is no way for us to get money to buy fertiliser. In fact, a bag was even 20,000 naira, some were selling for 17,000 and 16,000 and there is no way for us to get money and there is no food in the home. What made me happy here was the assistance from people.'

This response shows how participants were able to present their vulnerability visually and reflect it in the best way possible without any imposition. These are two of the beauties and strengths of the PM: its flexibility, and the fact that it allows participants to be immersed in the process. Further, the PM enabled participants to identify key needs and resources and place them in order of priority.

The PM was used to collect data from four inquiry groups per study site, one comparator group per site and eight semi-structured interviews per study site. Individuals shared their experiences freely without feeling intimidated because they were grouped according to their sex and within a particular age bracket. Similarly, respondents were equally grouped according to their religious affiliation. This approach made it easy for them to relate their experiences and even prompt each other to give more information on their pains, losses and their present-day lived experiences. The approach also reduced the power dynamics that would have been experienced if the groups were of mixed sexes. My experience shows that, when respondents are mixed, men always dominate the interview space and women tend to hold back.

River of Life

The River of Life was one aspect of the PM used in trying to understand intersecting vulnerabilities experienced by religious minorities living in poverty in the shadows of COVID-19 in Plateau State. Through the method, both researchers and respondents learn about the experiences of individuals in small groups. These groups are carefully selected and a demonstration of a river of life is presented to them. The group is then asked to imagine their life as a fast-moving river. In the river, there are rocks and obstacles that they have to pass through.

Respondents watched carefully the demonstration of the River/Road of Life and the matrix ranking to understand this new method of data collection and were eventually happy that the process was participatory. The River of Life exercise was very exciting, though many were sceptical at the beginning of the exercise. Once they were taken through the exercise and were asked to use objects of their choice to draw a river or road expressing moments of distress, endurance and relief, they loosened up and felt happy to create such images on their own. As described above, there were lots of innovations and approaches to narrating lived experiences by those interviewed. In Miango some of the women preferred the use of the road of life, while others the river of life, and to one it was a deep pond of despair. What this shows is that the method was well understood and so easy to adapt to describe various situations they are passing through in their lives. One of the respondents who utilized the metaphor of the River of Life claimed that because of the happiness she had in her life, she started out with pebbles and flowers and suddenly had stones and a few sticks throughout. It is clear from her River of Life presentation how she can convey both joy and pain. She said:

> 'Here is my own river of life first I was happy with my life I do irrigation farming and cultivate many crops that is how we take care of our needs then suddenly another life sets in which is the COVID-19 and attacks on our village. We ran and came to the city with my family, my husband went out to fend for us and they killed him till today we don't know what they did with the dead body.'

The research team conducted two inquiry groups in Miango and two in Jos North. The PM was used in both sites. There were between eight to ten respondents in each group, in both study sites. The researchers worked in pairs and according to the sex of the respondents – two men were assigned to the male group and two women to the female group. The interview was preceded by an introduction of the research team, the scope of the project and what the findings will be used for. Participants were asked if they were comfortable continuing, and verbal consent to take photographs was elicited. Participants were given room to introduce themselves, ask questions and ask to express themselves freely.

The researchers played complementary roles – note-taking, observing the exercise and assisting with the ranking interpretation. Participants in each group were allowed to choose the items they want to describe their situation at each point in their life. Some used roads, others a river, just whatever made them comfortable. Participants were also asked to go outside and pick sticks, stones, leaves, grass and whatever they want to use to describe their experiences. They were handed cardboards, markers, sticky note pads and Sellotape. An example of the exercise was collectively done with them, taking them through each step and allowing them to make contributions, ask questions and make comments. This greatly helped them to put people at ease, and they were soon eagerly waiting to do theirs. Once they were given the materials, they all concentrated.

The challenges they faced especially during the period of COVID-19 dominated the presentations. Most of the respondents expressed the challenges and problems they encountered eloquently while narrating their River and Road of Life, many said they were able to overcome the challenges with the help of individuals, religious groups, and civil society support. Government intervention was conspicuously absent from almost all of the presentations. The majority of responders remained sceptical of COVID-19's existence and impact, as well as the lockdown and its consequences, especially in light of the ongoing attacks on people's lives and livelihoods. When the assailants moved during the lockdown with seemingly no pushback from formal authorities, it made people believe that the lockdown was part of a conspiracy by government and international accomplices to lower the population, or worse, to exterminate the Black race. Part of the COVID-19 conspiracy that has gained wide acceptability, particularly in northern Nigeria, is that the vaccine is a birth control mechanism, that once you receive it you become impotent and have no reversal. And that the population of northern Nigeria will reduce when men and women become impotent.[4]

Matrix ranking

Matrix ranking is a PM that allows respondents to classify and prioritize their stated challenges and facilitating factors, and place them in order of preference. This method is effective for prioritizing potential community interventions. Participants were guided through the Matrix rating procedure, which involved ranking the problems and enablers they had identified in the River/Road of Life activity. Individually, the respondents sketched their river of life; when they returned to the group, they presented and discussed each river, and identified all of the challenges and enablers collectively. These issues were then gathered together, and they all agreed on which ones to include in the ranking chart. Using the beans, each respondent then presented the degree of their difficulty. The group discussed the problem with the largest total, as well as the enabler with the highest total. Other, lower-ranking concerns were explored, and they are equally important. The group's reaction after viewing the visual representation of the ranking confirms the essential importance of the PM in helping the group identify and prioritize difficulties. One of the respondents in the Jos North inquiry group was delighted:

> 'This is actually amazing, see the way the problems affected us from top to bottom. See how we all did our problems and the ranking.'

They placed the challenges horizontally at the top and their names vertically to the left in two matrices – one for challenges and one for enablers. Participants were given a maximum of three black-eyed beans to put in a box to indicate the severity of their challenge. The enablers were subjected to the same activity, with the addition of kidney beans. They all chorused and agreed on the seriousness of the situation whenever three beans were dropped. They all worked together to overcome the difficulties and facilitators. The researchers carefully observed and listened to how the respondents discussed their difficulties and how they all supported one another in recounting their low points and what they did to regain strength and stability.

In the ranking of difficulties, instability and the loss of a source of income came out on top. This is hardly surprising given that several settlements in Miango have been subjected to unprovoked attacks by herders and unknown gunmen who attack at night without offering any opposition because security personnel are absent or, worse, come hours or days later. For the enablers, family support, belief in God, hope and a desire to forgive were all important factors in restoring harmony. Prayer and faith in God revealed a sense of helplessness shared by the majority of respondents, who believe there is nothing they can do and nowhere they can turn for assistance. A response from one of the participants, a widow, captured below shows a situation of helplessness:

> 'I put my trust in God, He is providing all my needs, in good times or bad times I am not going anywhere till I see the end ... What comforted me was prayers, if not I would not be able to live in my village, what made us strong is prayer.'

As they finished the rating, several of the responders expressed themselves openly and empathized with one another. Throughout the rating, there were times of expressing sobriety and moments of laughter. They were giving context to the ranks by raising observations. They claimed, for example, that family support is a facilitator, but that trust in God is the most powerful. At the conclusion of the ranking exercise, participants thanked the researchers for taking the time to listen to their tales. I believe this is because they felt powerful while telling their tales, and the process helped them to participate and see the impact of COVID-19 and the marginalization they face as a group.

Reflections on using PM

The PM goes beyond data collection by allowing respondents to reflect on some of the challenges that have negatively impacted them, as well as what helps them build resilience. Participants at each study site validated each other's presence by nodding their heads or chorusing 'Yes', 'True' and 'Sure' as talks progressed. Additional oral interviews allowed them to go into greater depth about what they go through and have to deal with on a daily basis. The researchers did not make any suggestions or try to remind the responders of other topics, allowing the free flow of information and conversation. As the river/road and pond were displayed, the difficulties flowed organically. This made the rankings simple for both male and female responders. The whole process was practical, participatory and fun. The conversations were recorded, transcribed and translated.

What were the challenges?

The PM, while entertaining and revealing, is not without its flaws. It's a long procedure that necessitates the researcher's ability to keep the team engaged and ensure that the enthusiasm is maintained. This was accomplished by ensuring that responders remained engaged throughout the process. At each stage of the process, the facilitator needed to pay attention to who was talking too much and overshadowing the voices of others, as well as kindly urging individuals who appeared to be withdrawn to speak. Another area where the researcher's competence is required is paying close attention to the diverse participants as they tell their own experiences. As a researcher, I had to intervene swiftly to demonstrate empathy and, where necessary, interfere to soothe the responder. When times of empathy and interjections are protracted, it also demands attention to pick up on the issues that may need to be followed up on swiftly. Another issue is obtaining the required number of participants as well as all of the essential requirements in terms of age and socio-economic position; as a result, some of the respondents in this study do not fit into the age range grouping. This is partly due to the fact that a majority of uneducated people do not retain exact records of their birth dates and rely on guesswork when recounting events, seasons or catastrophes.

It's also difficult to find the correct setting. To get the most out of the responses, the activity must be conducted in a well-organized atmosphere free of noise and interruption. In Miango, for example, the community hall was adjacent to a football field. There was so much noise there that it was interfering with the recordings. The boys in the field were instructed to decrease their voices several times, only to return louder. In Jos North, the area available to the women's group was somewhat limited in comparison to the male responders. Furthermore, the respondents require a secure environment in which they can openly relate their experiences without drawing attention to the entire procedure. In general, the procedure went smoothly.

Reflections on using these methods to understand the impact of COVID-19 on religious minorities

The PM has real-world strengths that we saw in action when collecting data in Bassa LGA and Jos North LGA to investigate and comprehend the impact of COVID-19 on Nigeria's minorities. It is especially valuable for describing religious minorities' inequities and how they've got worse since the pandemic. Because of its participatory nature, marginalized communities can collectively construct and synthesize daily lived experiences. Also, unlike other data-gathering approaches, the PM provides a superior manner of doing vulnerability research in general without disadvantaging respondents. The PM provides a platform for marginalized and vulnerable people to actively participate in the collection of data on problems that matter to them. No matter what degree of knowledge the respondents have, the process is basic and easy to explain. Some of the respondents in this study – for example, in Jos North, the Comparator group, and even the inquiry group – have no formal education, but the practical approach and their participation allowed them to express themselves freely while also being satisfied with the outcome of their engagement. The categorization of respondents by sex, age, religion and socio-economic level served to attenuate power dynamics and other social barriers that could have hampered the free flow of interaction. The PM also allows members of the community to participate actively in the development of knowledge.

PM research offers favourable results when conducted with the community's help, cooperation and engagement since the respondents' concerns are captured and the level of impact is ranked by collectively. The researcher conducts analysis based on the people's perceived needs, rather than on pre-structured and coordinated issues seeking affirmation from respondents. Through visualization – such as the River of Life and ranking tables – and narratives that follow each participant's reason for their choice, this method allows for the preservation of marginalized voices, giving respondents a sense of connection to the data and, as a result, any report that results from the findings. Also, respondents' capacity is strengthened as a result of their participation in the exercises, and they so become an integral part of knowledge creation. This in and of itself empowers participants, placing them in charge of the information they get and so making them a part of the proposed solution.

Furthermore, the PM adds to the qualitative data collection process. It gives people the freedom to analyse, report and rate situations that affect them. It enables responders to interpret and prioritize their problems. Participants in this study were able to capture such hardship and neglect narratives in their River of Life exercise. The exercise provided them with a safe venue to express themselves in front of a non-judgmental audience, as well as a temporary support group.

What makes the PM different from other methods in the study of marginalized groups?

The PM is based on the idea of collective engagement and the production of shared knowledge. All participants require is initial assistance in outlining the process, after which they will take over and own the process. This act of ownership allows respondents in Plateau State's two study sites, Jos North and Miango, who have suffered the double impact of government neglect and unprovoked attacks during the lockdown to have a voice and be more vocal while remembering traumatic experiences of marginalization and exclusion that have increased with the pandemics. In Jos North, for example, female Muslims interacted freely because the method allowed women who are religious minorities even within their religious groupings and victims of gender discrimination to express themselves. Similarly, because responses were chosen from the same inquiry group, the in-depth interview added to the process. The respondents were eager to explain their problems in further detail, and one of the Miango respondents appreciated me for selecting her to provide more information. Perhaps the PM was designed to make respondents feel special.

In comparison to other methods, the PM allows respondents to express themselves far more freely. Other approaches take a diagnostic approach, in which the searchlight and other indications are already configured for respondents ahead of time. Respondents contemplate, list, rank and discuss their topics in the PM. As a result, their findings are unique to the community. This is due to the fact that they have been given time to reflect, and what is conveyed is the lived reality of these oppressed groups. In the sense that problems and solutions are self-identified, the PM provides a sense of self-fulfilment. Respondents selected their concerns without any prompting or suggestions for this study and offered them for ranking. Each respondent assigned a number of items based on severity, and the group totalled up and agreed on the results, further illustrating the degree of the impact.

Learning about encroachments on FoRB during the pandemic

Participants were able to highlight incidences of religious discrimination and violence using the River of Life, including unjustified attacks on Miango villages, security concerns, an increase in spousal abuse, child labour, malnutrition and crimes, all of which increased during the lockdowns. Furthermore, the lack of social services and welfare programmes to assist vulnerable populations, notably women, exacerbated the situation. One of the respondents (LS, 37, female, Miango) explained the scenario:

> 'life was fun at that time but now the issues of Fulani [attacks] have scattered everything and the life is not fun any more, you cannot go out and look for something to help you take care of your needs and any time you go out your mind is not at peace you can meet them at any time because they don't have a particular time of going out because they aim to cause harm, so you have to do anything close to the house. You can't go into the bush because even if it is for firewood, you can cut and sell and get money but now, we cannot go into the bush.'

The majority of respondents felt marginalized as a result of the government's delayed response to crises and in meeting their needs. Many people described how the suffering became terrible as a result of the government's pandemic lockdowns. They were unable to go out in search of food for a period of time during the lockdown. Furthermore, promises made by the government to offer social support and palliatives to the populations in both research sites were never fulfilled. A small number of people, religious organizations and civil society organizations backed them up. For two key reasons, respondents were sceptical of the government's handling of the COVID-19 lockdown. The first was that, while they were unable to travel during the lockdown, they were subjected to continual attacks within their villages. These attacks were more common when some of the lockdowns were not in place. One respondent described his trauma, in which his elder brother was killed first, followed by his father a few months later; as a result, he has become the family's breadwinner and is a student at the state polytechnic.

The second reason was the prohibition on religious gatherings, which many people objected to because they saw it as a tactic to limit worship and communion with God. Despite the fact that certain organizations protested by defying government lockdown orders and holding Juma'at prayers, the situation did not go well, and the authorities reacted quickly to discipline the defaulters. Respondents agreed that when people rebelled against government directives not to worship in the congregation or the regulation to provide social distance within the mosque during the lockdown, the government acted quickly by enforcing the COVID-19 restrictions, but when others are attacked in their sleep and on their farms, it takes longer for the government to show up and come to their aid. The aforementioned assertion is one of the reasons why religious minorities blame the government's inaction and see it as deliberate complacency; others believe the government is well positioned to protect lives and livelihoods but chose not to do so.

The PM assisted in bringing to light the intersecting challenges that many marginalized groups face on a daily basis. These are both external and internal. It is external when one group is pitted against another, and internal when women in their groups are frequently subjected to other forms of marginalization and exclusion in competitive and difficult situations. Often, the power dynamics at work in society work against the marginalized group, even when authorities claim marginalization does not exist. While recounting their experiences before, during and after the COVID-19 lockdowns, the majority of respondents stated that their conditions continue to deteriorate with no hope of improvement. According to one of the respondents:

> The distribution of palliatives has been politicized. We learnt it is given to party faithful through party leaders. The women leader will collect and give only to those she feels are her friends and loyalist, forgetting the fact that we are more affected by COVID. (Female respondent, Jos North, 2021)

Because of the politicization of the distribution process, only those with access to power have access to even the most basic necessities of life. And those who do not have access continue to suffer. The situation of the women we interacted with during data collection demonstrates that, even when civil society organizations and NGOs step in to help mitigate the effects of the pandemic, they frequently target men to receive assistance as household heads. This long cultural approach and belief about men being household heads places women in a doubly disadvantageous position, as they are unable to provide for their own and their children's needs. As a result, women in these communities face multiple forms of marginalization, first as women and then as religious minorities, poor women, minority ethnic groups and so on.

Conclusion

The PM approach to data collection allowed for the expression of a wide range of viewpoints. In this study, the PM advocates for marginalized groups, empowers them and provides them with a voice. Respondents acquire ownership of the findings as a result of their participation in the process of knowledge production. They collectively presented challenges and enablers, and then ranked and discussed them. The careful recruitment and grouping of respondents based on sex, religion, age groupings and socio-economic status removes some forms of social barriers that could affect the data collection process, allowing marginalized communities and groups freely to express their concerns, group them and rank them accordingly. Similarly, respondents were able to bring their own perspectives and words to the table thanks to the PM. In addition, because the group operated as a pseudo support group with almost all members sharing a similar experience, the right grouping of responders allowed them to express sensitive issues freely. Communities' needs and priorities can be determined with this method, allowing for authentic and genuine interventions.

Despite the fact that religious marginalization existed prior to independence, the country's return to civilian rule in 1999 appears to have heightened rivalry for political control of the country's political and economic resources. Such competitions culminate in a never-ending cycle of violence, with the religious minority on the receiving end of it all the time. Participants in this survey believed that their communities were being targeted because of the rising attacks on minority religious communities in the face of the pandemic lockdown, as well as a lack of proactive efforts to protect life and property. The PM used the River and Road of Life to express the dynamics of marginalized communities and their lived experiences.

Notes

[1] The majority tribes are the Hausa-Fulani, Igbo and Yoruba, while the minority ones are people of different ethnic groups found in the northern and southern parts of Nigeria. See Galadima (2010).

[2] On ethnic minorities in Nigeria, see Suberu (1996).

[3] Operation Safe Haven (OSH) is the military task force set up to maintain peace in Plateau State. The force has its operational command in Jos. The multi-task force is in charge of security of lives and properties in Plateau, Bauchi and parts of southern Kaduna. See more on OSH at: https://www.globalsecurity.org/military/world/war/op-safe-haven.htm

[4] Part of the COVID-19 conspiracy theory that has gained wide acceptability particularly in northern Nigeria is that the vaccine is a birth control mechanism, that once you receive it, you become irreversibly impotent, and that the population of northern Nigeria will reduce when men and women become sterile.

References

Ager, A., Stark, L. and Potts, A. (2010) Participative Ranking Methodology: A Brief Guide. Available at: http://www.cpcnetwork.org/wp-content/uploads/2014/04/37.-PRM-manual_v1.1.pdf.

Alubo, O. (2006) *Ethnic Conflicts and Citizenship in the Central Region of Nigeria*, Ibadan: Programme on Ethnic and Federal Studies (PEFS), Department of Political Science, University of Ibadan.

Best, S.G. (2007) *Conflict and Peace Building in Plateau State, Nigeria*, Ibadan: Spectrum Books Limited.

Dayil, P.B. (2015) Ethno-Religious Conflict and Gender in Nigeria's Middle Belt, PhD African Studies (Gender and Development) thesis, University of Birmingham, United Kingdom.

Dayil, P.B. (2016) My Personal Encounter Conducting Fieldwork in Northern Nigeria: The Encounters, Challenges and How to Overcome Them. Available at: https://cgd.leeds.ac.uk/2016/04/13/challenges-of-fieldwork-in-northern-nigeria-and-how-to-overcome-them/.

European Asylum Support Office (EASO) (2021) Nigeria Security Situation: Country of Origin Information Report. Available at: https://reliefweb.int/sites/reliefweb.int/files/resources/2021_06_EASO_COI_Report_Nigeria_Security_situation.pdf

Falola, T. (1998) Violence in Nigeria: The Crisis of Religious Politics and Secular Ideologies, Rochester, NY: University of Rochester Press.

Galadima, J.D. (2010) *Brothers against Brothers: The Press, Identity Politics and Conflict Management in Northern Nigeria*, Jos: Selidan Publishers.

Gwamna, J.D. (2010) *Religion and Politics in Nigeria*, Jos: Africa Christian Textbooks.

Howard, J., Para-Mallam, O., Dayil, P.B., Best, K., Mang, G., Abubakar, D., Muazu, R., Sabo, A., Joshua, S., Saeel, S., Hayap, P., Danfulani-Tsilpi, C., Samuel, C., Katung, K,. Saulawa, H., Yakassai, M,. Babangida, K. and Galla, A. (2021) Understanding Intersecting Vulnerabilities Experienced by Religious Minorities Living in Poverty in the Shadows of COVID-19, CREID Intersections Series; Religious Inequalities and COVID-19, Coalition for Religious Equality and Inclusive Development, Brighton: Institute of Development Studies, DOI: 10.19088/CREID.2021.012

Howard, J., Para-Mallam, O., Dayil, P.B. and Hayab, Philip (2021) Vulnerability and Poverty during COVID-19: Religious Minorities in Nigeria, Policy Briefing 6, Coalition for Religious Equality and Inclusive Development, Brighton: Institute of Development Studies, DOI: 10.19088/CREID.2021.013

HRW (Human Rights Watch) (2005) 'Revenge in the name of religion: the cycle of violence in Plateau and Kano states'. Vol. 17 (8a) May. New York.

HRW (Human Rights Watch) (2011) 'Nigeria: new wave of violence leaves 200 dead', 27 January, http://www.hrw.org/en/news/2011/01/27/nigeria-new-wave-violence-leaves-200-dead

ICG (International Crisis Group) (2012) 'Curbing violence in Nigeria (I): the Jos crisis', Africa Report No.196, 17 December, https://www.crisisgroup.org/africa/west-africa/nigeria/curbing-violence-nigeria-i-jos-crisis

Jimoh, A.M., Abuh, A., Ahovi, I.A., Akhaine, S. and Adunola, S. (2021) 'Govt places Jos on a 24-hour indefinite curfew'. Available at: https://guardian.ng/news/govt-places-jos-on-24-hour-indefinite-curfew/

Kastfelt, N. (1994) *Religion and Politics in Nigeria: A Study in Middle-Belt Christianity*, London: British Academic Press.

Krause, J. (2011) A Deadly Cycle: Ethno-Religious Conflicts in Jos, Plateau State, Nigeria, Geneva: Geneva Declaration Secretariat.

Kukah, M. (2021) 'What Kukah told US congress committee on foreign affairs'. Available at: https://www.thecable.ng/full-text-what-kukah-told-us-congress-committee.

Logams, P.C. (2004) *The Middle Belt Movement in Nigerian Political Development: A Study in Political Identity, 1949–1967*, Abuja: Centre for Middle Belt Studies.

Nnoli, O. (1980) *Ethnic Politics in Nigeria*, Enugu: Fourth Dimension.

Owete, F. (2014) 'Northern minorities protest "marginalization" by Hausa-Fulani', *Premium Times*, 27 May 2014. Available at: https://www.premiumtimesng.com/news/161512-northern-minorities-protest-marginalization-hausa-fulani.html

Pak, A., Adegboye, O.A., Adekunle, A.I., Rahman, K.M., McBryde, E.S., and Eisen, D.P. (2020) 'Economic Consequences of the COVID-19 Outbreak: The Need for Epidemic Preparedness', *Frontiers in Public Health*, 8: 241, https://doi.org/10.3389/fpubh.2020.00241

Pérouse de Montclos, M. (ed.) (2014) Boko Haram: Islamism, Politics, security and the State in Nigeria. West African Politics and Society series, vol. 2. Ibadan: African Studies Centre (ASC)/Institut Français de Recherche en Afrique (IFRA)

Rindap, M.R., and Auwal, M.I.M. (2014) 'Ethnic minorities and the Nigerian state', *International Journal of Arts and Humanities*, 3(3), 89–101.

Shobayo, I. (2020) 'Tragic lockdown: gunmen terrorise Plateau communities', Nigerian Tribune Online, 27 April 2020. Available at: https://tribuneonlineng.com/tragic-lockdown-gunmen-terrorise-plateau-communities/.

Suberu, R.T. (1996) *Ethnic Minority Conflicts and Governance in Nigeria*, Ibadan: Spectrum Books.

Tanko, A. (2021) Nigeria's Security Crises – Five Different Threats. Available at: https://www.bbc.com/news/world-africa-57860993.

Turaki, Y. (1993) *The British Colonial Legacy in Northern Nigeria: A Social and Ethical Analysis of the Colonial and Post-Colonial Society and Politics in Nigeria*, Jos: Challenge Press.

Vellturo, M. (2020) Religious Freedom Conditions in Nigeria in 2020. Country Update: Nigeria. December 2020. United States Commission on International Religious Freedom. Available at: https://www.justice.gov/eoir/page/file/1345386/download.

6

Applying Participatory Methodologies in Understanding the Impact of the COVID-19 Epidemic on Religious Communities in Nigeria

Henry Gyang Mang

This chapter discusses the fieldwork experiences of using participatory methods in studying religious minorities in Plateau State, Nigeria, during the COVID-19 epidemic period. The research, conducted for CREID between February and April 2021, among communities perpetually vulnerable to violent conflict and now the COVID-19 epidemic, helped provide an insight into their experiences and coping mechanisms. This chapter is primarily a discussion of the author's experience while using specifically the 'River (or Road) of Life' and the Participatory Rural Appraisal (PRA) matrix ranking with a group of Christian men. The team also used focus group interviews (FGDs) and semi-structured interviews (SSIs), and so was able to see first-hand the unique values of the participatory methods relative to the FGDs and SSIs. The uniqueness of the participatory methods is in their intentionality towards making the respondent create a more vivid picture of their experiences using the picturesque details that they themselves created. Furthermore, the PRA matrix ranking provides a minor but efficiently clear set of quantities, which can postulate a mixed-method approach. More interestingly, the study brought the researcher to the acknowledgement of his subjectivity in the research, and how the field helps researchers to overcome these subjectivities.

Introduction

In Nigeria, as with most developing countries, the disconnect between marginalized groups and state systems makes religion and religious organizations influential gatekeepers. In fact, a journalist in one of Nigeria's influential economic daily's summarily puts it thus:

> The sad reality faced by most Nigerians is the need for them to provide their own electric power supply, security, basic health care, quality education, good shelter, basic means of transportation and other essential services for themselves with little or no government support whatsoever. Nearly every social or public goods that should be a dividend of good governance and provided for a large number of Nigerians are privately sought-after by only those few Nigerians who can afford it. This has widened the social equality gap between the rich and the poor. (Victor, 2021)

A few others such as Elias, 2020, Agbormbai, 2021 and Utomi, 2021 have noted this and the agency of religion in the political manipulation of the populace. Religion has been the major gatekeeper in Nigeria's politics and society; politicians and government agents have for long used religious organizations and their leaders for access most especially to their poor adherents. These gatekeepers transmit both information and opportunity to their congregation, thus providing access to politicians. Without a doubt, religion (primarily Christianity and Islam) has been a major instrument in conflicts, political determinations and power-sharing in Nigeria.

It is in this gatekeeping process that even within the religions, marginalization occurs based on class, ethnic relationships or even geography. In many cases, religious minorities emerge due to the idiosyncrasies of identities such as noted above, and so even within religions there are quite a number of uncomfortable relationships and discontents among followers. This is not necessarily novel information, as quite a number of studies have been carried out looking at access and opportunity within marginalized groups in general and religiously marginalized groups specifically (Malik, 2002; Silimane, 2003, Hasan and Hasan, 2013; Oza, 2020).

This CREID project, comprising a concurrent study (in India and Nigeria) of religious inequalities and their intersections with other inequalities (class, caste, gender, age) in the context of COVID-19, was aimed at understanding the impact of the epidemic on communities already impacted by other challenges, in order to develop policy recommendations for responses which are sensitive to the experiences of these affected groups.

The fieldwork activities were conducted in Kaduna and Plateau states (both in Nigeria's north), between 2 and 5 March 2021. The author conducted fieldwork in Plateau State, where two local government areas, Jos North, which is the state's urban capital, and Bassa, an adjacent and more rurally based local government area compared to Jos North, were chosen.[1]

Plateau State has since 2001 been embroiled in a series of inter-religious, inter-ethnic and resource-based conflicts.[2] At various times, these conflict labels have been known to intersect, leading to what has come to be termed the 'Plateau Crisis'. Although the state is predominantly Christian in population and identity, it is located within the largely Muslim north of Nigeria. There is, however, a reasonably large population of Muslims living within the state.[3] Bassa LGA is mostly rural, although it headquarters of the country's second biggest army division. It comprises predominantly Christian autochthonous ethnic groups: the Buji, Irigwe, Kitche (Rukuba), and Pengana. Also living among these groups are a reasonably large population of Fulani and Hausa communities who are predominantly Muslim. Since 2001 there has also been a lot of conflict in Bassa between the mainly Christian farmers and the mainly Muslim cattle herders.

This chapter focuses on my own experience with the findings related to the inquiries with Christian men in Miango, Bassa LGA, although the whole study in Plateau State also included another local government area, Jos North. The study also comprised inquiries with Christian women, and Muslim men and women. Particular attention for this chapter will focus on Bassa, where my fieldwork was conducted among Irigwe Christian men, because my religious and gender identities were the same as theirs.

Methodology

The team in Bassa used three instruments. The first was a two-pronged approach using two inquiry group methods: the 'River (or Road) of Life' and the PRA matrix ranking. The team then conducted comparator focus group discussions with participants from the earlier inquiry group sessions. Lastly, the team conducted semi-structured interviews with two participants from the comparator focus group discussions. Two researchers were assigned to each inquiry group, FGD or semi-structured interview. While one researcher was facilitating the process, the other researcher was taking a record of the proceedings.

'River (or Road) of Life'

The 'River (or Road) of Life' instrument is an inquiry group method that generates the respondents' lived experiences through symbolism. The illustration of a 'river' or 'road' represents the lived experience of the respondent, over a period of time. In the case of this study, this comprised the one and a half years from the beginning of the COVID-19 outbreak.

The team used prompting questions similar to those in focus group discussions; however, their uniqueness was that they didn't generate debate as with the focus groups, but rather generated detailed personal experiences of the respondents. This was a big change for me specifically as a researcher, who has been used to using detailed question guides, to now use simple prompting questions which elicited varied and sometimes deep experiences. We used simple questions such as:

- What are the most important challenges you have experienced in your daily life starting from before the pandemic, and during it?
- What factors have helped you to cope?

In the facilitation process, the team leader gave an example, using a big flipchart, of a river/road running across the board, and he/she in agreement with the respondents agreed on the river/road to be the symbol of their movement in life from before the COVID-19 pandemic to the present. The symbols they drew along the 'road' represented their lived experiences, issues such as relationships with people, groups/organizations, events and situations they found themselves in, all of which characterized either positive or negative experiences.

All respondents were given large cardboard sheets and markers. They were also encouraged to improvise by using objects like rocks, sticks, leaves and so on, to further illuminate their experiences. They were then allowed between 10 and 20 minutes for drawing and setting their process. After everyone had finished drawing, each participant was in turn given the opportunity to present their river/road and narrate their story within five minutes. However, depending on how elaborate their narration was, some took up to 20 minutes.

Furthermore, the facilitator asked the following:

- What exactly did each symbol represent in your life?
- What were the critical moments, for example health, farming, work, business and so on?

The facilitator then wrote down the key points as they emerged into two lists:

1. Challenges
2. Enablers

The 'Road of Life' instrument presented quite a novel and interesting approach for in-depth qualitative focus group methods. Unlike the conventional focus group interviews, in which various points of view are elicited through heightened discussions among the group, the Road of Life requires the individuals to make a picturesque view of their life's passage within the given period. In the case of the session among Christian men in Bassa, all the men had a commonality of challenges ranging from narratives of violence and death due to conflict in their communities to discussions of their fears about not being able to provide for their families during those times. As noted earlier, there has been a high frequency of violence between farmers and livestock herdsmen, and this led to hard times in most communities within Bassa, most especially in terms of basic needs, finances, health and livelihood, and then the COVID-19 outbreak, leading to lockdowns, increased these insecurities.

However, even within all these, the respondents had some positive experiences. One common positive was the fact that the COVID-19 experience forced them to interact with family (both extended and nuclear) more than ever before. Another was an increased devotion to their Christian faith.

Now although all of this information can be acquired through a conventional focus group discussion, it was very noticeable that more passion and emotion were exuded by respondents while discussing their individual sketches of the 'Road of Life' than it would have been with an FGD. Also, unlike the conventional FGD, the listeners didn't have the option of interjecting but were encouraged to hold back and relate to the others' comments when presenting their own 'Road of Life'.

I also realized during the session that I had come into the field with a major bias, perceiving that the group we were dealing with, being from a rural area, and mostly non-formally (or only partially) educated, would be apprehensive of putting pen (or marker) to paper. This flawed presumption was totally wrong, because although most of the respondents were not formally educated, they easily grasped the concept of the 'Road of Life', and within the 15 minutes they had all understood the process and followed it passionately.

Three issues took centre stage in their 'Roads of Life':

1. Violence and death
2. The lockdowns
3. Religion

Violence and death

The long history of violence between the mainly Muslim herders and mainly Christian farmers in the area featured regularly in the respondents' descriptions and narratives during the 'Road of Life' session, where they described either their own experiences of loss within the family or those of others they knew. There were also discussions on the loss of property, farm produce or businesses due to the violence. Every respondent had an emotional experience when explaining that aspect of his 'Road of Life'. In one particular case, a respondent who had lost both a brother and father due to an attack during the COVID-19 lockdowns broke into tears while describing how he now has the responsibility of his brother's children, and with help coming from nowhere, he only 'looked onto God and neighbours'. This episode brought tears to a number of the other participants, who tried to calm him down, and we had to take a break for a bit, to calm down. However, interestingly, he showed a high sense of upliftment when he subsequently moved along in his 'Road of Life' description to the present time, which he described his family trying to reorganize and forge ahead with life. He noted that being able to go back into farming with his family members was one of his greatest joys, because it helped him both physically, emotionally and economically, considering that he now had to carry the added burden of his brother's children. In his words:

> 'During the lockdowns, when we were forced to stay indoors, and the attacks then continued leading to the death of my brother and father, I felt as if the world was just coming to an end, I asked myself why God would allow such a thing to happen, how can I cope with my brothers children? I knew I couldn't question God, and somewhere inside me, I was telling myself that it will be over. Now I'm back to teaching in the primary school, and my brothers children are doing OK. God has given me rest.' (He uses the word 'salama', which in Hausa means 'granted peace'.)[4]

An interesting thing I noted in his narrative was the way in which his 'Road of Life' revolved around church, death and the responsibilities ahead. I had asked them if the events had made them question their beliefs in God, and the general response was no; however, a few admitted that they had begun to drink alcohol more during the lockdowns.

For me, the emotional responses were quite unexpected: considering that the men came in high spirits and had started on a high note, the particular images they drew, which depicted dead bodies or coffins, brought a lot of memories. The activity of drawing the events of their 'Road of Life' was quite unique; the respondents' sense of creativity and their emotions as they described their life experiences during the period made me realize how powerful the inquiry group instrument is as a qualitative research tool. Indulging the respondents in not just discussion but in a creative activity that they could further elaborate on provided a much deeper and wider picture than conventional focus group methods.

Table 6.1: Bassa, Plateau State, Nigeria: PRA matrix ranking for Christian men (challenges)

Names	Lack of income	Ethnic violence	Domestic violence	Church & lockdown restraints	No (access to) education	No safety measures	Lack of health facilities	Lack of mobility
Anonymous	3 beans	1 bean	0 beans	1 bean	3 beans	3 beans	2 beans	2 beans
Anonymous	3 beans	3 beans	3 beans	2 beans	3 beans	3 beans	1 bean	3 beans
Anonymous	3 beans	3 beans	3 beans	2 beans	2 beans	3 beans	2 beans	2 beans
Anonymous	3 beans	4 beans	3 beans	2 beans	1 bean	3 beans	1 bean	2 beans
Anonymous	3 beans	3 beans	3 beans	2 beans	3 beans	3 beans	1 bean	3 beans
Anonymous	3 beans	3 beans	3 beans	2 beans	2 beans	3 beans	1 bean	3 beans
Anonymous	3 beans	2 beans	1 bean	2 beans	2 beans	3 beans	1 bean	3 beans
Anonymous	3 beans	3 beans	1 bean	2 beans	3 beans	3 beans	1 bean	3 beans
Total	24	22	16	15	19	24	10	21

Table 6.2: Bassa, Plateau State, Nigeria: PRA matrix ranking for Christian men (enablers)

Names	Unity within families	Personal upliftment	Individual increase in faith	Decreased violence	Better sales of harvests such as vegetables	Rest and increased wellbeing	Increased childbirth
Anonymous	3 beans	2 beans	3 beans	2 beans	3 beans	1 bean	0 beans
Anonymous	2 beans	3 beans	3 beans	3 beans	3 beans	3 beans	0 beans
Anonymous	2 beans	2 beans	3 beans	2 beans	3 beans	3 beans	3 beans
Anonymous	1 bean	3 beans	3 beans	2 beans	3 beans	1 bean	0 beans
Anonymous	2 beans	1 bean	3 beans	2 beans	3 beans	1 bean	0 beans
Anonymous	2 beans	2 beans	3 beans	3 beans	3 beans	2 beans	2 beans
Anonymous	1 bean	2 beans	3 beans	2 beans	3 beans	2 beans	3 beans
Anonymous	2 beans	2 beans	3 beans	3 beans	3 beans	2 beans	1 bean
Total	15	17	24	19	15	15	9

There is an ethical issue, however. As noted earlier, one of the respondents became highly emotional, and this also radiated to some other members of the group. We had to take a break, and allow the emotions to simmer. Furthermore, in order not to infuse too much trauma we changed the questioning to generate a more positive outlook, asking if there were more positive experiences during and after the lockdowns. Interestingly, quite a number of their responses from here on helped to calm them down and, in some cases, bring about a bit of laughter.

The lockdowns

One of the reasons why this particular discussion brought up a lot of interest was that it helped to provide a clear understanding of the fact that most of the respondents, and also probably most people within their communities, were oblivious of the general essence of the lockdowns, but they were not oblivious of the impact of the lockdowns on their livelihoods. In their views, none of the respondents believed they had personally experienced a COVID-19 death, as no one in their communities had died in any manner that presented as that. In fact, as one respondent in the focus group interview stated, 'We have never seen anyone with COVID-19. Sometimes on our phone (through social media) we saw dead bodies being carried out of hospitals. They said it came from China, but we didn't believe it will come to Africa, and God protected us.'

The view that the disease was rather far away from them seemed to be the generally accepted perception among the men: even when they heard of COVID-19 killing prominent Nigerians, it further instilled the idea that it was not a poor man's or local disease but one that seemed to affect mainly the rich, who had money to travel to places like China.

Furthermore, information concerning the pandemic seemed just like other government propaganda on the radio or other media. Thus they experienced the pandemic as quite distant from them, and the lockdowns seemed unnecessary. However, there was a clear agreement among all of the respondents during the session that attacks by suspected herdsmen escalated during the lockdowns.

Another emotionally charged issue had to do with lockdown restrictions on churches and other religious groups. One respondent was very bitter about the fact that during the lockdowns the Plateau State governor banned the celebration of Easter, forcing churches to close. The people of Miango annually combine their cultural day with the Easter period, and this meant no celebration in 2020. However, to their dismay, the same State Governor was alleged to have allowed Muslims to celebrate Ramadan, which came a few weeks later. The group was so angry about this in both individual comments and affirmations during the session. This sparked off a lot of questions about the Christian faith of the state governor, with one respondent jocularly saying:

> 'It is possible that he [the governor] has covertly converted to Islam and is only pretending to be Christian so that he is not impeached as governor. He seems to favour Muslims more, he gave them political leadership in Jos North and also even with our legislative seat. I don't trust him.'

Religion plays a significant role in the politics of Plateau State, and any action by political leaders could be misconstrued by people of one faith as favouring the other. This transpired in quite a few ways during the COVID-19 lockdowns, as seen with the case of festivals above, and even in issues relating to the sharing of food and other commodities as palliatives during the lockdowns some groups assumed that sharing was done to favour others more than them, and the blame was aimed mainly at the government.

Religion

Religion also presented an interesting emotional perspective during the 'Road of Life' sessions. While discussing their experiences during the lockdowns, a good number noted that they had not been regular churchgoers before COVID-19; however, the lockdowns and apparently the apocalyptic news about COVID-19, motivated quite a number of them to reinvigorate their pursuit of faith. Although devotion was limited by the lockdown, their personal and family devotions greatly increased. Most respondents were clear on their renewed devotion while discussing it in their 'Road of Life'. One respondent, though, in the focus group discussions presented quite a contrary view. He noted that at a point during the lockdowns he was angry with God.

> 'Why would God, after allowing such a terrible thing like COVID-19, leading to lockdowns, then allow Fulani to attack and kill people? For me, God has not been fair, bad things and bad people everywhere, and some people are now saying that going to church will help us?'

Many people had to rethink their religious values during the lockdown. Among the groups interviewed for this work, most respondents feared the apocalyptic nature of the COVID-19 events, but even at that, some questioned the intentions of God in allowing this alongside an already existent crisis of conflict, poverty and other disease.

PRA matrix rankings

The PRA matrix rankings are used to assess and study the preferences of participants for a particular issue or issues over others. In this case study, the PRA matrix ranking was done in relation to the challenges and enablers the respondents faced during the peak periods of the COVID-19 pandemic (see Tables 6.1 and 6.2).

The facilitators drew two matrix boards, one representing challenges while the other represented enablers. On each board the names of the participants were written down on the left column, while along the top row of the matrix table the various possible issues which posed as possible challenges or enablers were listed. The participants were asked one by one, to choose on a scale from 0 to 3, which signified how important each of these challenges or enablers was for them. They were each given a handful of beans and asked to use either none for the unimportance of the challenge or enabler or, at the most, three beans to signify how important the challenge or enabler was. Here, the more the beans, the more important the issue was.

The various quantities of bean seeds placed by each participant for the different challenges or enablers were totalled and, based on these quantities, the priority challenges and enablers were figured out from the quantities provided. As seen from the two images acquired from the PRA matrix ranking for Christian men in Bassa, lack of income and safety were the biggest challenges, followed by ethnic violence and the lack of mobility. On the other hand, views on domestic violence and issues related to health were less challenging. The facilitator tried to encourage further discussion on why domestic violence was less of a challenge, and a respondent noted that those issues were usually short-term and commonly resolved domestically, so did not present a major challenge. While this was the perspective of the men's group, that of the women was quite different. In the women's view, issues on domestic violence and those related to health were rated higher in the matrix. One can understand why domestic violence was a bigger challenge for women than for men. Most times the men were the perpetrators of domestic violence and in most cases they cared less for the larger health of the family, and so they would rather push away such incidents from their memories, while, in contrast, women who live with the bruises and the responsibility for health take it more to heart. That is why such issues were usually short-term for the men, and more long-term for the women.

Enablers

All respondents were in common agreement that the news of the emergence of COVID-19, and the events that followed, were quite terrifying to many. These fears led many to rethink their worldviews, and many became religious. In response to why they became more religious, one respondent noted: 'We thought the world was coming to an end ... this has never happened before, and the news about deaths kept on getting worse, so we were preparing for the end-time.' Interestingly, although they complained about poverty, most respondents talked about the experience of 'lack' in a lockdown as teaching 'prudence and contentment', and although there was anxiety about what to eat and other basic needs, it also gave them a break from paying the children's school fees, buying new clothes or even having to travel.

Other interesting enablers were the fact that they had time for retrospection, and also it was an opportunity to bond with family more, especially for the male respondents. The lockdown seemed to have fostered new family ties. While the enablers are more introspective and ephemeral, they seemed to have quite an impact on the worldviews of many of the respondents. A number of them noted that they had greatly reduced their drinking and had thought up ways to supplement their incomes, just in case they found themselves again in another tight situation similar to the lockdowns.

It is quite interesting to note that in both inquiry group sessions the respondents were highly motivated to talk after the activities they had either done themselves or had helped to do. For instance, during the 'Road of Life' the respondents were more interested in providing the narrative based on what they drew along their 'Road of Life'; in most cases, their drawings followed the sequence of the events of their lives during the period, and so when verbalizing that, they were able to make further visualizations. In the matrix rankings on the other hand, respondents found it easier to explain reasons why they had allocated more bean seeds to any particular challenge or enabler with more emphasis than if they were asked to simply respond to verbal rankings. The motivation seems to have come from the fact that they had been instructed to place the bean seeds based on their convictions. Therefore, when asked to explain why there seemed to be more emphasis on one rather than the other, they would not contradict themselves, but rather emphasise why they seemed to agree on one issue rather than another.

The uniqueness of these inquiry groups over a simple focus group discussion is the fact that they helped the respondents to further probe into their inner conscious minds to bring out some recessive memories, which would have been missed in an ordinary FGD.

FGDs and SSIs

A focus group interview was conducted with a different group of Christian men, mostly from different villages from those who were involved in the Inquiry Group Session. The FGD was held using a semi-structured interview outline which aided the interviewer to ask questions related to lived experiences of the respondents before, during and after the COVID-19 lockdowns. The transcript was submitted as part of the fieldwork data. The two main differences between the data obtained and experiences of the respondents in the inquiry group sessions and the focus group session were that the responses from the 'Road of Life' were quite detailed, and could provide more insight on the individual interviews with each respondent. The River of Life exercise also elicited a high level of emotional responses, which would hardly have come from a focus group discussion.

Two SSIs were also held with Christian men in Bassa, one with a respondent from the inquiry group session – a university undergraduate – and another with a respondent from the FGD – a farmer. This enabled the researchers to gain views from two differing perspectives. The two transcripts were submitted as part of the fieldwork data. In a sense, one noticed that the participatory inquiries elicited more emotion from respondents and therefore more perspectives in description than the FGDs or even the key informant interviews.

Significance of the use of inquiry group methods

The use of the 'Road of Life' and the PRA matrix ranking were eye-openers for me. I had never encountered this approach, and I was a bit apprehensive at first, especially when considering the 'Road of Life' for the men, because I had imagined that the respondents, being African men, would come with the perspective that being made to draw on a piece of cardboard was too juvenile and demeaning for them. But I was totally wrong. I realized that the concept was not only grasped easily by them but also interested them. I had come with some bias and, although not uncommon, it is important to appreciate its impact on research and how much it should be avoided. Just because they were from rural backgrounds, I had assumed they wouldn't grasp the concepts.

The inquiry group sessions have a way of extracting emotions from the respondents' narratives, which other instruments such as the SSIs and FGDs might not. For instance, I have often observed that in an SSI the respondent might seem restrained or tend to be very careful with his/her responses; also during the focus group, which could be less inhibiting in terms of responses when arguments or varying points of view are made, there still arises the tendency for superficial responses for the sake of argument. However, the 'Road of Life' deliberately drives the respondent to provide more emotive responses without inhibitions from other respondents, thereby expressing them in more detail when providing a narrative for his/her drawings. Likewise, the PRA matrix ranking generates the emotional magnitude of the respondent towards particular issues. By ranking emotions towards an issue one can quantify the levels at which the respondent finds the issue impacting him/her and their immediate community. Furthermore, it interestingly has a relatively small but clear set of quantitative values, which makes it something similar to a mixed-method approach.

Conclusion

The use of the 'Road of Life' and the PRA matrix ranking were eye-openers. Although we were initially a bit apprehensive about using it with the male respondents, they surprisingly grasped the concept and appreciated it in a manner we had least expected. The discovery in the study that the COVID-19 period encouraged respondents to be more religious, is not surprising, in that the choice to hold on to religion as a primary has arisen from the fear of losing paradise after the losses experienced on earth due to the disconnect between these marginalized groups and government, and furthermore between them and their parent religious groups. Most respondents seemed oblivious of government presence and appreciated religion more from their personal experiences rather than its larger structure. In their views, if COVID-19 portended the end of the world, then 'Heaven' became the final (and most optimistic) option.

Notes

[1] Nigerian states are further divided into local government areas (LGAs), most of which are created on the basis of population size, ethnic clumping or for purposes of gerrymandering.
[2] Plateau State lies between latitude 08°24′N and longitude 008°32′ and 010°38′ east, with coordinates: 9°10′N 9°45′E. Located centrally, within Nigeria, Plateau State is bounded by Kaduna State in the west, Nassarawa State to the south, Taraba State to the east and Bauchi to the north.
[3] I discuss this dynamic in Mang (2012).
[4] This respondent is a primary school teacher in one of the remote villages of Bassa that was attacked by the Fulani in August 2020.

References

Agbormbai, E. (2021) The Poverty–Conflict Nexus and the Activities of Boko Haram in Northeast Nigeria. ScholarWorks. Available at: https://scholarworks.waldenu.edu/cgi/viewcontent.cgi?article=12239&context=dissertations

Elias, P. (2020) 'Why Nigeria's efforts to support poor people fail, and what can be done about it', *The Conversation*. Available at: https://theconversation.com/why-nigerias-efforts-to-support-poor-people-fail-and-what-can-be-done-about-it-137122

Hasan, Z., and Hasan, M. (2013) 'Minorities at the Margins', in *India: Social Development Report 2012: Minorities at the Margins*. New Delhi: Oxford University Press.

Malik, I.H. (2002) 'Religious minorities in Pakistan'. Refworld. Available at: https://www.refworld.org/docid/469cbfc30.html

Mang, H.G. (2012) 'Minorities as a political majority: power and reciprocity within and outside the small geographic boundaries of a north-central Nigerian state', in M. Fois and A. Pes, (eds), *Politics and Minorities in Africa*. Nova Collectanea Africana, Cagliari: Centro di Studi Africani Sardegna (CSAS), pp 273–94.

Oza, P. (2020) 'Religion, culture and the process of marginalization', SSRN, 4 August. Available at: https://ssrn.com/abstract=3644854 or http://dx.doi.org/10.2139/ssrn.3644854

Silimane, S. (2003) 'Recognizing minorities in Africa'. Minority Rights Group. Available at: https://minorityrights.org/wp-content/uploads/old-site-downloads/download-43-Recognizing-Minorities-in-Africa.pdf

Utomi, P. (2021) *'Nigeria under Buhari is most miserable place to live on earth – political economy professor, Pat Utomi'*, *Sahara Reporters.* Available at: /article/nigerias-government-http://saharareporters.com/2021/12/13/nigeria-under-buhari-most-miserable-place-live-earth—political-economy-professor-pat.

Victor, A. (2021) 'Nigeria's government disconnected from the people', Businessday NG. Available at: https://businessday.ng/opinion disconnected-from-the-people/

7

Working with Survivors of Trauma: Using Participatory Ranking to Explore the Experiences of Izala Women in Northern Nigeria

Fatima Suleiman

I am the regional coordinator of the Women, Peace and Security network, and Director of the Islamic Counselling Initiative of Nigeria (ICIN), which works to promote interfaith dialogue among marginalized religious minority groups, with a particular focus on women. In Nigeria there is a lot of gender-based discrimination and violence, and, as a woman growing up in this context, this severely impacted my self-esteem. In my career, and as a Nigerian woman, I am passionate to redress this imbalance through work to increase women's awareness of their rights, to build their capacity and to promote women's education and participation in governance. This has not been without resistance, as seen through the National Assembly's recent dismissal of the Gender Bills, legislation I have been working for over the past decade. In Wase, Plateau State, northern Nigeria, women are not allowed to vote or to be voted for. I am working to ensure women's greater participation in the 2023 Nigerian national elections and to protest against this injustice. In Nigeria women are marginalized, and, knowing this, I believe we shouldn't just sit on the fence. If women were given equal rights to men, I believe Nigeria would be a better place, and there would be less violence. Women deserve a seat at the table. My role, my passion, is to create awareness among marginalized Nigerian women of their rights, and to mobilize for action. I am a storyteller, a researcher, a facilitator and an activist.

Introduction

In this chapter I will explore my experiences of using participatory methodologies, including focus group discussions (FGDs) and participatory ranking methodologies (PRM), to understand the experiences of Izala Muslim women in Wase, northern Nigeria, as part of research funded by the Coalition for Religious Equality and Inclusive Development (CREID). Izalas are a minority sect within Islam, and a Muslim minority among the Sunni Muslim majority in Nigeria. The aim of the research was to understand how being a woman and a member of a religious minority accentuates experiences of marginality, and to see how the experiences of Izala women differed from those of Izala men, and from Christian women. The idea behind the use of participatory methodologies was to enable the voices of the women to be heard through the study, to reveal their perceptions of discrimination and violence in the course of their everyday interactions.

Context

ICIN has worked with Izala women from rural communities as part of previous work mapping the intersection of poverty and religious marginality for development. This work revealed Izalas, one of the largest Islamic minorities in Nigeria, to be also one of the most socially and economically marginalized groups. Izala Society, formally Jamaʿat Izalatul Bid a Wa Iqamatis Sunnah (Society for the Removal of Innovation and Re-Establishment of the Sunnah), also called JIBWIS, is an Islamic movement originally established in northern Nigeria to fight what it sees as the *bid'a* (innovation) practised by the Sufi brotherhoods. Izalas are a reclusive sect, and Izala women, in particular, are not permitted to intermingle with other religious groups, including other Muslim women.

Izala doctrine sees women as purely domestic figures. Izala women are not permitted to be educated, to leave the house unsupervised or without wearing a hijab, to work or to access healthcare unless the provider is female. Given the prohibition on intermingling outside of the Izala sect, and the restriction on the formal education of Izala women, this essentially precludes all healthcare access. Izalas are also distinct from other Muslim sects in that they don't celebrate occasions such as weddings, births or social festivals. They are consequently a controversial and highly marginalized group within Nigeria.

Due to this marginalization, it would not have been possible to conduct this research with the Izala women without the use of participatory methods, or without the trust that I have built with the community through over 14 years of engagement with religious minorities in rural Wase; this, for an isolated and reclusive minority group, was a crucial enabling factor for the research.

Method

The research with CREID was not my first time employing participatory methods – I have used them previously for a visual study with UN Women to understand the prevalence of gender-based violence (GBV) in my region. This also was not without its challenges, as for women affected by GBV, it is generally taboo to talk about it. This cultural taboo made other forms of research inquiry impossible, since victims would not speak out, particularly in public/group settings. We worked with the International Federation of Women Lawyers (FIDA) to connect affected families with a lawyer to advocate on their behalf, but, due to this taboo, the families mostly refused: they said they didn't need legal help. We therefore had to approach victims individually, to interview them individually and confidentially, to create anonymized video testimonies to try and understand the women's experiences. The objective was to establish a baseline for further sensitization work across the region to break the permissive culture of silence around GBV.

For the CREID study, focus groups and participatory ranking exercises were used to understand the perceptions and experiences of Izala women in Wase, compared with women from the majority Christian and Muslim religions, and from Izala men.

Thirty women and ten men were selected from across a variety of backgrounds. They had all lived in Wase for over a decade, and the group included teachers, housewives and nurses. The economic realities of the participants ranged from very poor to low- and middle-income earners, who were largely involved in some form of trade, as well as a number of farmers. The participants included a mix of those married, widowed and single, and FGDs were separated according to gender and faith to encourage open discussion.

Having studied the participatory ranking method, we modified it to suit our context and the participants. For example, we were very conscious of cultural nuances, and we took care to use objects that could not be construed to be religiously demeaning.

The rationale behind using the participatory method was to capture, as widely as possible, the 'voices' of Izala Muslim women, to reveal their perceptions of discrimination and violence in the course of their everyday interactions.

During their individual FGD, the Izala women were asked to identify the greatest threats facing them, both in scale and in depth. The group then ranked these threats to determine which were the most concerning and limiting to them. The threats that the group identified were then used within the FGDs with Christian women, Christian men and non-Izala Muslim men as points of discussion, to ascertain to what extent they agreed with the Izala women's ranking.

After the research, we found that PRM helped us highlight key findings while providing the opportunity for deeper analysis. The women were also able to engage and discuss their opinions and experiences during the FGDs, which was an additional advantage compared with alternative research methodologies, such as individual interviews, surveys or questionnaires, since it helped to create a common understanding for the participants. We noticed it also helped us to develop culturally relevant indicators in administering our questions in a structured manner, enabled the results to be swiftly consolidated and then enabled these to be used to develop action plans seeking to address the identified priorities.

While quantitative and qualitative methodologies are often placed in opposition to one another, the PRM helped us to draw on the strengths of each.

What are the greatest threats facing poor Izala Muslim women?

Our PRM focused on providing qualitative data, with some additional quantitative data through the use of participatory ranking and closed follow-up questions. The participants from all of the groups – Izala women, Christian women, Christian men and non-Izala Muslim men (who were used as comparators) – were encouraged to discuss how the threats affected them and which threats they believed to be the greatest.

Ranked in order of importance, we were able to highlight five key threats. These are presented in the table below. The numbers represent how many people in the group felt that the threat was of high concern.

The PRM helped us to understand cultural and religious indicators and where to place them. In ICIN we now routinely use PRM to understand issues and develop plans of action accordingly (see Table 7.1):

> 'This was the second time I was using the Participatory Ranking Methodology (PRM) for my work as a researcher. When the Lead

Table 7.1: Participatory ranking exercise with Izala women in northern Nigeria

S/N	Threats	FGD – Izala women (20)
1.	Gender discrimination within community	19
2.	Discrimination based on religious identity	18
3.	Restricted dress, mobility	15
4.	Lack of access to work	13
5.	Forced marriages, sexual harassment and bullying	11

Researcher for this work said we were to use PRM I was a little apprehensive, but I told myself, this may be the best opportunity to really test PRM as a "mixed methods" approach, and it turned out a huge success given the diverse nature of the respondents when we were drafting the questions and when we were doing the counting and ranking.' (Prince Charles Dickson PhD)

'As the name suggests, apart from just being participatory, the combined use of both quantitative and qualitative methods in a singular study like this was a learning for me. Especially how we fused our desk review and key informant interviews.' (Translator)

PRM has helped to categorically confirm issues, and it has also been useful to challenge perspectives of participants:

'I have now seen that despite our inequalities we can engage and be engaged by other stakeholders especially with the style that Fatima Suleiman and her team used.' (Izala woman)

'I have never been part of this type of research. It has been almost one year, and the way I see Izala women has changed considerably.' (Christian woman)

'It was good they took us away and gave us privacy to talk about our problems in an environment and with a team we could trust. We spoke freely and were able to identify our problems and suggest solutions that we understand and believe can work.' (Participant)

'I was very concerned how the method will help overcome or apply religious and culturally sensitive indices but the engagement that the participation allowed was an ice breaker.' (Participant)

This PRM method has therefore contributed towards our organizational aim of empowering marginalized voices, helping to raise awareness of other experiences and perspectives.

Challenges

The Izala ideology and doctrine presented many challenges in conducting the research with women in Wase. Izala customs and traditions are infused and influenced by centuries-old patriarchal rules, restricting access of women to public spaces, community service or transport, unless accompanied by a male relative. Women are not to be seen or heard outside of the home, while the practice of *Purdah* mandates the separation of the sexes. Under Izala doctrine, women are excluded from working, and celebrations for weddings, births and cultural festivals are prohibited. This further serves to accentuate the social marginalization of this minority Islamic sect in Nigeria.

Due to the restrictions on the engagement of Izala women, I conducted separate focus groups to navigate this challenge – if I had not done so, or if I had just tried to conduct a survey, interviews or similar, Izala women would not have participated; they would not have spoken. The assurance of the confidentiality of the space was also key (a point I emphasized during the prelude to the discussions) because the women were afraid to speak out and to share their experiences, for fear of their being broadcast to the wider community. Bringing the women together in a participatory focus group for the participatory ranking exercise helped to engender a feeling of trust; the Izala women shared similar backgrounds, experiences and identities. This group space provided an enabling environment for the women to connect and to feel encouraged to share their experiences, to tell their story and thereby to identify and rank key issues facing the community. Yet it was important for me to establish from the offset that we would not be providing solutions to their problems: we were sharing experiences to form a story, to construct a narrative which could, hopefully, be used for change, so that their daughters and future generations of Izala women would not have to share in their experiences of discrimination. To raise awareness of the fact that they do have rights and they can have rights, and access to education. That this could lead to further future discussions within Wase which could make things better.

For me, as a facilitator, a women's rights activist and a Muslim, I was confronted by the Izala ideology: the assertion that as Izala women they felt they were not permitted to receive a Western education, despite the fact that Islamic teaching encourages the pursuit of education; the power dynamics between Izala men and women, where it was felt that the men had the power to do everything, including to beat their wives, and the women had the power to do nothing – they were not to be seen or heard (*Purdah*); the conception that women are not allowed to pursue a livelihood outside of the home. I understood these expressions to be a cultural exercise of patriarchy.

There were also language barriers to the research. There are a plurality of languages spoken in northern Nigeria, and while I understand the main dialect, Hausa, a few of the participants spoke local dialects I did not understand. We therefore needed to work with four different interpreters across the different focus groups. The interpreters worked to capture the women's experiences on flipcharts, and we also recorded, transcribed and translated the discussions. Within each FGD each woman had the space to talk about her experiences, to be listened to and witnessed. The discussion was guided by prompting questions organized into themes, and due to the nature of some of the issues raised, including emotional accounts of rape by security agents, once the recorder was turned off we offered subsequent support in the form of counselling.

I do a lot of counselling because so many women from Wase have been affected by violent conflict, and they have issues around breaking their silence; they feel it doesn't make a difference if they speak or not. Group participatory research is effective in working with trauma-affected groups because of the mutual support network created which transcends the period of study. For this research, it did make a difference. We have also been able to connect the women to other support groups for better livelihoods, and some of them have been able to assimilate into other communities to begin their lives all over again, despite losing their families and their children.

Conclusion

It is important for me for research to be linked to action, particularly working at the intersection of women's rights and trauma. The earlier participatory research I conducted with women affected by GBV laid the groundwork for more open discussion, and for a clinic for victims, in collaboration with FIDA. For my work with the Izalas, this led to an interfaith sensitization dialogue, with creative elements and cookery, which was broadcast on the local radio and via social media. Izala women are not only secluded but also misunderstood for how they dress, and in the two years following the research with CREID I have convened an annual sensitization discussion and Q&A, bringing together women of different faiths, including Christians, Muslims and Jewish women, to ask questions and share their experiences of discrimination in order to challenge persistent stereotypes and misunderstandings: to open up new ground for women of all faiths. The more open discussion there is, the greater the awareness, the tolerance and the acceptance between faith groups. Even some of the Izala women from the CREID focus group attended the discussion, which was a breakthrough in view of the taboo within Izala doctrine on intermingling beyond the Izala sect.

The research created more discussions, and it got me thinking – how can we best support women from minorities? From the CREID research we discovered that, for Izala women in particular, they in many instances lack an understanding of their rights, and this can even lead to violent conflict. If minority women, who already experience exclusion and discrimination, don't have a basic education, they don't understand the meaning of a better life for their children: if I don't go to school and my child doesn't go to school, what does he become tomorrow? He is already marginalized due to his faith, and it is easier for him to be indoctrinated by ideologists to take up arms. I have employed participatory methods in subsequent research to interrogate this causal link – particularly the indoctrination of, and countering the incidence of, violent extremism among young women. When you have a woman with a basic education, who knows her rights, she wants to give her child an education. She wants to see that the child goes to school and becomes a doctor, a lawyer, a teacher, an architect ... And we would have a better region. The research consequently led to a lot of discussions and to changes for some of the participants involved: some of the women began to take adult education classes, two are now facilitators in a project working with victims of rape to speak about their experiences and break the silence and another two are working in a rights and advocacy organization based in Abuja.

Often the emphasis within research is on funding and the need to generate more revenue to address particular needs. Instead, for this participatory research, one of the key findings was the importance of mentoring: women mentoring other women, to facilitate, advise and support each other through the challenges of GBV, conflict and discrimination. This is the pathway to greater inclusivity in Nigeria.

Appendix – the participative ranking methodology (PRM)

We used the participative ranking methodology (PRM), a participatory 'mixed methods' approach to data collection, in which a group of knowledgeable participants are guided in generating responses to a specific question or set of questions. It is a 'mixed methods' approach, drawing on both quantitative and qualitative methodologies to generate rich, contextualized data that can nonetheless be quantified, ranked and compared across or within groups. We chose this method, although it was largely a first for us, because we noticed it promotes an engaged and participatory process and was going to be better for engagement with Izala women than other methods, such as individual interviews, surveys or questionnaires, given the cultural, doctrinal and pragmatic strictures faced by Izala women.

Method

PRM builds on the tradition of participative rapid appraisal (PRA) methods. Indeed, the PRA acronym can be used to recall and present the key steps in use of the method: Pile, Rank, Account. These steps are described below.

Pile

The basic process of PRM is very similar to that of an open-ended focus group discussion: the facilitator, or moderator, first defines the scope of the research question for the participants, and then works to elicit responses from the individuals in the group. However, instead of relying on a note-taker to capture the key features of discussion, PRM uses objects that are selected by participants to represent key themes of their discussion.

This selection process was iterative, where, through group dialogue, the facilitator works with participants to negotiate which object represents which theme. Depending on the tendencies of the group and the sensitivity of the research question, the moderator may need to prompt participants to elicit feedback and responses on specific issues. As participants' responses are linked to specific themes or topics, objects representing these issues are 'piled' in front of the group.

Rank

The facilitator then defines a continuum along which participants can rank the importance of the issues represented by each of the objects in the pile. This can simply be a line drawn on the ground with a heel. Participants are then encouraged to place objects along the continuum in an order that reflects their relative importance. When an individual places an object, the facilitator asks others if they agree with its positioning, inviting others to reposition it as appropriate. Adjusting the positions of objects continues until a final ordering is agreed among the group.

Account

At each step of the process, responses are recorded. This includes recording all of the responses free-listed in the 'pile' section, as well as the final 'rank' of each agreed afterwards. Crucially, however, the note-taker records the reasons stated by every participant – their 'account' for the positioning of any object. These accounts – generally expressed as clear, propositional statements – often provide a rich insight into local circumstances, attitudes and challenges.

References

Ager, A., Stark, L. and Potts, A. (2010) *Participative Ranking Methodology: A Brief Guide, Program on Forced Migration and Health, Mailman School of Public Health*, New York: Columbia University Press.

Ben Amara, R. (2013) The Izala Movement in Nigeria: Its Split, Relationship to Sufis and Perception of Sharīʿa Re-Implementation. PhD thesis, University of Bayreuth. Available at: https://epub.uni-bayreuth.de/id/eprint/101/

Suleiman, F. (forthcoming) Sharing the Experiences of Members of Religiously Excluded Groups – Intersecting Inequalities in Everyday Life. CREID Intersection Series: Religious Inequalities and Gender, Coalition for Religious Equality and Inclusive Development, Brighton: Institute of Development Studies.

Iraq

8

Facilitating Peer Research for Freedom of Religion or Belief in Iraq

Sofya Shahab

Introduction

Within this chapter I explore the experiences of accompanying activists as peer researchers through processes of participatory research with women and men from religious minorities in Iraq and the Kurdistan Region of Iraq (KRI). Rather than detailing the research process and results, my focus is therefore on methods of supporting peer researchers from within participating communities to conduct, analyse and present their research and how these methods can be used to further understandings of intersecting inequalities among marginalized groups in Iraq. The research approach and overarching questions were designed by my colleague Mariz Tadros at the Institute of Development Studies, while we worked together to facilitate the trainings and to accompany our colleagues in Iraq throughout the research process. For those we accompanied, applying participatory approaches and undertaking peer research was an entirely new experience, a majority having backgrounds either within the NGO/development sectors or as women's rights activists. In exploring the intersection of gender and religious marginalization through the Coalition for Religious Equality and Inclusive Development (CREID) we therefore worked alongside activists who also belonged to religious minorities in Iraq including the Kaka'i, Sabean Mandean, Shabak, Yazidi and Christian (Syriac Orthodox and Chaldean) communities, recognizing the contribution they would bring to the research. We additionally approached Baha'i and Turkman Shia activists whom we also hoped to include; however, they did not have the capacity to participate in the research at this time. Through partnering with these researchers, we also aimed to 'move away from an extractive model social research' and empower them to affect positive social change within their communities.[1]

The diverse and complex history of Iraq means that it is home to a large number of different ethnic and religious groups. However, recent conflicts including the terrorist campaign undertaken by Daesh from 2014 to 2017 has meant that these populations are under threat and experiencing a rapid decline in their numbers in Iraq and KRI. Recent estimates have put the population of Iraq at 37,548,000 (UN, 2016), approximately 99 per cent of whom are Muslim – 60–65 per cent Shia and 32–37 per cent Sunni (including a majority of the Kurdish population) (Minority Rights Group). Prior to Daesh it was estimated that in Iraq there remained about 350,000 Christians, 500,000 Yezidis, 200,000 Kaka'i, under 5,000 Sabean Mandeans and a small number of Baha'i (Minority Rights Group). While the Iraqi constitution highlights that 'Iraq is a country of multiple nationalities, religions, and sects' (Article 3, 2005[2]) enshrining principles of non-discrimination and the equality of all Iraqis, as well as making provisions for the protection of the Turkmen and Syriac languages alongside the national languages of Arabic and Kurdish, these rights as guaranteed by the constitution are not mirrored in the everyday realities of Iraq's minorities (UNPO, 2013).

This was most clearly evidenced through the targeted campaigns of Daesh against these populations and their desire to eradicate these histories, cultures and peoples from their so-called 'caliphate'. As part of their devastating campaign, Daesh undertook mass genocidal pogroms that included the slaughter, enslavement and forced exodus of thousands of innocent civilians with a focus on those belonging to religious minorities – most especially Yazidi communities, followed by Christians, then Turkmen and Shabaks, as well as Kaka'i communities, although their history of hiding their identity meant they were less visible and therefore not targeted to the same extent (Knell, 2017). With the attack on Sinjar on 3 August 2014 thousands of Yezidis were massacred, their bodies dumped in mass graves, while tens of thousands were forced to flee their homes and left without food or water amid scorching temperatures (Cetorelli et al, 2017; UNAMI/OHCHR, 2014). Those who were unable to escape were tortured, forced to convert to Islam or killed, while young women and girls were taken into slavery, forced into marriages and raped (UNHRC, 2016). Such targeted persecution was not limited to the Yazidi community – although they were the most numerous and devastated by these acts; Christians were given the ultimatum to leave their homes, remain as second-class citizens and pay the *jizya* tax or face execution – some by crucifixion (USCIRF, 2016). Christian, as well as smaller numbers of Shabak and Turkmen, girls were also kidnapped, many never to be heard from again (UNAMI/OHCHR 2014). Alongside these humanitarian atrocities, Daesh also sought to cleanse the region of the diverse and ancient heritage of these communities, through the destruction of tangible sites and preclusion of intangible practices (Isakhan and Shahab, 2020). Such acts have been declared a genocide against the Yazidi and Christian communities by a number of state governments including the European Parliament, the US House of Representatives and the British Parliament, multilateral bodies and NGOs (CR, 2016; EP, 2016; Hansard, 2016).

Although Daesh have been driven from the frontlines, and the territories they took reclaimed, through research led by members of these targeted communities it is possible to unravel the different forms of ongoing marginalization that continue to constitute the everyday experiences of peoples – particularly women – who belong to these groups. As part of the research process, peer researchers who belonged to religious minority communities in Iraq and KRI were identified through networks of women's rights activists, including the Hammurabi Human Rights Organization and the Gender Studies and Information Organization. Rather than undertaking participatory research directly within the communities ourselves, we invited these identified individuals to participate in a workshop about the project and methods so that they would be equipped to facilitate peer research within their own communities. Participants in the training workshop therefore included: three Yazidi women from Essyan and Sharya camps and one Yazidi woman from Bashiqa; one Chaldean Catholic woman from Mosul currently living in Erbil and one Syriac Orthodox Christian man from Hamdaniya; one Shabak woman from Bartella; one Turkman Shia man from Bartella; one Sabean Mandean woman from Erbil; and one Kaka'i woman from Erbil. The three young Yazidi women from internally displaced persons camps chose to work together in the production of their report, as did the two Christian participants.

During the workshop we explored what it means to undertake participatory approaches, as well as the specific methods – participatory ranking and focus group discussions (FGDs) – that would be employed by the researchers within their communities during this project. We additionally discussed the research questions and objectives in understanding the particular challenges faced by women from religious minorities, because they are women and belong to a minority. The focus was therefore on how the experiences of FGD participants differed from the experiences of men in their community, alongside how they differ from the experiences of women more generally in Iraq and KRI. A majority of the women participants opted to undertake two focus groups with the women in their communities and to identify and train a male research assistant to conduct two focus groups with the men. In one case the researcher – from the Kaka'i community – chose to lead all four FGDs with the male and female Kaka'i participants.

Rationale for research

In undertaking such research, especially in a context where there is ongoing displacement, insecurity and trauma related to religious marginalization, utilizing peer research enabled us to remain sensitive to the needs, interests and priorities of those we were working alongside. This is because the participatory approach we employed centred community members as colleagues and researchers of their and their communities' experiences. As a result, the focus was on 'conducting research "with and for" the subjects of the research' and mitigating power balances that traditionally arise within the research process (Institute for Community Studies, n.d.). Positioning women activists as lead researchers in the project who know and are known for their work within their communities, also enabled the inclusion of participants in the focus groups who are at the margins of their community, and whose voices are often overlooked and participation deterred. For example, one component of the research was undertaken with Yazidi Survivors and was facilitated and led by a Yazidi woman who is herself a Survivor. For the peer researchers themselves who may also have been overlooked and silenced alongside their communities the opportunity to share their concerns and be heard was integral: 'This was a dream for me, that one day I would write about oppressed women and write about our suffering, and I felt that my dream had come true' (Yazidi researcher from Essyan camp). Collaborating with those who had been most marginalized was therefore a means of empowerment, highlighting their thoughts, experiences and challenges, while evidence has additionally indicated that participating in peer research can assist in employability and build self-esteem and confidence (Dowling, 2016; Thomas-Hughes, 2018; Dixon, Ward and Blower, 2019).

The civil war in Iraq from 2003 to 2011 and rise of Daesh have brought the issue of religious freedom to the fore in Iraq. However, the silence from communities other than Yezidis regarding the women and girls kidnapped by Daesh suggests there is still a great deal of sensitivity related to the targeting and discrimination they have experienced. This silence is evident both within the minority communities themselves and in how they present themselves externally. Histories of persecution have also contributed to some minorities – most notably the Kaka'i – cultivating a more insular approach to their religious practice and discourse regarding what they share with outsiders (although this is now becoming a point of contention within the Kaka'i community). As a result, employing participatory methods that sought to position members of the communities as partners in the research was integral to ensuring trust and legitimacy among participants, so that they felt confident in openly discussing and sharing their experiences relating to FoRB and religious/gender marginalization. As the Assyrian researchers described, the process of peer research provided a unique opportunity 'for the participants to share their challenges and experiences through a comfortable environment given that we, as researchers, belong to the same community and this increased confidence and trust both in the sharing of personal stories and also in how this research would be used to benefit their communities'. This was because the issues discussed within the focus groups were also issues experienced by the researchers and reduced the likelihood of misunderstandings arising. Through an empathetic approach and the sharing of their own personal examples, the researchers were therefore able to cultivate a safe space which – as well as generating knowledge for understanding and action by ensuring the research was relevant to participants – was in some instances personally and collectively therapeutic. Enabling an honest discussion of challenges usually hidden in silence, there additionally arose opportunities for the solidarity required to counter oppression. This was built into the rationale for working with peer researchers, especially those with a background in activism and strong connections to the community, to enable the taking forward of the findings by and for local community actors once the research process had concluded.

Alongside greater community acceptance for the research being undertaken, through a recognition of the expertise and knowledge that the peer researchers brought to the process we were able to foreground analysis by the peer researchers within the reports they produced (Macaulay et al, 1999: 774). This approach highlighted the voices of marginalized groups where they contributed 'their experiences, their everyday knowledge, and their ability into the research process and thereby gain[ed] new perspectives and insights' (Bergold and Thomas, 2012: 202). Having researchers from within the community lead in the analysis and writing of their research reports gave a greater depth of nuance and understanding to the research and also allowed for connections between experiences and events to be made in new ways. Undertaking the research process within multiple communities and bringing the researchers together in their exploration of FoRB allowed for shared learning between groups by creating prompts with regards to points of similarity and divergence. While the focus was on conducting the research with small groups in each community and on foregrounding individual personal stories rather than generalizing or homogenizing experiences across a community, through an investigation into the intersections of gender and religious marginalization, as well as local applicability, the learnings and recommendations from these communities may also have broader policy and programmatic relevance taking account of 'local priorities, processes and perspectives' (Cornwall and Jewkes, 1995: 1667).

Although we sought to position peer researchers as colleagues and partners within the research process, there were some areas where collaboration was more limited. As Cornwall and Jewkes have noted, while

> [p]articipatory research is theoretically situated at the collegiate level of participation[,] [s]crutiny of practice reveals that this level is rarely, if ever, achieved ... in many cases, people are 'participated' in a process which lies outside their ultimate control. Researchers continue to set the agendas and take responsibility for analysis and representation of outcomes. (Cornwall and Jewkes, 1995: 1669)

Within the project certain elements of the research were indeed set – mainly with regard to the overall focus on the intersections of religious and gender marginalization and the methodological approach. This diminished opportunities for participants to identify the broader topics and research themes that were most relevant to them needing to be addressed. However, within this overarching framing we sought to enable room for adaptation according to the various contexts of each community and to identify priority needs. Through research plans submitted by the peer researchers there was therefore the opportunity to tailor the research as they saw necessary with regards to the formation and make-up of the focus groups, how they would employ and structure the methodological approach and the core questions and topics that would be discussed. The peer researchers were additionally responsible for the analysis of the findings and were the lead authors of their reports, to ensure that their knowledge, representation and interpretation were foregrounded.

In response to this way of working, we positioned the research process and partnership as a form of accompaniment whereby working alongside the peer researchers was a collaborative learning process. This allowed us to become 'an ally, an advisor, an enabler, and maybe a partner, to users undertaking research' (Bergold and Thomas, 2012: 203). We were therefore there to provide support and assistance, especially for those who were inexperienced in conducting peer research, but also to learn from and adapt the research approach according to the knowledge of the researchers and through their analysis of the research findings. As well as allowing for in-depth explorations of the particular challenges facing participants due to their religious and gender identities, the project therefore also enabled a process of participatory learning regarding the strengths and limitations of different methods for accompanying peer researchers. This mode of accompaniment as a methodological approach in peer research is examined in further detail in the section below. Initially focusing on the importance of establishing trust in the research process and building relationships between facilitators and researchers to enable two-way open and honest dialogue and feedback. It then goes on to explore modelling as a tool for training peer researchers before assessing how accompaniment was practised within the design, piloting analysis and writing of the research reports.

Accompaniment

Trust and relationship-building

One of the key challenges we experienced in establishing the research project in Iraq was the initial process of identifying participants. The onset of COVID-19 and subsequent lockdowns and travel bans prevented the international travel required to maintain and establish relationships with potential partners and participants in the time preceding the research period. While in some circumstances it did prove possible to undertake participatory research by adopting online and distance-based methods, these adaptations were predominantly successful in situations where there were pre-existing relationships (Hall, Gaved and Sargent, 2021: 12). Furthermore, the type of research we were seeking to undertake, around sensitive subjects relating to freedom of religion and belief specifically drawing upon examples of people's lived experiences, meant that this research could not be captured by digital methods or surveys, or through online meetings or phone calls. Rather, it necessitated face-to-face and group interaction to generate a sense of collectivity and solidarity among focus group participants. Similarly, it was also important for the workshop for the peer researchers to be conducted in person in order to build group relationships, ensure clear communication and model the methods the peer researchers would be using within the FGDs. In seeking to reach those who were most marginalized due to their religion, gender, class, wealth and education, there was also the risk that in seeking to conduct research online due to restrictions arising from COVID-19 we would preclude these groups from participating as a result of needing access to networks, internet and communications devices. Additionally, as Hall, Gaved and Sargent have noted, during a global pandemic such as that encountered throughout 2020 and 2021, it may also be necessary to 'reflect on whether data collection is absolutely necessary during what is arguably a highly stressful and uncertain period in many people's lives, and if so, ensuring the methods used provide positive psychological and wellbeing benefit to participants' (Hall, Gaved and Sargent, 2021: 12). For these reasons, rather than adapting the workshop and research to online formats, we decided to wait until it would be possible for peer researchers and participants to meet in person. The drawback of this was that this put the project under tight time constraints, making it more challenging to build deep trust and reflexive, flexible and iterative modes of working.

Conducting participatory research on the intersections of gender and FoRB required a foundation of trust, both between participants in the FGDs and the peer researchers and between the peer researchers and Mariz and myself as facilitators in the research process. This was because, although the peer researchers may be known and trusted by the community prior to the FGDs, in order to ensure honest and open dialogue regarding the topics being covered and genuine feedback into the research process – and therefore a strong collaboration between us and the peer researchers – the peer researchers needed to be confident in our reasons for facilitating the research, the approach being devised and how the research would be used. Only if they had a secure knowledge and understanding of these elements would we be able to receive their full buy-in and therefore the buy-in of the participants in the FGDs and to enable them to carry forward the research and findings after the reports had been completed. Traditionally, '[t]his trust must be allowed to develop; it builds on long-term, honest relationships that are characterized by closeness, empathy, and emotional involvement' (Bergold and Thomas, 2012: 203). However, as there had not been opportunities to establish trust between us and the peer researchers over a sustained period of time, a core focus during the initial workshop was to cultivate these relationships and understandings.

To facilitate collaboration and trust from the outset, Mariz and I positioned ourselves as facilitators journeying and learning alongside participants. Rather than a top-down approach, we sought to invite, recognize and build upon the strengths of the peer researchers. As a result, we requested their input, listening carefully to their concerns and suggestions and together discussed ways of addressing or incorporating these. In this, a core element of our role was to create a safe space in which participants felt comfortable and open to share their learnings and experiences. To enable this, the first two days of the five-day workshop were almost entirely based around getting to know one another, our positionalities, histories and experiences. As part of this process, we also sought to co-construct the workshop design and environment with the participants. One of the ways in which this was achieved was through working together to develop the guidelines and expectations for the workshop. To assist with this, participants were asked to reflect on and answer four questions:

> In the context of this workshop –
> What does safety look and feel like?
> What does presence look and feel like?
> What does kindness look and feel like?
> What does courage look and feel like?

They were then invited to share their responses within groups of three and to use them as a base for community guidelines. We then took each group's responses to create an overarching statement which read:

During this workshop we agree to –

- Create a space of safety by ensuring that everyone in the room feels a sense of security and comfort to speak up or to observe in silence. We

trust that we can – and will be encouraged to – share our thoughts and ideas without fear of judgement or criticism.
- Be present in order to reach the goals of the workshop and research project as a journey on which we are embarking on, and aim to complete, together. That we will give equal opportunity to everyone to express themselves and that we will listen to what we have to say. That we will attend all the sessions we can and enter into the room in a spirit of learning, recognizing and respecting the knowledge that each of us has to share.
- Show kindness to one another through understanding and compassion, recognizing all of our shared humanity. That we will create space for everyone, treating each person as the precious diamond they are.

The other key means by which we cultivated a safe space and started to establish trust was through the River of Life exercise, as it enabled the peer researchers to begin to know one another. This involved participants using the analogy of a river to illustrate the story of their lives and the journey they had been on so far – incorporating tributaries for periods of growth and opportunities, bends for new directions they had taken, as well as waterfalls, rapids and boulders for the challenges they encountered. Once they had finished their drawings, each participant was invited – if they wished – to share their river with the rest of the group in the workshop. Through the Rivers of Life exercise and the sharing of individual journeys and experiences it was possible to contextualize and personalize the lived experiences and implications of broader political events. For example, one of the researchers described the displacement of the Shabak community from Mosul due to the persecution they had faced there. By humanizing her story and the struggles she had faced, she served to distance such events from political contestations. In a particularly moving moment, on completing her River of Life, the other participants put politics aside and spontaneously applauded the Shabaki researcher in recognition of her strength and all she had achieved in advancing the rights of women in her community.

Modelling

Alongside building trust, another aspect of the co-generation of workshop guidelines and Rivers of Life exercise was to model ways in which the peer researchers themselves could establish a safe space for the participants in the focus groups to share their experiences. While they were not expected to undertake these activities directly within the FGDs, through the questions for the guidelines we were able to emphasize and reflect on the elements important in shaping an atmosphere of comfort and security and by sharing and listening to each person give their personal history within the Rivers of Life, to practise attentively holding space for one another. In this way, the training workshop was built around a process of modelling in order to familiarize the researchers with the approach, methods and principles they would use in the FGDs by embedding them within the workshop design.

Within the workshop we also used modelling by working through simulations of the research methods with the peer researchers. This was most important with regards to the participatory ranking exercise, as it was an entirely new method for all the researchers. As a result, I took on the role of facilitator for the exercise and invited the rest of the group to share the biggest challenges they faced in their daily lives, as well as also sharing some prompts with them which included education, healthcare, transportation and employment. Once we had together curated a list of key challenges on a flipchart, each participant was invited to order them according to their own perspectives from the most to the least important. Within this task I also modelled different ways in which this might be done, and we discussed the advantages and disadvantages of each option. This included asking each participant to write their own list in a notebook, numbering the challenges on the flipchart or using objects to represent each of the challenges, which the participants could order according to their rankings. They were also invited to give a brief explanation for their ranking. Along with enabling the researchers to practise using the research methods, this worked to help identify core topics which the researchers would then cover within their FGDs beyond those which had already been put forward as standardized across all research countries and communities.

In establishing some topics that needed to be covered from the outset this was one area in which a more hierarchical approach was applied. The need for these topics was to allow for some forms of standardization and cross-country comparison between the research groups. However, each standardized topic was discussed in depth with the researchers, to ensure they understood why it was important to include and that we had their agreement to incorporate it within the FGDs. They were then also invited to include their own challenges which they had identified during the workshop according to the specific contexts of their communities or to add any other challenges that arose during the FGDs. Bringing the researchers together from across the different ethno-religious groups assisted in the identification of the topics which were most applicable within the Iraqi context, as well as where their experiences may diverge from other groups and those from the majority. This was because they were able to work together to identify areas of marginalization and to assess whether these were found within their own communities. As a result, alongside co-creating a list of themes to be introduced in the FGDs if not raised by the participants, it also allowed for the peer researchers to begin to understand the analysis process by drawing on their knowledge to consider points of differentiation for other groups in terms of access to services, resources and opportunities and the reasons for these.

Through the participatory ranking exercise and FGD simulations, we drew on specific examples to ensure clarity and also to model for the peer researchers how they might also ensure the participants understood what was being asked during the FGDs. When facilitating the focus groups we requested the peer researchers to focus on three things – specific examples of marginalization, the reasons behind this marginalization and the impact it had had. We therefore gave a range of examples as to what this might look like 'XX, you mentioned that it can be difficult for Yazidi girls to travel to Mosul for university. Do you know of a specific incident where this has been the case?' and to encourage the peer researchers to draw on and share examples from their own experiences as a form of modelling for FGD participants. They could then potentially use an example such as 'When my sister went to the hospital because she is Christian and does not wear a headscarf the receptionist said the doctor was busy and could not see her, but when another woman came who was Muslim she was taken straight in. In this way my sister does not get as good treatment or care as other women.'

This process of modelling was useful in helping the peer researchers practise and understand the research approach and focus. However, despite taking the time to reflect as a group at the micro-level with regards to the workshop – checking in each day as to whether expectations had been met and questions answered – it would also have been beneficial to apply this form of reflection at the macro-level. This would have allowed us to explicitly reflect together on how the workshop had been designed and why we were doing the things we were doing in the way we were doing them. As a result, we would have been able to directly make the link between the modelling system we sought to employ and the participatory research methods the peer researchers would be engaging with in their communities. Rather than relying on these techniques to be implicitly observed and carried forward, we therefore could have deliberately illustrated the means through which we were building a sense of community and collaboration and facilitating a space where each person felt their perspective was valued and important to share.

Design

In the process of accompaniment the core approach was to recognize and accept the strengths of the researchers – particularly with regard to their connections to and knowledge of their communities, and their ability to deepen analysis through their own understandings and experiences of the situations discussed within the focus groups – as well as to recognize what might be new or different for them in undertaking a research project and to support them with those gaps. For this reason, we employed templates that provided questions to help guide participants through the process of developing their research plans and reports but which still left space for them to design the FGDs as they thought would best suit their communities. This was particularly with regards to the considerations that would ensure the participants felt comfortable and free to speak for example through the demographic make-up of each FGD. Alongside the template for the research plan, I met with each researcher individually to review their plans and to help them explore the specific details of how they would go about the research, the rationale and contextual basis for their approach, the obstacles they might encounter and how they could overcome them.

Piloting

The first FGD was used almost as a pilot to trial the methods with the researchers and participants and to assist in guiding what might be useful in the next rounds. Before the first FGD occurred, I consequently ensured I was available for one-to-one meetings with the researchers to discuss any concerns they might have and to review the methods particularly in relation to the participatory ranking exercise. However, it was only those peer researchers who had never facilitated or been involved in FGDs who took up this opportunity while the other peer researchers all indicated that they were confident and comfortable with the approach. This might also have been a reflection on age – those who accepted the additional support were also those who corresponded with the youngest of the peer researchers – as well as the cultural context, in which it is unusual to ask for help. In recognition of this it might therefore have been useful to set these meetings as required rather than to pose them as optional.

To get a sense of the degree to which the workshop had been successful and the peer researchers took to the process, and to input into the reflections on the first FGDs, we also reviewed a copy of each of the transcripts from the first FGD for each group in order to be able to discuss in more depth with the researchers how they might wish to proceed. From the transcripts we provided individual written feedback and held a group discussion with the peer researchers to draw out the common challenges encountered within the first FGDs and how these might be addressed. For example, for each point a participant raises the peer researcher might also inquire as to what happened, where and when it happened, how the subject felt, what the impact on them was and how would this have been different if they had not been of their religious group and if they had not been a woman. This also supported the peer researchers in being able to focus on how the challenges discussed were different from those faced by all women in Iraq and from those faced by all people in their community, regardless of gender, in order to understand how religion and gender intersect to mean that people are treated a specific way.

Writing

Recognizing the knowledge and expertise the peer researchers brought to the analysis of the challenges discussed during the FGDs and participatory ranking sessions, the peer researchers also undertook the writing of individual research reports documenting their findings with regard to experiences of marginalization resulting from gender and religious affiliation within their communities. Writing can be a solitary endeavour, and even though the FGDs involved multiple peer researchers, the production of the report was predominantly undertaken individually. This had practical benefits in terms of timelines, by streamlining the analysis and report-writing process, but it meant that it was less of a participatory process. To draw on the knowledge of the community participants more broadly it would have been useful to involve those who were interested and willing more thoroughly in the analysis and recommendations within the report. This might have led to points of divergence or disagreement but also to a potentially more informative report that did not rely wholly on the predominant interpretation of one person – even from within the community – with their own positionality, which may have influenced their analysis. In reviewing the drafts of the reports written by the researchers, I began to notice that it was those who were younger and less experienced who appeared to connect with the process and understand the approach we were seeking more thoroughly. This may have been because they were more open to learning and setting aside their own expectations – relying predominantly on what we had cultivated together in the workshop space rather than past experiences of leading or facilitating FGDs.

Despite the challenges to a participatory model of report writing, the production of the reports was taken to be an iterative process. This meant that the reports for each community were written by the researchers from that community, but with some guidance from us – mostly in the form of questions – as a means of drawing out the researchers' knowledge. Although this feedback had mostly been provided through written comments, where I did have the opportunity to meet in person with each of the researchers to review their reports, I found that being able to orally ask questions, clarify and probe was incomparable as an approach to drawing out their analysis and depth of understanding. This may have been in part because the peer researchers took the knowledge that they had for granted, assuming that these elements would also be known to others and therefore not necessary to include in as much detail.

Learning

Identifying the right researchers

In engaging in participatory approaches through peer researchers and undertaking a study that relates to FoRB, finding the right researchers who understood the approach, would engage with the methods and belonged to the same community (both in terms of religion and location) as the FGD participants was integral. This was particularly the case for working with sensitive issues such as gender-based violence. Taking the time to meet and engage with potential collaborators prior to the outset of the project would therefore have been useful in establishing strong relationships and beginning the process of reflecting on different positionalities and how they might impact on the research outcomes. As well as being part of a specific community – for example, a religious minority – it can also be necessary for the peer researchers to attend to other intersecting identities and privileges, especially with regard to authority that may make inclusivity and participation more challenging. In this way it is not so much the experience of the researcher in matters relating to FoRB and women's rights as their ability to connect with people and to make them feel confident in sharing personal details about their lives and experiences that allows a greater insight into the everyday lived experiences of those from religious minorities and how these experiences impact their right to freely identify with and practise their beliefs.

Co-constructing research questions

Employing participatory research methods allowed space for peer researchers to input the areas and themes that they deemed relevant to FoRB among their communities that should be covered during the focus group discussions. This knowledge of the peer researchers and inclusion within the research design, enabled focus groups to be tailored around those issues most pressing to each specific group – while also incorporating responses to common themes across the group in order to draw out similarities and differences. Through participatory methods it was therefore possible to develop a deeper and more nuanced understanding of FoRB as it related to each community.

Leaving preconceptions behind

At the same time as recognizing the knowledge and experience of the peer researchers and incorporating that within the research process, for the participatory approach to be successful in enhancing knowledge and understandings of FoRB within the everyday lived realities of participants at times it is also necessary for the peer researchers to set aside their preconceptions and expectations with regards to their communities' experiences in relation to FoRB. As such, it is necessary for the peer researchers to also approach the research as a learning process, in which each individual participant is an expert in elucidating and analysing their own experiences in relation to FoRB, and that these experiences and understandings may differ from those of other participants and the peer researchers. For the peer researchers it was therefore also an opportunity to learn and understand more about their communities, especially those who are most marginalized, so that 'with this kind of research approach we [the researchers] learned about the greatest threats in scale and depth facing Assyrian men and women from their own perspectives, with a focus on the unique vulnerabilities facing Assyrian women' (Assyrian researchers in conversation with the author). Part of the value of this form of research is therefore that it illuminates individual perspectives and readings of FoRB as it holds meaning and importance for individuals in their daily interactions and also to highlight various differences within communities so that the peer researchers, through this broader understanding, might take account of this within advocacy, NGO and education initiatives with which they are connected, enhancing the potential impacts of such research. As the Assyrian researchers went on to note,

> 'We as researchers also got to know the brave and patient people who believe in themselves and their nationality. Despite these challenges and hearts full of sorrow and fear of the future, the participants were ready to face these difficulties to preserve their rights and defend their identity, which [... made] us more confident in our abilities in facing challenges and threats and preserving our rights.'

Peer support network

One of the strengths in utilizing participatory approaches and peer researchers to undertake this research was that it enabled an iterative process of learning from one another, about the challenges we encountered and the ways in which they may be overcome. However, while the peer researchers were connected through the workshop and also participated in a number of online meetings together, it would have been helpful to cultivate this network further to create more formal spaces for shared reflections. While some of these relationships were established through informal mentoring between some of the peer researchers, this could have been enhanced through group learning circles that deliberately made space for reflection and were built into the process. Although most of the researchers were working with different communities, coming together in this way might also have allowed for greater discussion and depth in drawing out insights from the FGDs in relation to FoRB. Through focusing together on overlaps and divergences between experiences, the specificities of FoRB according to each community and the reasons behind it, as well as the means of addressing injustices, might have become more obvious.

Participatory writing

As noted, while the research process was built around participation and collaboration, the analysis and writing of such research can be a relatively solitary process. Therefore peer-support networks could also be strengthened in the latter stages of the research process. This would enable peer researchers to further develop opportunities to learn and reflect together by incorporating a writing workshop where researchers can work on their reports receiving direct inputs and support, as well as presenting their findings and potentially gleaning insights from each other. These reports could also be presented to willing FGD participants for their reflections before being finalized. This would enable a process of checks to be undertaken with community members to help further analysis of how FoRB intersects with gender in experiences of marginalization.

Conclusion

Using participatory methods enables us to glean new insights into FoRB and religious inequalities in three key ways. First, through putting peer researchers at the centre of the research process, it allows for greater nuance in relation to people's experiences of FoRB as the researchers are themselves from each of the communities included in the study and only undertook research within their own community. As such, they were able to draw upon their own knowledge and experiences to help identify core themes in relation to FoRB for inclusion within the FGDs that were particularly pertinent to their community and which an external researcher may be unaware of. Second, the focus of participatory methods in building trust and creating safe spaces for researchers and participants allowed for sensitive topics in relation to FoRB and experiences of marginalization – and especially gender-based violence – to be discussed more openly within FGDs. This was also enabled through the use of peer researchers which resisted a potentially voyeuristic or judgemental tone to discussions around these issues. Third, employing participatory methods gave space for an enhanced focus on the everyday lived realities of individuals as they perceive matters relating to FoRB as having impacted on their encounters and experiences. As a result, participatory methods assisted in furthering understandings of how people relate and respond to intersecting experiences of marginalization and the very real impacts that religious discrimination therefore has on their lives.

Within this study, participatory methods were also especially relevant as a means of empowering communities and individuals who have experienced marginalization as a result of their gender and/or religious belief. Through a process of engaging with communities as actors within the research, valuing not just their responses but also their inputs to the process itself and their analysis of the findings, individual and community agency was foregrounded. In this way, rather than being represented by others, their voices and experiences were highlighted and incorporated at length within the reports. This is especially pertinent with regard to FoRB as it is most often those who have official standing, such as religious leaders, who are requested to engage with these matters and to comment on behalf of others. It is also worth noting that the lead researchers for each of the reports were women from within the communities who were responsible for training male researchers who could lead the male FGDs, so that as well as democratizing the research in terms of participation and leadership by moving away from 'expert' representatives (who are also predominantly male) the research also worked to highlight women's voices and perspectives regardless of research and educational background and experience.

By utilizing participatory methods, communities were also able to feel more confident in the research as they had a greater degree of ownership over it. Unlike with an extractive model, through participating in this form of research, communities are also then more likely to be encouraged to directly address the challenges they face with regard to FoRB. Finally, during the process of undertaking this research it was found that it is rare for people – especially women – to have the opportunity to discuss their experiences of marginalization due to their gender and religion. However, through a process of talking, listening and understanding, some participants gained a greater sense of solidarity through the knowledge that they were not alone or to blame for such incidences. As such, the form of the research and the topics it addressed in relation to religious and gender marginalization allowed the FGDs for some of the participants to become spaces of healing.

Notes

[1] https://icstudies.org.uk/about-us/what-peer-research
[2] Available at: https://www.constituteproject.org/constitution/Iraq_2005.pdf?lang=en

References

Anon. (2005) 'Iraq 2005 Constitution – Constitute'. Available at: https://www.constituteproject.org/constitution/Iraq_2005?lang=en.

Anon. (n.d.) 'What is peer research?' *Institute for Community Studies*. Available at: https://icstudies.org.uk/about-us/what-peer-research

Bergold J., and Thomas, S. (2012) 'Participatory research methods: a methodological approach in motion'. *Forum Qualitative Sozialforschung / Forum: Qualitative Social Research*, 13(1). https://doi.org/10.17169/fqs-13.1.1801

Cetorelli, V., Sasson, I., Shabila, N. and Burnham, G. (2017) 'ISIS' Yazidi genocide: demographic evidence of the killings and kidnapping', *Foreign Affairs*, 8 June.

Cornwall, A., and Jewkes, R. (1995) 'What is participatory research?' *Social Science and Medicine*, 41(12):1667–76. doi: 10.1016/0277-9536(95)00127-S.

CR (2016) 'Genocide in the Middle East'. *Congressional Record: Proceedings and Debates of the 114th Congress, Second Session* 162 (40):H1303-D252.

Dixon, J., Ward, J. and Blower, S. (2019) ' "They sat and actually listened to what we think about the care system": the use of participation, consultation, peer research and co-production to raise the voices of young people in and leaving care in England', *Child Care in Practice*, 25(1): 6–21. https://doi.org/10.1080/13575279.2018.1521380.

Dowling, S. (2016) ' "Finally someone who doesn't judge me!" Evaluation of peer research method for the YOLO study: transitions and outcomes for care leavers with mental health and/or intellectual disabilities'. Evaluation report, Belfast: Queens University Belfast.

European Parliament (2016) 'Joint Motion for a Resolution on the Systematic Mass Murder of Religious Minorities by the so-called ISIS/Daesh'. In.: European Parliament. Available at: https://www.europarl.europa.eu/doceo/document/RC-8-2016-0149_EN.html.

Hall, J., Gaved, M. and Sargent, J. (2021) 'Participatory research approaches in times of COVID-19: a narrative literature review'. *International Journal of Qualitative Methods*, 20: 1–15. doi:10.1177/16094069211010087

Hansard (2016) 'Daesh: genocide of minorities'. *UK Parliament* 608.

Isakhan, B., and Shahab, S. (2020) 'The Islamic State's destruction of Yazidi heritage: responses, resilience and re-emergence after genocide'. *Journal of Social Archaeology* 20(1): 3–25.

Knell, Y. (2017) 'Iraq's minorities fear for their future'. *BBC News*, 22 September.

Macaulay, A., Commanda, L., Freeman, W., Gibson, N., McCabe, M., Robbins, C. and Twohig, P. (1999) 'Participatory research maximises community and lay involvement'. *BMJ: British Medical Journal* 319(7212): 774–8.

Minority Rights Group (2018) 'Iraq – World Directory of Minorities and Indigenous Peoples'. Available at: https://minorityrights.org/country/iraq/

Thomas-Hughes, H. (2018) Critical Conversations with Community Researchers – Making Co-Production Happen? Bristol: University of Bristol and AHRC Connected Communities. Event report. Available at: https://connected-communities.org/index.php/ project_resources/connected-communities-catalyst-fund-reports-2016-18/

UN (2016) 'UNdata | Country Profile | Iraq'. Available at: (https://data.un.org/CountryProfile.aspx/_Docs/CountryProfile.aspx?crName=Iraq

UNAMI/OHCHR (2014) 'Report on the Protection of Civilians in the Armed Conflict in Iraq: 6 July to 10 September 2014', in United Nations Assistance Mission for Iraq/ Office of the United Nations High Commissioner for Human Rights.

UNHRC (2016) '"They Came to Destroy": ISIS crimes against the Yazidis'. United Nations Human Rights Council, Office of the High Commissioner for Human Rights: Independent International Commission of Inquiry on the Syrian Arab Republic, Independent International Commission of Inquiry. Report: A/HRC/32/CRP.2, 15 June.

UNPO (2013) UNPO: European Parliament Urges Protection for Iraqi Turkmen. Available at: (https://www.unpo.org/article/15643)

USCIRF (2016) Annual Report, Washington, DC: Commission on International Religious Freedom.

9

Participatory Learning and Action (PLA) and Reflective Practices: Training Teachers to Become Effective Promoters of Freedom of Religion or Belief Principles in Education

Yusra Mahdi

Introduction

In Iraq, education has not succeeded in promoting pluralism and inclusion of religious minorities (Osman, 2015). It has rather had the opposite impact. One reason is that it has failed to acknowledge the presence of other religions and ethnicities, contributing to strengthened stereotypes and eventually the marginalization of individuals from minority religions.

This is the case with the subject of religious education (or Islamic education), whose curriculum follows exclusively the Muslim view, lacking the promotion of 'an inclusive discourse that transcends the communal segmentation of Iraqi society and the associated binaries of sameness and otherness' (Osman, 2015).

In December 2019, the Coalition for Religious Equality and Inclusive Development (CREID) programme launched a project to reform religious education (RE) with the aim of fostering pluralism and appreciation of diversity among the young generations in the name of freedom of religion and belief (FoRB). The project sought to improve poor religious education standards, which the country scoping phase (Lapcha, 2019) had identified as a core contributor to the marginalization of minorities. More specifically, it addressed religious inequalities through introducing a new pro-pluralism religious education curriculum.

However, it was found that the curriculum alone would not lead to the expected change if teachers, learners and other stakeholders didn't develop specific competencies and mindsets to take it forward and sustain its impact. Accordingly, participatory pedagogy approaches were conducted during the March 2021 Teachers Training programme with primary school teachers to promote pluralism, respect for diversity and other religious equality principles.

Background

At an education policy level and since the establishment of the education system in 1921, minorities in Iraq saw their rights violated and discriminated. The current state policy mandates that Islam is the official and only religion taught in the school national curriculum.[1] So, while Muslim students are taught and graded in RE, minority students cannot attend. Instead, they are supposed to learn about their own religion outside school, whether in churches, temples or other places of worship. However, there is no public obligation or support in the process of doing so. The result is that minority religions are not known by Muslim students, while minority students feel different and discriminated against by law (Barany, 2013). This seems to suggest that there is a connection between how the education system presents minorities and the marginalization they suffer in the society, as illustrated in Figure 9.1.

The underlying assumption of the project is that, by involving in curriculum development and religiously diverse stakeholders, as well as by training teachers, the cycle can be broken by improving awareness as well as response to religious inequalities (Figure 9.2).

In most recent years, the Iraqi education system has suffered further setbacks because of the COVID-19 pandemic, which led the Ministry of Education (MoE) to adopt measures that include limited school attendance, the temporary removal of some subjects from the curriculum (including RE) and a shift to distance learning. Critics of the MoE's plan stressed that the distance learning plan did not account for the technical difficulties and internet cuts affecting both learners and teachers. Furthermore, not involving teachers in the decision-making process and the non-participatory approach left them unmotivated and demoralized. Figure 9.3 summarizes the main challenges met by the project.

Purpose of this chapter

This chapter seeks to share insights and lesson learned from using participatory methods for the Teachers Training programme, such as participatory learning and action (PLA) and reflective practices, to facilitate the acquisition of religious equality values by teachers, enabling them to translate such values into their classroom practice, and eventually empower teachers to become

Figure 9.1: Cycle of discrimination against religious minorities in Iraq

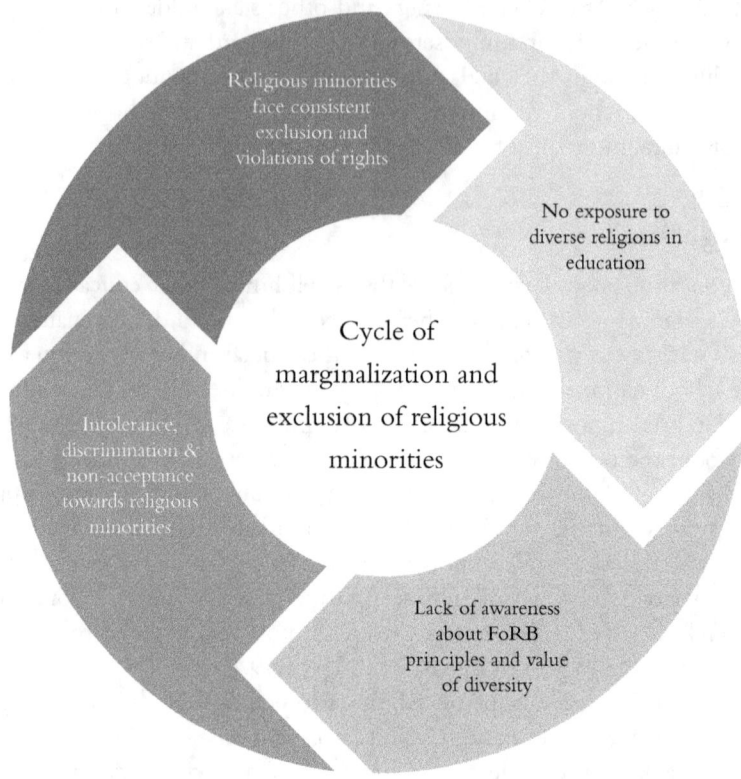

Figure 9.2: Theory of change

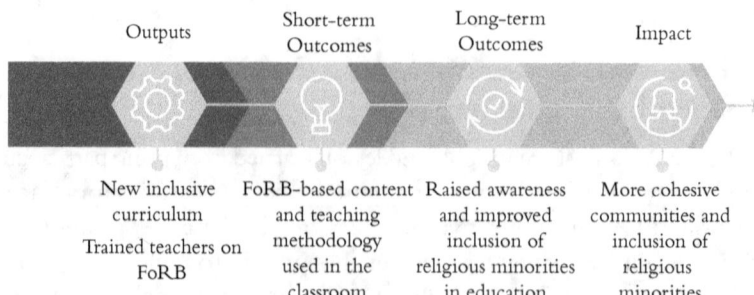

Figure 9.3: Emerging challenges

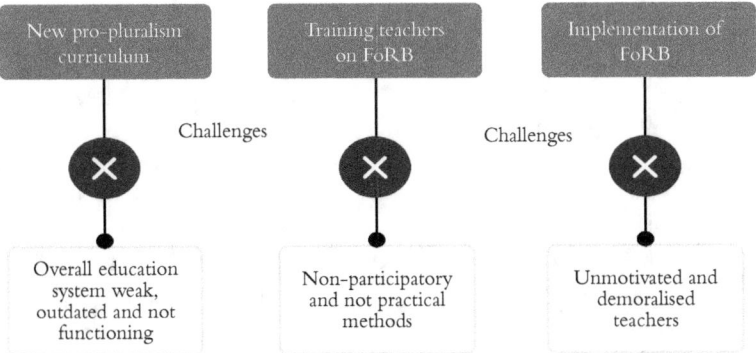

agents of change (IDS, n.d.). The aim is to put forward the benefits of using participatory methods to address the aforementioned challenges (Figure 9.4), where evidence showed:

- using PLA enabled trainee teachers' improved acquisition of practical knowledge and new content;
- reflective practice empowered trainee teachers and made them deliver new ideas.

Research methodology

The training programme was conducted with RE teachers from three Iraqi provinces (Dhi Qar, Anbar and Baghdad). The sample of teachers were selected from the schools taking part in the implementation of the new pro-pluralism curriculum, which include a total of 43 teachers (31 females and 12 males). The trainers of the programme were selected based on their experience in curriculum development and capacity building of educators. Workshops used a hybrid method, combining concurrent online delivery and in-person attendance. Course content included the new pro-pluralism RE curriculum and FoRB values such as diversity and pluralism, which were delivered using brainstorming sessions with interactive discussions. Additionally, participants were trained on different pedagogical methods and educational learning theories that promote teaching and development of learning based on varying levels of complexity, from basic knowledge and comprehension to advanced evaluation and creation.[2]

There are two components to the methodological approach. As explained in the diagram (Figure 9.4), one is to train and expose teachers to concepts

Figure 9.4: Emerging challenges and learning

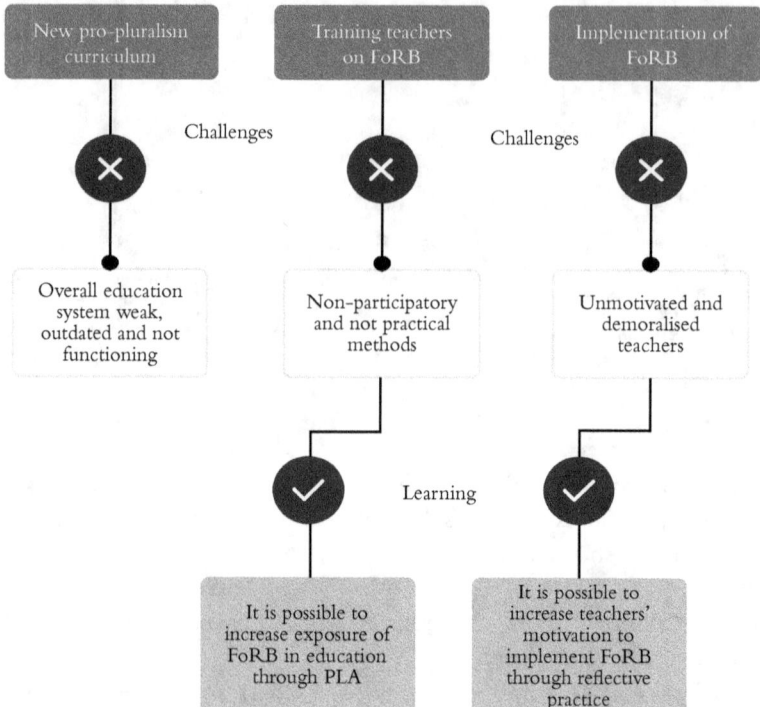

of FoRB through PLA, and the other is to encourage teachers to become decision-makers and agents in the implementation of FoRB through reflective practice. Thus, the approach relied on:

- PLA being the means, where the focus is on teamwork and collaborations between participants to enhance experiential learning and skills development in FoRB principles;
- reflective practice being the end, where the emphasis is on empowering participants to become directly involved in deciding and developing processes for implementation of FoRB.

PLA is an approach that fosters learning through participation (group analysis) and action (practical implementation). The approach was chosen for the Teachers Training programme because of its recognized ability to help translate theory into practice and acquire skills to adapt to diverse settings. This responded well to the request made by participants to receive support with adapting theory to everyday contexts, to the shifting and uncertain situation in the Iraq education system and to our beliefs that teaching is a practical activity and that learning is a social experience.

Figure 9.5: Kolb's Experiential Learning Cycle

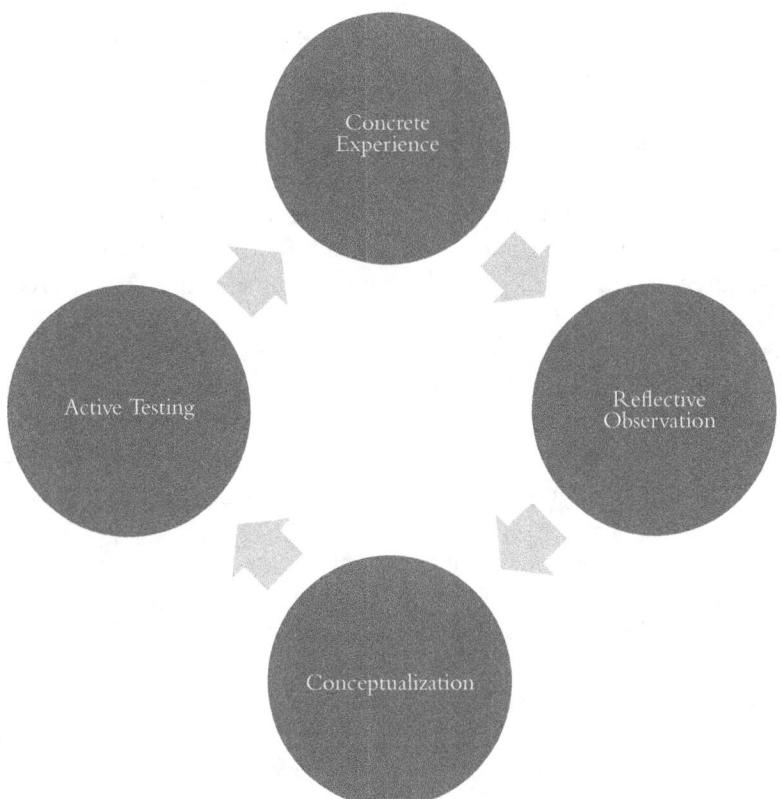

Microteaching, which is an example of a participatory training method based on action, is regarded as effective for translating theoretical knowledge into practice and for acquiring the flexibility needed to teach in challenging and changing circumstances. Introduced in 1960 by Dwight W. Allen for the purpose of improving teacher training at Stanford University (USA), this method works by providing teacher trainees with a pre-implementation experience and a practical understanding of the teaching and learning process in a controlled environment.

This pre-implementation experience through microteaching followed an experiential learning cycle, where 'knowledge is created through the transformation of experience' (Figure 9.5). In the first stage, participants are introduced to the new experience through microteaching, and examples of this will be discussed in the next section. Next, they get a chance to reflect on the new experience through feedback and observation. This contributes to the formation of new concepts and changing beliefs that will finally facilitate the testing of these new experiences in the world around them.

Changing teachers' beliefs is an extensively debated and complex issue, which reaches beyond the scope of this chapter. However, one of the approaches which have proved efficient in shifting teachers' beliefs is reflective practice (Stuart et al, 2009). Reflective practice is an approach that includes methods and techniques that help individuals and groups reflect on their experiences and actions to engage in a process of continuous learning and review of new concepts and conclusions. Reflection enables the recognition of the assumptions, frameworks and patterns of thought and behaviour that shape our thinking and action, which in turn can nurture greater self-awareness, imagination and creativity. For example, teachers were encouraged to express their ideas and experiences within groups of their peers. This was to help transform their way of thinking for both personal change and collective development. In this sense, reflection is a pathway to a paradigm shift in teachers' minds. Furthermore, this approach is different from other approaches because it takes development from a bottom-up perspective, where teachers are empowered to address the constraints they face in their society.

To trigger reflection and empowerment among participants, scenario-based exercises were used. It is a technique that can also contribute to better interaction and engagement with the concepts of the training. Research has shown that scenario-based training can be more motivating than instructional training. For reflective practice, the premise of the method is that participants are provided the opportunity to put their learning into practice through a problem-driven understanding and utilizing storytelling to explore solutions. The scenario-based exercise consisted of describing the situation and telling the story using STAR behavioural test. Participants are required to structure their story by discussing the situation, task, action and result (STAR) of the situation, describing:

Situation: Participants describe a specific situation that has happened in the past. Details are given about what happened, when and where, and who was involved in the event.
Task: Participants state what their role was in the situation or what goal they were working towards.
Action: Participants describe the course of actions taken to address the situation, what was done and what specific steps were taken.
Result: In this final stage, participants articulate the outcomes of the actions: what they accomplished and what they learned.

The next sections will provide examples and evaluations for: (1) the use of microteaching under PLA; and (2) the use of scenario-based exercises under reflective practice.

Acquiring practical skills through microteaching

The new experience that participants of the training programme were exposed to was the application of concepts of religious diversity and pluralism through enhanced participatory pedagogy. This was a new approach to how they normally teach Islamic education (which often involves rote learning). Participants were informed that the microteaching exercise will provide the opportunity for them to familiarize themselves with the concepts and methods, reflect on it with peers, modify and adapt ideas to fit their personal experiences and, finally, test it in a controlled space before the actual implementation in classrooms.

In addition, the method enabled trainers of the programme to bring the concepts of the new pro-pluralism curriculum closer to the understanding of trainee teachers. We made it clear to teachers that we were not expecting them to take the new curriculum and teach it immediately in their classrooms before they themselves understood and were familiar with its concepts. Participants were first introduced to the curriculum's four chapters and the intended learning outcomes.

Following the exposure to the concepts and values of FoRB and pluralism, microteaching provided the opportunity for participants to practise, thus internalizing the knowledge and skills acquired. To this end, a sample group of nine participants were selected and given the two tasks. It was not possible to engage all 43 teachers in the microteaching exercise due to limited time and capacity of the training programme. However, this indirectly and unintentionally contributed to participants who were not involved to be a control group. The impact of this will be discussed in the final reflections and conclusion section of this chapter.

First, to take part in a micro-lesson planning group exercise, the sample group of participants were invited to develop short lessons which made use of the newly acquired concepts and values. Participants were given Chapter 1 of the curriculum to integrate in their lessons (Box 9.1). Second, they were asked to deliver the lessons to their peers, who assumed the role of their students. Eventually, the teachers received feedback from the trainers, the project coordinator and the teacher trainees they had taught, used an observation sheet (see Appendix).

Microteaching succeeded in helping the trainees make sense of the theory they were initially exposed to, and in letting them assess its feasibility in practice while taking into consideration the context and their own beliefs and ability as teachers. Furthermore, participants used the exercise to apply concepts of pluralism in innovative ways, integrating them into diverse subjects. The following are examples of how teachers experimented applying concepts of FoRB in Arabic language, geography and physics (Box 9.2).

Box 9.1: Chapter 1 of the new pro-pluralism curriculum

Title of chapter

'For every kind a lovely pair'

Concepts

1. Diversity in the surroundings.

This concept highlights that diversity is present around us, in our food, colours, languages and more. It encourages learners to look for diversity in their context.

2. Diversity is a cosmic phenomenon.

This concept highlights the essence of diversity and pluralism and encourages learners to think theoretically about it as a universal idea.

3. Diversity in cultures

This concept brings learners' attention to the diversity in cultures, awareness and religions. It encourages learners to recognize different components of their society.

Values

Dignity of human beings

This value stressed the unity of human beings: no matter how different we are, we are all humans with rights and responsibilities.

Learning outcomes

This chapter seeks to develop the idea of diversity in the minds of learners so that they become accustomed to it as a universal and cultural value that surrounds them from all sides.

All trainees stated that this was the most useful training activity, as it made them understand in-depth the new teaching methodology and FoRB values. As anticipated, it was the practical implementation and the social experience (group learning as opposite to individual learning) which made a difference in comparison to other traditional theoretical

Box 9.2: Case studies of Freedom of Religion or Belief application through microteaching methods

Case study 1: Integrating FoRB with Arabic language

HUDA, female teacher from Baghdad

HUDA chose to present a micro-lesson about the Arabic language. She started by reminding learners about the previous lesson and that today they will learn about the pluralism of letters together giving meaning to words, taking learners on a journey of understanding the beauty of diversity in the surroundings.

'We are going to learn about the diversity of words in the Arabic language. Can we call it a word, if it does not have plural letters? So, when we add different letters together, doesn't that give a word meaning? I will give you an example: can we remove a letter from the alphabet? Can we discriminate against one letter, let say "D" and say we don't want to include it in our words? No, because that will take away from the meaning and beauty of words. Therefore, it is the diversity around us that gives us meaning, the diversity in our society and country.'

Case study 2: Integrating FoRB with history

SAJA, female teacher from Baghdad

SAJA decided to start her history lesson with a question to learners and introduced them to concepts of diversity in cultures.

'Let me ask you a question. If we were to travel outside of Iraq now, would we encounter different cultures?' Learner reply: 'Yes, if we go to India, we will get to know their culture, Hinduism.' Teacher: 'Correct, now let's think about the countries that are closer to us, such as Emirates, Kuwait and Oman, do they not have different cultural dress? So, the diversity of cultures, how did it come about, through history? Over time different cultures evolved and now they are part of different countries' heritage. When you go back home, I want you to ask your parents about heritage, for example what is Nowruz, what other cultures are there in Iraq?'

Case study 3: Integrating FoRB with physics

BAAN, female teacher from Anbar

BAAN introduces the lesson about physical changes and described to learners that we can make different shapes of things, but it does not take away from their original properties, linking it to the concept of human dignity.

> 'Today, we are going to learn about physical changes. I brought with me some learning materials to help you understand things better. Here I have some clay. I want you all to make a shape with it. Make any shape you want, animal, flower, ball.'
>
> She collects all the shapes from the learners. 'So, now you've chosen to make different shapes and forms with your clay. But do you think that this changed the properties and substance of the clay? No, all these shapes have the same properties as the original clay. In our world, we also have different religions, and people are free to choose different beliefs. But does this change the fact they are human beings? Does it take away from their dignity as human beings? We are just different shapes and forms, but we are all originally humans. I have some rice and some lentils here. I am going to mix them together now. By mixing them, am I changing the substance of any of them?' Learners reply: 'No, they still look the same.' 'So, if we mix with other cultures and religions, do you think that will change our human components? This is something for you to think about as part of homework.'

teacher training programmes. As one of the trainees stated, 'The practical application of what we learned during the training, the work groups that were formed and the lessons that were implemented by the trainees had a great role in equipping us with the skills and knowledge needed to teach the new programme.'

Furthermore, during Question-and-Answer sessions, participants expressed that the emphasis should not be on books alone, but on values that go beyond the classroom and can be applied to learners' daily activities and experiences.

One teacher stated: 'Inculcating values needs to be not just through textbooks ... it needs to be through experience and practicality; Not just RE, Arabic language, these values the teacher can deliver in all classrooms.'

Perhaps, the feedback from participants provided the indication that the frontal lecturing at the beginning of the training was not as effective for understanding the concepts. For example, when the trainers used the first day solely for narrating the theories and ideas in the curriculum, we found that participants were confused about the purpose of the training during the initial Question-and-Answer session.

It was only when microteaching was conducted that participants became more engaged and enthusiastic about integrating the concepts in their lessons. This was particularly noticeable when comparing results with participants who did not take part in the microteaching exercise. We found that those who did not get the chance to practically apply the new concepts were still not sure about the feasibility of the project and its curriculum. Some even questioned the approach of the trainer, stating that it is too complex for teachers to understand: 'You [trainer] presented this book to us, but we still don't have a solid and clear idea about it.'

Box 9.3: Case studies about scenarios from teachers' personal experiences

Case study 4: Role-play of discrimination against colour of skin

RAWA, female teacher from Baghdad

RAWA decided to present the scenario from her personal experience in the form of role-play, with assistance from two of her peers.

'Hello, class. I want to share with you an incident that happened to one of your classmates and I want stress that it was wrong. ZAINAB, can you stand up? What did you say to your friend SAJA? You said that she has dark skin and you made fun of her! Do you think this is right, class? Look how upset you made your friend SAJA. We don't make fun of people just because they are different from us. We are beautiful because we are different. Now can you apologize to your friend SAJA.'

RAWA ended the scene and continued by saying that this had actually happened in one of her classrooms. She added that she wanted to empower her student who suffered from the incident by making her class leader. Now she is happy and has lots of friends, including the girl who made fun of her.

Case study 5: Scenario of exclusion of Christian student from Islamic Education

SUZAN, female teacher from Baghdad

SUZAN shared that she had a student who was from the Christian faith but her class did not know this, because the student was new and not known to her new peers. During the Islamic Education lessons, she would leave the classroom because non-Muslim students are not obliged to attend.

'This made my students ask me about Nadia's action, so I explained to them that Nadia is from a different religion. But soon I started noticing that her classmates were treating her differently. They were excluding her from their play and activities. So I decided that in the next Islamic education lesson, Nadia would teach her classmates about her religion and she would attend any time she wants. Her classmates were very interested in knowing more about her culture, rituals and holidays. Now she is happy at school and looks forward to share her ideas in every Islamic education lesson.'

Therefore, it is recognized that more emphasis should be placed on enhancing microteaching and lesson planning as a means for the effective implementation of FoRB concepts. Referring back to Figure 9.5 and Kolb's Learning Cycle, it is not sufficient to participate in an experience for learning to happen. It is necessary to reflect on the experience to make decisions and formulate concepts which can then be applied to new situations. This learning must then be tested out in new situations. Hence, the participant must make the link between the theory and action by planning, acting out, reflecting and relating it back to the theory (Kolb, 1984).

Developing new mindset through reflective practices

The training programme stimulated teachers' reflection using the scenario-based exercise. For this, each participant was asked to recall a situation where they had had to deal with conflict resolution in their classrooms. Before the exercise, trainees were introduced to the concept of 'Managing conflict' from the new pro-pluralism curriculum.

Trainees were divided into groups of three and asked to each share a scenario of conflict from their experiences. They were instructed to use the STAR method to help them articulate and reflect on the story or scenario. This method was also useful for facilitators to measure the competencies of participants, as the stories they share indicated their abilities in managing the conflict from start to end. The exercise encouraged teachers to reflect on the significance of their role, the impact they can have on learners' behaviour and, most importantly, on their understanding of and position towards difference. Teachers shared different examples of scenarios where they had to deal with a conflict associated with an act of discrimination against a student from minority groups.

While the scenario shared by Suzan implies the acceptance of a minority student's religious belief, this is an individual case that does not solve the overarching problem of the systematic exclusion of religious minorities from RE. The fact remains that the teacher here is still not obliged by policy to include information about a non-Muslim faith in her lesson. Therefore, realistically the approach in this scenario may not be feasible or replicable in other classrooms, as it is not backed by a concrete policy or action from the school's management or education authority. Nevertheless, we cannot ignore that the attitude shared in the scenario has contributed to enhanced awareness about the necessity of religious equality and pluralism in education settings.

At the end of the exercise, participants received feedback from the trainers for each scenario, highlighting key factors contributing to best practices and key classroom management competencies.

Allowing trainees to apply the concepts of the programme through reflection on their own experiences boosted their confidence and morale in becoming the decision-makers in their classrooms and contributing to effective change. In post-training feedback forms, many participants mentioned that this was one of the main benefits of the programme: "Confidence in oneself was one of the main benefits, recognizing the importance of the work we do. Recognizing the role of the learner and student".

In other words, reflective practice in the form of participation as an end, is the process of meaningful participation with peers, where development emerges when their confidence and competence are built up. In this process, their peers were able to give their feedback and encourage critical thinking in situations (telling of scenarios). Therefore, in this peer-supported reflection, participation becomes a process of achieving greater individual fulfilment, personal development, self-awareness and empowerment for decision-making.

Conclusion

Religious education in Iraq is contributing to the exclusion of religious minorities by not teaching religiously diverse content or values pertaining to religious equality that are relevant in today's world and indeed, to the country's diverse tapestry of religious communities. This has further marginalized religious minorities and the lack of awareness about their rights has subjected them to a cycle of endless discrimination, misconceptions and violations. The CREID programme in Iraq seeks to rectify this by addressing the poor RE standards in Iraqi schools and to implement a new pro-pluralism curriculum that seeks to raise awareness about principles of religious equality, and hence contribute to greater social cohesion and inclusivity.

During the implementation phase of the project, it was found that in the beginning teachers were not actively engaging with concepts of religious diversity and equality, because the focus was only on the acquisition of theoretical knowledge: in other words, the content of the curriculum. Subsequently, lessons from the Teachers Training programme stimulated the need for a shift to adopting more participatory methods. This is when teachers' acquisition of practical knowledge and reflection on their own personal experiences became a significant milestone in the application of FoRB concepts and principles of religious equality in education.

For this, microteaching and scenario-based sessions showed that when teachers have the opportunity to apply concepts of the pro-pluralism curriculum in their own practice, learn from peers and reflect on their practice, they become more empowered and motivated to promote principles of religious diversity.

However, there were several challenges associated with the implementation of such participatory methods. First, it was found that there was not enough time and limited capacity to include all participants of the training in the exercises. Thus it was difficult to measure the impact on all trainees. Those who did not take part in the microteaching and scenario-based sessions expressed confusion and lack of understanding towards the concepts and purpose of the new pro-pluralism curriculum. Yet this can be considered as an indication for the effectiveness of the PLA approach and reflective practice in enhancing teaching about FoRB principles.

In addition, it is recognized that this is not enough to end the cycle of systematic exclusion of religious minorities in education. Educators may be able to reflect on their own experience and change some behaviours in their classroom, by including stories promoting pluralism and diversity, but this alone will not solve the institutional discrimination that does not provide a parallel religious education system for non-Muslim learners. However, perhaps it is important to recognize the effectiveness of peer support changing teachers' mindsets and experiences in challenging discrimination against minorities.

Nevertheless, the assumption is that through improving knowledge and raising awareness among teachers, we can enhance action towards recognizing the rights of minorities. Therefore, CREID's approach in Iraq is aimed at empowering key stakeholders such as teachers, and working towards changing mindsets, not merely changing curricula, for the effective promotion of FoRB principles in education.

Appendix – Observation sheets
1. Scoring rubric

Item	0 Not applicable	1 Poor	2 Acceptable	3 Good
Introduction	Objectives were not stated	Objectives were not clearly stated	Objectives stated at some point of the lesson	Objectives clearly stated at the start
Teacher's knowledge of content	No knowledge of subject	Limited knowledge of the content	Some knowledge of the content	Deep knowledge of the content
Concepts' explanation	No explanation provided	Limited explanation provided	Some explanation provided	Clear explanation provided
Teacher checks students' understanding and provides clarification	No attempts made	Limited attempts to check but without providing clarification	Some attempts to check and clarification provided	Ongoing eliciting attempts with clear clarification provided
Teacher provides correction and feedback	No correction or feedback provided	Limited correction without feedback provided	Some correction and feedback provided	Formative correction and positive feedback provided

Item	0 Not applicable	1 Poor	2 Acceptable	3 Good
Activities	No activity conducted	Activities are not clear and without instructions	Activities are appropriate with some instructions	Activities are effective stimulating interactive with clear instructions.
Materials	No material used	Limited use of teaching materials	Some teaching materials used	Creative use of teaching materials engaging learners
Teacher's method of assessing students' learning	No method used to assess students' learning	Limited and judgemental methods used to assess students' learning	Some non-judgemental methods used to assess students' learning	Non-judgemental methods used to assess students' learning
Classroom atmosphere	Lesson not delivered	Tense atmosphere making learners anxious	Pleasant atmosphere allowing learners to be relaxed and at ease	Conducive atmosphere allowing learners to be engaged and at ease
Classroom management	Lesson not delivered	Chaotic management where learners speak over each other with no leadership	Teacher able to manage learners and somewhat in control of outcomes	Teacher in control able to lead with positive attitude and disciplined approach
Students' reactions	No student reaction	Students not engaging with activities, showing frustration or boredom	Students engaging to some extent with activities, asking questions	Students actively participating and engaging in activities throughout the lesson
Level of students' understanding of content	No measurement of student understanding	Students show poor understanding of content and don't understand questions	Students show some signs of understanding of content answering correctly most questions	Students respond to all questions, nodding along as they engage with content

Item	0 Not applicable	1 Poor	2 Acceptable	3 Good
Overall	Lesson was not delivered	Session has no benefit to learners and does not achieve any of the outcomes	Session meets some of its outcomes and objectives with beneficial assessment	Session meets all learning outcomes, objectives and both teacher and students benefit from experience

Name of Observer: ....

Name of Teacher being observed: ....

Name of School/Location: ....

Date of Micro-lesson .... \ .... \ ....

2. Micro-lesson observation sheet

Instructions: Please rate the teacher's behaviour in each component on a scale of 0–3, with 3 being the highest rating. This form is intended for use in conjunction with a standard evaluation criterion (Scoring Rubric). Please also provide an explanation of each score.

Items and criteria	0	1	2	3	Explain your rating
1. Introduction (for example, objectives are stated)					
2. Teacher's knowledge of content (for example, solid, deep)					
3. Explanation of concepts (for example, clear, linear)					
4. Teacher checks students' understanding and provides clarification (for example, ongoing, eliciting)					
5. Teacher provides correction and feedback (for example, positives first, formative)					
6. Activities (for example, effective, appropriate, creative, stimulating, clear instructions)					
7. Materials (for example, effective, appropriate, creative)					

8. Teacher's method of assessing students' learning (for example, appropriate, practical, non-judgemental)

9. Classroom atmosphere (for example, pleasant, conducive)

10. Classroom management (for example, positive discipline)

11. Students' reaction (for example, active, participatory)

12. Level of students' understanding of content

13. Overall

Notes

[1] Throughout Iraq's history of curriculum development, and since the establishment of its educational system in 1921, the leadership has been criticised for using RE for indoctrination and asserting the superiority of one group over the other, as well as the 'complete disregard of Iraq's ethnic, religious and linguistic diversity'. For example, dating back to the time of Sati' al-Husari in 1921, where the curriculum's 'emphasis on Arab nationalist indoctrination was seen as propagating obliviousness to special considerations for minorities, and this was evident in Al-Husari's objection to "opening teacher-training colleges in Mosul and Hillah where the majority of the students might be Christian or Shi'i, fearing a consolidation of communal spirit' (Al-Khoei Foundation, 2020).

[2] Bloom's (1956) Taxonomy hierarchical model was introduced to trainee teachers, which classifies learning objectives for students, from recalling facts to producing new and original work. Source: Ruhl (2021)

References

Al-Khoei Foundation (2020) 'Religious Education Reform in Iraq: Islamic Education Curriculum Analysis', unpublished paper for CREID.

Barany, L. (2013) 'Teaching of religious education in Iraqi state schools and the status of minorities in Iraq: a critical review', University of Duhok; International Journal of Arts and Sciences, 6(4): 451–66.

Bloom, B.S. (1956) *Taxonomy of Educational Objectives*. Vol. 1: *Cognitive Domain*, New York: David McKay & Co.

DDI: STAR method, Available at: https://www.ddiworld.com/solutions/behavioral-interviewing/star-method

IDS (n.d.) Participatory Methods: Learn and Empower. Available at: https://www.participatorymethods.org/task/learn-and-empower

Jinan Hatem Issa and Hazri Jamil (2010) 'Overview of the education system in contemporary Iraq', European Journal of Social Sciences, 14(3): 360–68.

Kolb, D.A. (1984) *Experiential Learning: Experience as the Source of Learning and Development*, vol. 1, Englewood Cliffs, NJ: Prentice-Hall, p. 38.

Lapcha, H. (2019) CREID Country Scoping Report, Iraq: Al-Khoei Foundation.

Osman, K.F. (2015) *Sectarianism in Iraq; The Making of State and Nation since 1920*, New York: Routledge.

Ruhl, C. (2021) 'Bloom's Taxonomy of Learning'. Simply Psychology. Available at: https://simplypsychology.org/blooms-taxonomy.html

Stuart, J.S., Akyeampong, K. and Croft, A. (2009) *Key Issues in Teacher Education*, Basingstoke: Macmillan.

10

Embracing Emotion and Building Confidence: Using Participatory Methods with Yazidi Women in Iraq

Zeri Khairi Gadi

Introduction

Yazidi communities in Bashiqa and Bahzani, northern Iraq, have experienced significant marginalization on account of their religious identity, including in access to education, healthcare and employment. Zeri was invited to conduct participatory research as part of the Coalition for Religious Equality and Inclusive Development (CREID) in 2021 to gain increased understanding of how being a woman and a member of a religious minority may enhance experiences of marginality. The aim of this research was to explore how these intersecting inequalities impact women's positions and roles in relation to the state, social justice and development policy and practice. The research involved inquiries with religious minorities across Iraq, including Yazidis, Assyrians, Christians, Kakais, Shabak and Mandean communities.

Zeri conducted four group inquiry sessions with 50 Yazidis in Bashiqa and Bahzani: two groups were held for Yazidi women (26 in total), and two for Yazidi men (24 in total), in order to disaggregate experiences by gender and to conduct a comparative participatory ranking exercise of the key issues seen to be facing communities. The participants were between 18 and 60 years old and were asked, through open-ended questions, to share their experiences and rank the perceived severity of the challenges faced by Yazidis in Iraq. The discussions identified access to education, followed by religious discrimination, safety and security, access to healthcare and basic mobility and freedom as the primary challenges facing Yazidi women.

These barriers, as identified and ranked according to their priority by the research participants, in addition to the researcher's expertise, informed practical policy recommendations to redress the discrimination resulting from intersecting inequalities for Iraq's Yazidi women.[1]

Zeri speaks

When I was first invited to participate in the research with CREID, I was very excited to take part in such a special project with Yazidi women in Iraq. This is the first such project in Bashiqa to bring Yazidi women together to talk about the ongoing marginalization, discrimination and racism they face. Yet, while Yazidi women are oppressed, I believe they are also strong.

The process and method

Because of the oppression Yazidis face, it was not easy for me to find women to participate in this research who could express their feelings without fear or hesitation. I made several visits to local councils in Bashiqa, as well as some Yazidi organizations, in addition to making posts on social media (to closed groups for women in Bashiqa). The selection process was lengthy and rigorous. It was difficult to convince women to participate, I believe because they are afraid to discuss their feelings and problems with others. Iraq is dominated by the majority religion, Sunni Islam, and the participants have become accustomed to fear, and reticent to express themselves as an oppressed minority. This fear has become ingrained and is now being passed on to the next generation.

These concerns meant that it was necessary to meet with the Yazidi women in strict conditions of secrecy and confidentiality. It was important to provide full assurance that everything would be confidential and that there would be no pictures or mention of names in the published research. Thus they were not afraid to speak, provided the sessions were kept very confidential.

I started with a simple group discussion to establish ease and mutual trust, so that we could get to know each other. We agreed at the beginning that, as Yazidis, we are one united and interdependent family, and that the discussion would remain between us. This made the women feel comfortable and ready to share sensitive problems and wounds that they had always kept hidden within them. As they shared their experiences in these intimate, warm sessions, I observed that the participants felt they belonged to each other; there was a strong camaraderie born from suffering from the same problems. All participants had been exposed to discrimination, marginalization and racism, despite their different ages. I no longer felt that age played a significant role. Older women were discussing with younger girls the same types of problems and feelings.

At the beginning of the session we, as minority women, agreed first to identify problems, and then to discuss them. I believe this method was the best approach, since the participants were then ready to present their problems together on the board. The women managed to identify over 30 basic problems they face in their daily lives. After the participatory exercise, every woman ranked the problems, from the most important to the least important for her. I asked each woman to identify what she sees as the primary issue she faces. After completing this exercise, an extensive discussion ensued.

The discussions were emotional. I could sense deep sadness; despite being in their homeland, they were experiencing such problems only because of having a different religion. I noticed that, at the peak of the discussions, I didn't sense any fear of confrontation. Rather, I witnessed their overwhelming sadness as they opened up to each other and shared with each other very sensitive experiences which they had encountered in their lives.

I noticed how the women gained self-confidence in these vulnerable moments – they identified with each other, and together formed new networks and friendships. I felt proud of having been able to facilitate such a space filled with openness and trust: trust and the sense of community to say, 'Yes, I am a Yazidi woman who has been discriminated against, but I will not have this stop my dreams in and for my country and my homeland.'

I believe that these facilitated group inquiry sessions, which used open-ended questions and a participatory ranking exercise, are essential to understanding the experiences and challenges faced by minority communities, which have not been highlighted in such an intensive (or participatory) way before. The sessions were vital and special; they were the first ever held uniquely for women, bringing them together in such a beautiful and supportive way in Bashiqa in order to share their feelings and experiences as women, as Yazidis and as Iraqis. I believe this research was directly impactful for participants: they felt that someone cared for them and for their problems, that someone wanted to listen to and help them. The sessions also helped to reduce entrenched feelings of loneliness and marginalization, since participants saw their neighbours and friends were experiencing the very same situations and problems. Yet they had never previously discussed them together.

Following the ranking exercise, the discussion involved accounts of situations and problems that, in the modern era, we were shocked to still be facing. The group consensus found that some humans are still living in another world, a world of racism and discrimination which demeans individuals and minorities. This research revealed that Yazidi women face great challenges within Iraqi society, but that they are also resilient and resistant; they have not quit studying, for example, and seeking a better life.

Through this project, I have come to discover things that I never expected about the suffering of minorities in all respects in Iraq, including within government departments, in the marketplace and even in hospitals.

My learning

I was silent most of the time during the group inquiry sessions; I focused instead on listening. As a Yazidi woman, the challenges recounted were also challenges I myself face and have faced. It is true that, as a girl from the Yazidi minority, I have been very marginalized and discriminated against, but I have also discovered that women of my region in northern Iraq have been subjected to far greater marginalization due to their religious identity. I also discovered that the Yazidi minority is oppressed by the government in ways I didn't realize. I discovered that Yazidi women do not play a significant role in politics, due largely to fear.

During the discussions, I listened carefully to the participants' experiences and felt strange feelings that I had never felt before: that I was in a strange place, discussing issues which shouldn't be present in modern Iraqi society – enslavement, injustice and stark religious inequalities. The discussions were somewhat strange to me at first – I had not facilitated, or even participated, in such sessions before with such a large number of people. While it is typical to discuss issues with parents and friends, it was empowering to conduct sessions beyond these restricted networks. The participants, through shared experience, were afforded confidence to speak and participate. As a facilitator for these sessions, I also feel more powerful than before.

Today I feel emboldened to talk to a stranger from outside of my community, from another religion. Today I can stand with confidence and say that I am a Yazidi girl and, despite being discriminated against, I have never stopped pursuing my work and dreams. Today I have the power to defend myself, without fear or hesitation, when I face discrimination or when I feel marginalized. I have learned that fear of the majority has brought us to where we are today. I hope I also managed to transfer this feeling of power to the participants, who I also consider to be strong. The fact that they shared sensitive feelings and experiences with me, without fear, is in and of itself powerful and demonstrates this strength.

Today I have different feelings about minorities. I knew they had been unjustly treated prior to conducting this research, but I did not know the extent of the discrimination faced by minorities in Iraq. I was surprised to find that the different age groups who participated in the sessions suffer from very similar problems and are exposed to the same situations everywhere – whether in the market, in schools or in hospitals. Those who wish to criticize or belittle someone because of their religion have no regard for age. I noticed that women were almost unanimous regarding their hope for freedom and mobility, and their prioritization of this, compared to the male group inquiry sessions, as a key challenge facing Yazidi women.

Positionality

I did not conduct the sessions with Yazidi men. Instead, I selected a man to facilitate these sessions, cognizant that that this would make them feel more comfortable, rather than having a woman facilitate the discussion. Men would probably feel restricted or reserved about sharing their problems with me as a woman. I also know through experience that, in Bashiqa, there are things that men will only talk to men about. It was hoped therefore that the decision to elect a male facilitator would create an environment where the participants felt more comfortable to express their feelings. As an Iraqi I also know that Iraqi men believe that there are some things that men understand better than women. For example, when talking about politicians, they prefer to address a man rather than a woman. The male facilitator would therefore also allow them to overcome their shyness, and to speak freely and comfortably. I am sure that, if I had conducted those sessions, I would not have obtained the desired results. I also know that, traditionally, women in our society are very shy. Thus, they would probably not get good results if they were to moderate focus group sessions for men.

As a Yazidi woman from Bashiqa, this helped me to conduct the focus group discussions (FGDs) with the Yazidi women through established relationships of trust. Women in Bashiqa have great confidence in each other and always prefer to discuss sensitive issues with someone from within their own district. This assertion also applies to men in Bashiqa; therefore, using local facilitators was crucial for conducting this research – particularly due to the sensitivity of the issues being discussed. Local facilitators were also key from the perspective of language and accessibility: people from Bashiqa have a very unique dialect, and they prefer to talk to someone who uses their dialect, so they can express themselves better. This strategy therefore helped to obtain the most from this research.

Challenges

The focus group sessions faced a few challenges. For example, there were many illiterate women among the group. I therefore needed to help them prioritize challenges in the participatory ranking exercise. This challenge was also faced by the male facilitator of the groups with the Yazidi men.

A further challenge was that some women brought their friends or relatives to participate in the session. As the space was limited, I was not able to accommodate a larger number than expected, particularly in line with COVID-19 social distancing requirements. Carefully selecting the right venue helped to overcome this challenge. The number of women, which exceeded 12 per session, also had its pros and cons. Sometimes they would all talk to each other about their problems at the same time, and at times I also had to interrupt to allow every woman to have a chance to participate.

However, an advantage of the larger group sizes was that, as they shared their feelings and problems with each other, I saw how this seemed to have a therapeutic effect: it reduced their feelings of loneliness and isolation through the opportunity to explore and discuss shared experiences of pain and exclusion. When each woman heard the problems of the other women in the group, including those of her peers, friends or even neighbours, she then felt empowered to disclose her own experiences. Each woman therefore gained strength from the group. However, sometimes there were very personal and sensitive issues that the women were embarrassed to mention before such a large group. In future, to address this issue, it would have been better to ask the men and women if there were things they would like to talk about in private following the closure of the FGDs.

This project highlighted many feelings which had been buried within individuals, as well as identifying many problems that have yet to be solved. In the sessions, many women and men also tackled these problems: for example, the existence of a law that does not allow Yazidis to become judges. This law is a pressing problem for Yazidi society, since it directly exposes them to discrimination. While Yazidis may study and master the law as a discipline, this prohibition creates a discriminatory ceiling preventing their advancement to the top of the field, with broader implications for issues of justice for Yazidi communities. Further issues discussed include the educational curriculum, which the Yazidi minority is seeking to change, and the Yazidi Survivors Law – both of which have yet to be applied.[2] This project highlighted issues within Iraqi society that were somewhat buried.

The project revealed other surprising things for me as a Yazidi activist in Bashiqa. For example, I did not know that all Yazidi women were discriminated against for the most basic reasons – just for being a Yazidi, and a woman. It also became evident that all women in Bashiqa are exposed to discrimination, whether directly or indirectly.

Conclusion

In the end, I would like to send a word of thanks and a bunch of flowers to all those who contributed to this project; it is essential for Yazidi women to meet like this and to address collectively the problems they face. This research has led to a strengthening of the relationships among the women who participated. I did not expect the fantastic turnout and engagement in both the group inquiries with Yazidi women and men. This engagement and willingness to talk, to share experiences of suffering, particularly following displacement, reveals that Yazidis are sick of the discrimination they have faced. This project provided an outlet for this pain, and an opportunity to share it with others, and to find some relief.

Notes

[1] Zeri's experience of this process, working with the assistance of Hoshank Ghanim Elisa, Wissam Salim Hussin and Hori Khairi Jumaa, is recounted in the rest of this chapter, in the form of an edited interview, which was recorded, transcribed and translated, and sensitively synthesised and edited by Kathryn Cheeseman.

[2] For more information on the Yazidi Survivors Law see Beam (2021).

Reference

Beam, A.L. (2021) 'Yazidi Female Survivors Law of Iraq – full text English translation', *Ekurd Daily*, 4 March. Available at: https://ekurd.net/yazidi-female-survivors-law-2021-03-04.

Pakistan

11

Lessons Learned Using Participatory Methodologies in Exploring Intersectional Marginalization of Religious and Sectarian Minorities in Pakistan

Asad Shoaib and Jaffer Abbas Mirza

Introduction

This chapter examines the impact of participatory research methodology in effectively documenting the daily experiences of the religious and sectarian minority groups in terms of intersectional marginalization due to the intersection of faith, poverty and gender identities and how the intersection of these factors leads these communities down the economic and social ladder. Participatory methods were employed by the researchers to co-create knowledge with the targeted groups, placing them at the centre of knowledge creation to evaluate their vulnerabilities and instances of exclusion.[1] The participatory research was used to gather key information from the perspective of the local communities, whereas the interactive storytelling sessions were used to create a sense of belonging for the religious and sectarian minority groups for generating key information on social exclusion and intersectional marginalization.

The research was conducted in the semi-urban and urban locales of Lahore and Islamabad where Christian and Shia minority groups lived, to explore the context of structural and systemic marginalization faced by these minority groups in Pakistan. Pakistan is on the list of 'Countries of Particular Concern' on religious freedom (USCIRF, 2022). The idea of the independent Muslim country of Pakistan was conceptualized on account of intrinsic discriminatory politics of the Indian subcontinent, where Muslims were, despite their large population, considered a minority. Yet post-independence politics in Pakistan kept pushing the minority communities to the margins, and so the ideals of inclusive politics and egalitarian society remained largely unachieved. Pakistan is a diverse society comprising numerous religious and ethnolinguistic groups. The diversity, however, has shrunk lately with demographic changes. The population of religious minorities has constantly changed in Pakistan amid anti-minority structural and attitudinal biases (MRG, 2019). At the time of partition in 1947, almost 23 per cent of Pakistan's population was comprised of 'non-Muslim' citizens. Today the proportion of religious minorities has declined to less than 4 per cent.

Anti-Ahmadiyya riots, structural violence against Christian minority members while exploiting the legislative apparatus, forced conversion of Hindu and Christian girls, destruction of churches and temples and mob vigilantism and systematic bloodshed of Shias are some of the most explicit forms of violence that often make headlines.[2] However, some other forms of marginalization are embedded in Pakistani society that shape the minority identity in the country. Such forms of marginalization stem from the intersection of language, culture, economic inequality, religion and so on.

There has been a series of structured anti-minority politics that have shaped the conscience of the society. Anti-minority campaigns by organized groups can be publicly witnessed in the form of literature, messaging and/ or religious polemics.[3] Thousands of minority community members have fled the country in the wake of persecution, yet hundreds of thousands are still living in constant fear of persecution and threats. Some of the most highlighted cases have made international headlines, yet hundreds of them go unnoticed on a daily basis. Minority persecution comes in various shapes and forms and often manifests itself in most unnoticeable ways. It is highly important to learn about the hidden forms of persecution and marginalization because the minority communities have, over the years of persistent episodes of marginalization, internalized the very notions of persecution and marginalization. Therefore, this research on religious equality and intersectional marginalization is crucial to understand and explore the nature of marginalization of religious minorities in Pakistan, even in its most obscure and overlooked forms. The locales for this research are selected on the basis of a history of violence, poverty and their religious minority status.

The locale of the research was selected after robust consultative sessions with community members from Lahore and Islamabad, who identified social exclusion, violence against the minority groups and lack of access to public services, limited economic opportunities for the minority groups and endemic poverty. Early in the research process, Punjab province and Islamabad Capital Territory (ICT) were shortlisted for conducting the research. There were two important reasons to start with these two broad areas. First, both have a significant presence of a Christian community with a history of religious persecution. The second reason was based on operational viability and better resource mobilization. However, the selection of the research locales was the trickiest part of the current research project. The scoping research informed the selection process of the communities after visiting multiple communities through the conceptualization phase of the research. The relatively isolated minority communities were selected to minimize the risk of any potential conflict and to guarantee free mobility of the data collectors in the locale. The criterion for selecting a locale included three key factors significant for studying intersectional marginalization: poverty, history of conflict and a residential area of minority communities. All six shortlisted research sites satisfied all three conditions – that is, they are inhabited by the religious minority groups, have a history of conflict and can be considered as poor in terms of their livelihood practices and living conditions.

Participatory methodologies

Participatory action research (PAR) was employed to draw out insights about the intersection of religious identity and poverty in the experiences of marginalization of the religious minority groups. PAR combines two distinct research approaches: participatory research and action research. The adopted research approach engaged researchers and participants throughout the research process from the initial stage of the research leading up to the community development actions. The approach is considered unique for its applicability in issues concerning inequalities, oppression and social exclusion. It treats the participants as experts due to their lived experiences of the specific topic. By involving participants in the research process, PAR promotes the identification of actions desired by the participants to influence social change. For this project, the actions and changes proposed by the participants were used to inform the community uplifting projects facilitated by HIVE, a social innovation organization based in Islamabad.

This research combined more traditional qualitative research methods with participatory methods. Both qualitative and particularly participatory research methods allow the researchers to elicit rich and detailed accounts for conducting a robust qualitative analysis. Unlike quantitative methods such as survey research, the aim of the qualitative research is to analyse the in-depth meanings participants associate with the events, experiences and incidents that happen in their lives on a day-to-day basis. The employment of PAR helped to reduce the power asymmetries that traditionally occur between the researchers and the participants, enabling a process of mutual learning.

The first phase of the research involved qualitative but not participatory methods. A scoping study was carried out to explore the various intersections that caused marginalization in several minority communities. The scoping research was conducted to identify geographical areas for further in-depth research and project implementation of CREID.[4] It included multiple visits, informal conversations and structured interviews with locals, community and religious leaders and political representatives from union councils. The data was collected using interviews as a research tool. The interviews were structured to extract the perceptions about religious inequality, inclusive development and opportunities of intervention to improve the well-being status of the communities, who are otherwise living in extreme poverty and experience social exclusion.

Through the scoping research exercise, 24 in-depth interviews were conducted in five cities across Pakistan with: (1) faith-based leaders; (2) religious minority members; (3) representatives of civil society organizations; and (4) political representatives such as mayors and Union council chairmen. In addition to this, focus group discussions (FGDs) were held with the minority community leaders to understand their positions on intersectional marginalization. The questions that were designed for the in-depth interviews and FGDs aimed to explore ways that could bring about inter-faith harmony and achieve inclusive development across the various locales. During the FGDs, facilitators explained to the participants the concept of 'intersections' and 'intersectional marginalization' while elaborating the goal of the current research exercise. The researchers used examples from within the Pakistani society to explain what intersection meant here and how it might apply to various exclusion- and marginalization-related contexts.

Each FGD spanned several hours, during which participants discussed diverse themes of social exclusion, marginalization and inclusive development to shortlist the communities most impacted by the intersection of their religious identity and poverty in marginalization. As a result, communities were identified for conducting PAR research. As explained above, three basic premises were positioned to identify the research locales for CREID research and community intervention: economic status, minority status and the history of violence.

Storytelling

For the ongoing research, the lead researcher, and the HIVE core team had initially decided to collect data on intersectional marginalization and religious inequalities using structured survey and a focus group discussions (FGDs) guide.[5] However, the strategy was later changed after a thorough discussion with Shandana Khan.[6] After thorough deliberation and brainstorming, stories were specified as data collection tools. Humans are storytelling beings, and so this model of collecting data was followed to capture the extended and intricate experiential accounts of the participants. A new conversation-based data collection technique was strategized to exhibit more openness towards indigenous narrative rather than bombarding respondents with questions, anticipating that this technique could potentially prove to be counter-productive. Some of the researchers also felt that, since qualitative data collection is necessarily inductive, any prior structuring of the data collection methods can lead to an inflexibility in terms of responding to the emerging insights. This can therefore lead to a methodological 'tunnel vision' while making sense of the collected data. To address this potential issue, the research team devised a strategy to keep the storytelling sessions more participant-oriented, where participants took the lead while the researchers captured their responses using certain prompts and gentle guiding rather than floating definite questions. The researchers were the active listeners while the participants led the conversations about their own experiences. This method helped in capturing the lived experience of the participants in their own unique ways without influencing their versions by throwing at them the preconceived notions and questions.

The idea of storytelling was conceptualized to bring forth the extensive details around religious discrimination and inequalities embedded in the society. Researchers were directed to use vignettes and paralinguistic expressions to encourage the participants to continue and pour their hearts out without shying away from significant details. This, however, does not mean that the conversations we had with the respondents were completely open-ended and are not comparable. Rather, it specifies that the data collection technique was relatively open, and that it was more 'respondent-driven' than 'researcher-driven'. The prompts were used to kickstart the discussion and at times referred to an event or incident about inequality that may have happened to another participant, community in the same or different locale.

The data collectors were provided with a conversation guide to ensure they did not stray away from the main themes and can seek help from guides while engaging in conversations. However, the conversation guides were different from the semi-structured interviews in several ways. For instance, a conversation guide was based on prompts that included a similar response from another locale or participant, or another incident induced by intersectional marginalization. It did not necessarily have a particular sequence or a phrase that could influence a participant's version of truth related to intersectional marginalization. For instance, we asked them to share if they were ever subjected to police brutality or social exclusion based on their religious identity, poverty or both.

Largely, this approach helped to capture insights that were much more nuanced and diverse. A preference was given to the storytelling sessions over interviews under the premise that storytelling sessions would lead to the surfacing of individual *experiences* rather than the opinions of the participants. It is, therefore, established that experiences can be validated correctly whereas opinions are hard to be validated through cross-checking.

The conversation guide consisted of questions that steered the conversations through the storytelling sessions. The guide included themes pertaining to religious inequality and various intersections of marginalization. Broader themes emerged from the theory of intersectionality, and from literature on the marginalization of religious minorities in Pakistan. However, instead of policing the parameters of the questions, researchers were directed to use referential clues from within the responses that emerged from the stories. The broad conversation guide, however, included the prompters that aimed to probe the individual meanings participants associated with the intersections of marginalization. For instance, they were asked to share what living in this locality as a minority felt like, or how their identity as a minority shaped their everyday life, or simply how their religious identity had led to their marginalization. The prompts included probing about the following aspects of their experience:

- religious identity and marginalization based on religious identity
- economic status;
- gender;
- health;
- access to state institutions;
- access to employability;
- access to mobility;
- power or powerlessness;
- community association;
- political participation; and
- fear of participating in social life and persecution.

Instead of asking the participants direct questions, the researchers used the prompts to elaborate on what they meant by certain ideas such as exclusion and marginalization, inclusive development and political participation, just to give an impression of what they were looking for: the understanding of community practices through the community lens. Researchers were prohibited from creating meanings from the responses based on their own understanding and/or experiences. Instead, they were directed to listen to stories and probe each response to extract the meanings participants associated with these intersections. Each characteristic was further investigated in comparison with others. For instance, a response that claimed that marginalization was because of their religious identity was cross-checked against whether what the participant thought about marginalization, had their economic status been different from what it was then. The investigation of this kind helped the researchers to capture the data with clarity about the various intersections.

A key consideration was given to the positionality of the researchers to ensure that their bias and preconceptions did not impact the research findings. Although most of the researchers involved in this participatory research process belonged to the same communities, it was ensured that the researchers did not influence or control the flow of the storytelling sessions or of the deliberative exercises while conducting the matrix ranking. The researchers were particularly directed to keep their previous knowledge about the persecution and marginalization of the minority communities at bay in order to capture the new and experiential accounts through the eyes of the participants. Researchers completely alien to the situation would not have been able to steer the conversations using vignettes. The researchers were therefore grouped in pairs, with one of them belonging to the same locality and having similar religious identity. This helped to build a rapport with the participants of the storytelling sessions and matrix ranking; otherwise it would have been difficult for the 'outsiders' to collect the rich information that we did. Pairing the researchers from the same community also helped in navigating the local contexts the participants were referring to during the sessions.

Similarly, we placed a stringent emphasis on following ethical practices while engaging with the participants of the research. These included asking for written and verbal consent regarding the research study and recording of the storytelling sessions and interviews. At times the participants of the research did not allow us to record the conversations. All the researchers were directed to take utmost care of the recordings and share on the Google drive as soon as it was possible. Similarly, we placed a high value on the protection of gathered data, and nothing was shared with anyone except the core research team. The entire team pledged not to use any data whatsoever other than that recorded this research assignment.

Matrix ranking

The idea of matrix ranking was proposed to capture collective preferences for community uplifting projects later to be implemented as part of the final stage of PAR.

The team received training in matrix ranking through various mock ranking exercises, to acquaint them with the process. A brief matrix ranking template was developed by the lead researcher, keeping in view the aims of capturing intersectional marginalization and religious inequalities. However, this does not mean that researchers went into the field with the existing bias towards the sources of deprivation and set of preferences for community action. Rather, guidelines to conduct the matrix ranking group exercise were shared with all the researchers to enable them to clearly explain the process to the respondents. After the individual storytelling session, a group matrix ranking exercise was conducted in each locality where the participants of the storytelling sessions gathered. The matrix ranking sessions were not necessarily conducted on the same day as the interviews, but the participants of the matrix ranking remained the same, as they already knew what intersectional marginalization was and how it impacted their well-being.

The facilitator first explained the concept of matrix ranking to the participants and the entire idea of the exercise to reach a consensus-based conclusion as to what is the most important public service that is lacking and the source of vulnerability for the community. After thorough discussions among the participants on lack of access to public service and the most pressing sources of deprivation, a consensus was generated that led to the identification of the areas that needed most urgent intervention. The results of the matrix ranking, at a later stage, through a deliberative process with the community, translated into community uplifting projects including installation of water filtration plant in Joseph Colony, establishment of a medical clinic and installation of solar panels in Rimsha Colony in Islamabad.

Limitations of the research

This research activity, using participatory research methods, aimed to learn from the participants about how they ascribe meanings to marginalization based on their experience of everyday life in their current settings. It also aimed to collate these experiences to form a narrative that could inform a wider audience of the nuanced forms of marginalization emerging from embedded religious inequalities in Pakistan. Additionally, these sessions were conducted to enable dialogue around the most pressing issues minority communities faced and to identify community action projects. Individual narratives were recorded to explore the precise realities of minority life in Pakistan, especially with respect to Christian and Shia marginalization. The key challenge to this learning process was building trust with the participants in the research in the first place. HIVE's key informants and resource personnel helped the research team to enter the research areas. However, research of this kind requires in-depth exploration of various factors because of the complex nature of the issue.

Establishing rapport with the respondents requires a researcher to get involved in their everyday life to record, assess and validate the collected information. It may involve recurrent visits, spanning months, to establish a rapport with the respondents to win their trust and confidence. It is also important to note that the respondents from Joseph Colony could have shared more, had they been engaged in storytelling sessions outside their areas because of security concerns and a perpetual history of violence.

Rapport-building is an organic and dynamic process which leads to the in-depth exploration of intersectional marginalization. Researchers tried to establish rapport with the community by making recurrent visits and multiple conversational methods such as the use of vignettes as prompts. Researchers faced significant difficulties that impacted their movement across research areas. For instance, In Joseph Colony researchers were asked to leave by the female members of a household, citing the potential dangers, and were asked to delete the audio-recordings of the interview as well. Even in Mochi Gate, researchers faced issues in building rapport with the respondents initially, even though interlocutors belonged to the same community. Research of this scope aimed to better understand the very complex phenomenon of marginalization. This requires validation through researchers' observation of the processes, events and life patterns to reveal various factors that shape community life in a given socio-economic and cultural setting. Additionally, to understand these factors, it is necessary to engage with the community at a deeper level, which is only possible through continuous engagement with them.

> 'The settings (socio-economic and political) in which these (minority) communities live are extreme. Our job here is to look at what sorts of marginalization impede their well-being. It is indeed a huge responsibility; however, at the same time we need to make sure that our own imagination does not cloud the day-to-day experiences that shape life around here.' (Asad Shoaib – lead facilitator)

Another important challenge was to identify female researchers from these communities. Women, in general, face 'cultural' and religious barriers to acquiring education. As a result, more girls are out of school than boys (HRW, 2018). The repercussions of this attitude become more visible when one encounters the unavailability of female researchers. Religious minorities are also part of the same society where girls' education is discouraged. Moreover, the fear of persecution or forced conversions also prevent girls from Christian and Hindu families from accessing higher education (Maheshwary, 2020). As a result, finding female researchers from these communities becomes a significant challenge which we also faced during our research. Though we managed to find female researchers, it had halted the project for a few weeks.

Reflections on the use of participatory methods for understanding intersectional marginalization

The use of participatory methods, particularly the storytelling sessions, helped us to navigate the extent to which social exclusion and marginalization are shaping the lives of Christian and Shia minority communities in Lahore and Islamabad. The storytelling sessions uncovered the most detailed accounts of everyday persecution and marginalization that these communities experience. Storytelling and matrix ranking sessions enabled participants to meticulously explain and deliberate about how certain religious inequalities deprive them of exercising their agency, denying their voice against injustice and treating them as lesser humans. The participants of the matrix ranking were asked what they thought were the most pressing issues they faced in their localities that hinder their well-being. Here is one of the deliberative conversations that was recorded among two participants during a matrix ranking session in Youhanabad, Lahore.

Participant 1: Education is the only way to graduate out of poverty. You educate your kids and they land good jobs and make their families proud. But how do you educate them if schools do not provide equal treatment to our kids? How can they attain education?

Participant 2: Education is no doubt an important aspect, but we lack these basic amenities such as access to clean drinking water, or the sources for livelihood. Education comes later; first we need clean water to drink to avoid contracting water-borne diseases.

The storytelling process helped researchers to document the instances of deprivation, exclusion, marginalization and violence perpetrated on minority communities in their own unique understanding. Storytelling is different from other qualitative research techniques because it allocates more value to the participant experiences than researchers visualize. This method is focused on 'bottom up' knowledge creation where participants guide the conversations actively instead of being the passive respondents of questions that researchers deem significant. matrix ranking, too, is an interactive and iterative method that helps to navigate the importance participants attach to various forms of services while at the same time, highlighting the most important social and economic vulnerabilities and sources of deprivation. These participatory methods give prominence to individual understanding and experiences that researchers often lack while conducting research using other qualitative methods.

During this study, participants in the research exercise had differing degrees of responsiveness on questions. For instance, recalling about their experiences about marginalization, one participant would be responsive in assessing the connection between their economic status and marginalization while another would not. It varied between Shia and Christian communities. The Shia respondents showed a certain degree of uneasiness about being identified as poor during interviews, whereas Christian respondents showed no displeasure on the usage of words such as *Ghurbat* or *Ghareeb*.[7] The Shia population in Mochi gate, although financially weak/poor, feel humiliated when sharing their financial miseries and pretended to be doing well.

> 'We are not poor. Hussain is our guardian. Mola Ali [the fourth caliph and first imam of Shi'as] has held our hands. We just face issues from the Wahabis [anti-Shi'a polemics and violence]. How can the devotees of Mola Ali and Hussain remain poor?' (One of the respondents during a storytelling session in Mochi Gate, Lahore)

In contrast, most of the Christian participants thought that their weaker economic status was the cause of marginalization, whereas the Shia participants thought that their marginalization or selective targeting aimed to deprive the community of its intelligentsia such as doctors, traders, lawyers and professors. Noushan Ali Rana, a Lahore-based professional, explained that

> there are multiple factors [behind the genocide of Shi'as in Pakistan]. Religious [sectarian identity] is, of course, the prime reason. But there is also a political factor. If you see the target killings of Shi'as, the majority of the deceased were professionals or influential people [posted on some high-level positions in media, government and banks]. This is a well-thought strategy of marginalising Shi'a by killing their professionals and influential people. (Rana, 2020)

It was not possible to generalize the acceptability of certain marginalization-related aspects among those taking part in the research. It was observed that participants exhibited varying communicative priorities even within the same communities. However, the research exercise indicates that Christian respondents were more open in terms of referring to their experiences of social exclusion and fear of persecution. Shia participants, by contrast, seemed to have internalized the threat of violence, and consoled themselves by associating with the historic connotation of 'Husssainiyat vs. Yadiziyat'.[8] The research exercise established that the method of storytelling triggered the respondents to share intricate details about their experience of marginalization; however, the recorded contradictions within each interview also suggest that participants either exhibited a varying degree of openness to the researchers or had different ideas about marginalization and exclusion.

It is evident from the current research activity that both of the religious minorities studied face marginalization across the five research areas. However, the responses collated through the storytelling sessions reveal distinctive area-specific characteristics that shape marginalization and its implications differently for each religious minority. The Christian religious minority faces severe marginalization at Joseph Colony for several reasons. First, Joseph Colony is a small Christian settlement of around 130 households. It is surrounded by the factories of various kinds and some majority Muslim areas. Christians at Joseph Colony are the most vulnerable of all the research areas because of the prevalence of extreme poverty, non-existent public good provisions and the relatively small population in comparison with the other Christian settlements explored in this research. Members of the Christian community inhabiting Joseph Colony are more prone to communal violence and marginalization because of their low socio-economic status and smaller population in the area.

> 'My children were running for life with no clothes on, and this the most terrifying incidence I had to witness being Christian. The women had no dupatta in their necks, nor did they have their shoes on, everyone ran without any clothes on, and all this happened because we were Christians and Muslims burnt our town over a petty small issue.' (A Christian resident of Joseph Colony[9])

Youhanabad is an area with a similar socio-economic status to Joseph Colony. However, living in Youhanabad, although marred in endemic poverty, does not entail as much fear of violence as living as a Christian in Joseph Colony. Basic life-sustaining public goods are equally absent in both, Youhanabad and Joseph Colony.

Similarly, the fear of direct violence is relatively low in Bahar Colony, another majority Christian settlement, adjoining one of the upper-middle class vicinities of Lahore: Model Town. Majority of the Muslims residents of Model Town depend on Bahar Colony's Christian community for their low-paid menial chores such as sweeping, cleaning and home helps. Bahar Colony, too, is an impoverished community and the inhabiting Christian community faces marginalization of various forms, yet the frequency of incidents is much lower than the marginalization faced by the Christian community in Joseph Colony. Since it is peripheral to an upper-middle-class vicinity, access to public services – schools, hospitals, parks and clean drinking water filtration plants – is much easier than in both Joseph Colony and Youhanabad. Similar to Bahar Colony in terms of its close proximity to the upper-middle-class Muslim vicinity is 66 Quarters in Islamabad. A significant population of Christian community members from 66 Quarters are employed – mostly as sweepers for janitorial jobs – in Islamabad's Capital Development Authority (CDA) and are also in service in the nearby Muslim households. This is one of the causes to which the less frequent incidents of direct physical violence can be attributed. They are also able to access public goods such as parks, basic healthcare units and schools.

'We can independently disclose our identity and have religious freedom. However, if there are untoward conditions in the country and there are some attacks on churches then we will be restricted from going to the church and gather in some other way.' (A Christian resident of 66 Quarters, Islamabad, shared during the interview)

This and such other responses gesture towards the difference between the experiences of the ghettoized Christian community members and those who live closer to the urban middle-class neighbourhoods. Since the majority community living in the upper-middle-class neighbourhoods depend on the Christians for menial work, their experiences are 'better' than those in Youhanabad and Joseph Colony.

Mochi Gate in Lahore is a Shia residential area with a historical root dating back more than 400 years (Sheikh, 2018). It is one of the oldest urban settlements in the historic city of Lahore. Part of the walled city of Lahore, this area is a busy retailing hub with a considerable Sunni, Barelvi population.[10] The Sunni and Shia communities of Mochi Gate have co-existed since the earlier days of the settlement. They have over the years developed a co-existence model of non-interference in each other's sectarian faith. Another interesting reason for the relatively peaceful co-existence is the communal marriages that have taken place between both the communities.

'We do not experience any violence in the area as the area is majority Shia with some Sunni population. We have developed a mutual co-existence model without having to preach to each other. Both communities are supportive of each other. During Ashura processions, the Sunni community help in maintaining the security of the area. Inter-sect marriages are common in the area as they have been living here for more than 200 years.' (Custodian of a Shi'a congregation centre in Mochi Gate, Lahore)

Since the matrix ranking exercise aimed at prioritizing areas for a community action project, it was also instrumental in bringing to the surface the major sources of deprivation among the socially excluded groups. The participatory nature of the matrix ranking exercise helped the participants to exchange their viewpoints vigorously and deliberate on the direst sources of deprivation alongside exploring opportunities for community uplifting projects. The matrix ranking, as previously highlighted, was facilitated by the researchers whereas participants engaged energetically with each other to reach a consensus to finalize the community action projects. During the matrix ranking exercise, participants reflected on various dimensions of social exclusion and sources of deprivation while highlighting instances where they were subjected to feeling alienated, disgusted and vulnerable.

> 'We are called Churhas [dirty, a derogatory word used against Christians] in public space. The other day someone called me that. Of course some of our people do the cleaning stuff but that does not make us filthy. Does it? If we don't clean up the mess created by the rich people around, this city would stink like a heap of garbage. Such comments leave us frustrated and disgusted. I don't think we deserve this. Do we? You tell!' (A Christian respondent during one of the matrix ranking sessions)

This opportunity also provided them a platform to navigate their status within the society from a relational standpoint. Through the matrix ranking exercises, the participants were allowed to engage in deep conversations about the persecution and the underlying causes that lead to such persecution while detailing how these can be mitigated by uplifting the minority communities by adopting various solutions.

Conclusion

Freedom of Religious Belief (FoRB) is a difficult topic to explore in a country like Pakistan, where minorities have perpetually faced persecution at structural and attitudinal levels. Minorities, under the fear of persecution and social exclusion, restrain themselves from mentioning their plight as a result of political and social arrangements. The fear of being exposed keep the minority communities from expressing their day-to-day experiences with 'outsiders'. The current participatory exercise, however, enabled the minority community participants to express themselves freely because of its conversation-based approach. The conversations allowed the participants to candidly share their everyday experience of living among the majority Muslim communities. Instead of following and responding to the questions posed by the researchers during the interview-based models of inquiry, the participants were able to speak about their lived experiences with a greater degree of ease and comfort.

The initial rapport building, and the decision of assigning the data collection task to the researchers with a similar religious background, turned out to be an effective method, yet the conversation-styled data collection techniques proved to be pivotal in terms of recording the most intricate and experiential details of living in Pakistan as minority community members. Despite the richness of the data collected through the conversation-based participatory methods, the amount of time researchers spend in the field determines the extent to which participants are comfortable in sharing their lived experiences. Time plays a key role in building trust with the participants of the research. Even during the current research study, a few participants were initially reluctant to share their stories with the researchers, and refused to get their stories recorded. However, they felt at ease when our researchers visited them multiple times and built a considerable rapport through continuous engagement with them.

The research team at HIVE tried to develop as much rapport and understanding with the community members at each locale. It is highly recommended that future researchers studying intersectional marginalization in these locales spend more time in the community over a longer period to record more rigorous details of everyday life. It is also highly recommended that future research projects engage with the local community in the area using participatory research methods, which can help record important details of everyday life in terms of various groups – such as women, young groups and the elderly – within each community. The research team also identified the importance of working with the peer researchers (member of the religious minority community from the same locality with the lived experience of the issues under discussion) to improve the level of trust between the researchers and the community. Researchers who worked in pairs retrieved more rich stories than the individual, 'outsider' researchers. It is highly recommended to work with the peer researchers, accompanied by a highly trained researcher to bring out the nuanced experiences.

Another important learning was the comfortability of the participants to speak about instances of marginalization in a group setting. This was also observed during the matrix ranking exercises, where those taking part in the exercise engaged vehemently in rich discussions to reach a consensus. Although this practice is time-consuming, it provides better opportunities to the researchers not only to track the level of marginalization and persecution but also to gather important prompters for individual storytelling sessions.

Notes

[1] The whole data collection involved eight people who had facilitated in collecting stories, conducting and arranging interviews. These eight people consisted of males and females from Christian, Shi'a and Sunni backgrounds. The authors of this chapter, Asad Shoaib and Jaffer A. Mirza, belong to Sunni and Shi'a Muslim backgrounds respectively. Both authors are aware about the religious identities, power dynamics and privileges associated with them. Therefore, throughout the research, both researchers have thoroughly and consciously tried to be aware of their position of privilege and ensure that the inherent biases of the data collectors and note-takers do not impact the findings of the research. For this, we time and again had team conversations and debriefing sessions in which we emphasised multiple times the importance of maintaining our objectivity as much as we could.

[2] Reports on Anti-Ahmadiyyah Riots, 1953–1954. Digital Archive LUMS. Available at: https://archive.lums.edu.pk/anti-ahmaddiyah-reports/

3. Pakistan witnessed a new wave of anti-Shi'a campaign in Pakistan. See Mirza (2020a, 2020b); Annual review of anti-minority hatred and discrimination.
4. Coalition for Religious Equality and Inclusive Development (CREID) is a project initiated by the Institute of Development Studies to understand the intersectional marginalization faced by religious minority groups and how it impacts inclusive development. The research findings helped in drawing useful insights about the attitudinal bias and structural inequalities that religious minority groups faced. The research findings helped to design community action projects aiming at reducing such inequalities.
5. Asad Shoaib, the lead facilitator for this research, is an academic and a development researcher with more than seven years of field and desk experience of conducting primary and secondary research studies on diverse topics related to development. He led CREID in Pakistan with support from HIVE Pakistan. HIVE Pakistan is a research and innovation organization based in Pakistan. HIVE was the implementation partner of CREID in Pakistan.
6. Dr Shandana Khan Mohmand is a social scientist based at the Institute of Development Studies, University of Sussex.
7. *Ghurbat* and *ghareeb* mean 'poverty' and 'poor', respectively.
8. Hussainiyat and Yazidiyat are anecdotal constructs in Shia Islam where Prophet Muhammad's grandson, Hussain or Hussayn, is hailed as a protagonist in the battle of Karbala, a modern-day city in Iraq. In Shia Islam, it is part of the faith that Islam resurged after the Prophet's grandson sacrificed his life for standing upright for his principles. The antagonist of the story is Yazid, who was a coercive ruler and the second Caliph of the Umayyad Dynasty. This battle was fought in 680 between Yazid's army and Hussain's comrades, mostly his family members. Hussain was martyred in the battle. 'Hussainiyat is also a Manichaean concept in Shia philosophy in which Hussayn and his followers (Shias) are in continuous struggle against 'evil' Yazeed and his 'progeny' (in the shape of militant terrorist organizations that target Shias and their practices). Shias see or interpret the current violence they are facing as the continuation of the battle between right (Hussayn) and evil (Yazeed).
9. In 2013 a Muslim mob burned more than 100 Christian houses in Joseph Colony because of a false accusation of blasphemy. (Naeem, 2013). Since the incident, Christians in Joseph Colony have lived in constant fear of further attacks.
10. The Sunni Muslims of South Asia are divided into two major sub-sects, Deobandi and Barelvi, named after their places of origin in India in the nineteenth century. Barelvis believe in intercession between humans and Divine Grace. This consists of the intervention of an ascending, linked and unbroken chain of holy personages, reaching ultimately to the Prophet Muhammad, who intercedes on their behalf with Allah. Barelvis constitute the majority within the Sunni population of Pakistan.

References

HRW (Human Rights Watch) (2018) 'Shall I feed my daughter, or educate her?' Available at: https://www.hrw.org/report/2018/11/12/shall-i-feed-my-daughter-or-educate-her/barriers-girls-education-pakistan

Maheshwary, R.S. (2020) 'Poor Marginalised Hindu Women in Pakistan'. CREID Intersections Series, Coalition for Religious Equality and Inclusive Development, Brighton: Institute of Development Studies. DOI: 10.19088/CREID.2020.006

Mirza, J.A. (2020a) 'The changing landscape of anti-Shia politics in Pakistan', *The Diplomat*, 28 September. Available at: https://thediplomat.com/2020/09/the-changing-landscape-of-anti-shia-politics-in-pakistan/ (Accessed: March 25, 2023).

Mirza, J.A. (2020b) 'Religious minorities in "Naya Pakistan"', *The Diplomat*, 16 March. Available at: https://thediplomat.com/2020/03/religious-minorities-in-naya-pakistan/

MRG (Minority Rights Group) (2019) 'Pakistan – World Directory of Minorities and Indigenous Peoples'. Available at: https://minorityrights.org/country/pakistan/

Naeem, W. (2013) 'Joseph Colony attack: as bigotry rises, so do minorities' miseries', *The Express Tribune*, 10 March. Available at: https://tribune.com.pk/story/518887/joseph-colony-attack-as-bigotry-rises-so-do-minorities-miseries

Rana, N. A., (2020) 'Storytelling Mochi Gate, Lahore'. Interviewed by Syed Ali Abbas Zaidi and Asad Shoaib.

Sheikh, M. (2018) 'Harking back: The enigma that the name of "Mochi gate" presents', *DAWN.COM*, 9 September. Available at: https://www.dawn.com/news/1431768

USCIRF (United States Commission on International Religious Freedom) (2022) 'USCIRF releases new report highlighting religious freedom in Pakistan', 5 August. Available at: https://www.uscirf.gov/release-statements/uscirf-releases-new-report-highlighting-religious-freedom-pakistan

12

Using Participatory Research Methodology to Understand Daily Experiences of Religiously Marginalized Communities: A Case Study of Christians in Joseph Colony (Lahore) and Rimsha Colony (Islamabad) and Shi'as in Balti Basti (Karachi)

Maryam Kanwer and Jaffer Abbas Mirza

Introduction

The Ravadar project, an Urdu word which means a person who respects, recognizes and accepts others with openness, was envisioned as a platform to advocate and address issues of freedom of religion or belief (FoRB) through community interventions and development projects in the selected economically marginalized minority populated areas of Lahore, Islamabad and Karachi.[1] The project, supported by CREID under the 'coalition-building' theme, and implemented by HIVE Pakistan,[2] aims to study how these communities' experiences of marginalization and exclusion on a daily basis affect them, and to explore how engaging them in community development projects may promote inclusion and freedom of religion or belief (FoRB). The project has three components: community-led blogging, local minority coalition/formation of local (Ravadar) committees and community development projects. For this chapter we have identified three projects that were implemented in three different areas – that is, Joseph

Colony (Lahore), Rimsha Colony (Islamabad) and Balti Basti (Karachi). The project activities were conducted between June 2020 and March 2021.

We used participatory research methodology (PRM) to collect the stories and to document the daily experiences of the people living in the neighbourhoods being focused on, with the aim of understanding how persecution due to religious beliefs, when intersecting with poverty, gender and other identities, forms a complex connection and how it further pushes these communities to the end of the road.[3] Based on our learning, the current chapter discusses the participatory methods and steps used in these selected projects, highlights the effectiveness of the open/community-driven participatory methodologies particularly for engaging with marginalized communities and suggests that adding or incorporating action-based plans into research or consultations may strengthen the participatory methods.

Joseph Colony is a low-income Christian neighbourhood in Lahore, Pakistan, comprising more than 130 Christian households. It has a history of violence as over 150 homes were burned down by a mob of right-wing Sunnis in 2013 over a false blasphemy accusation (DAWN, 2013). The community continues to live in a state of fear of violence, and the members face discrimination. Amid this fearful living environment, traumatic history and poverty, access to clean water has been a huge issue for the community for around 20 years, according to the residents. Women face extra difficulty as they rely on the male members to fetch water for them due to lack of mobility as they don't have access to basic transport (the water plant was installed in a neighbouring Muslim majority area and it was risky even for men to access, due to the threat of violence).

Rimsha Colony is an informal Christian settlement located in sector H-9, Islamabad. In 2013 a Christian girl named Rimsha Masih, who was just 14, was falsely accused of committing 'blasphemy', and the situation became hostile for Christians (Associated Press of Ottawa, 2013). As a result, many had to flee the colony and some of them shifted to a nearby Christian settlement. The unofficial estimate suggests that there are more than 1,147 families, where 99 per cent of households are Christian.

Ameer Mauvia Sector, operates from this area. It is a prohibited anti-Shia militant outfit in Pakistan that has a long history of committing violence against the Shia community of Pakistan (Stanford University, 2012). Sipah-e-Sahaba Pakistan (SSP) and its militant offshoot Lashkar e Jhangvi have attacked several Shia public gatherings across Pakistan and in Karachi over the last two decades. One hundred and eighty Shia families, mostly settlers from Gilgit-Baltistan, are residing in Balti Basti. Previously, over 300 Shia families lived in the area, but due to security concerns and incidents of anti-Shia discrimination/violence half of the Shia population moved to other areas of Karachi.

Figure 12.1: Community mapping exercise among Christians of Rimsha Colony and Joseph Colony and Shi'as of Balti Basti

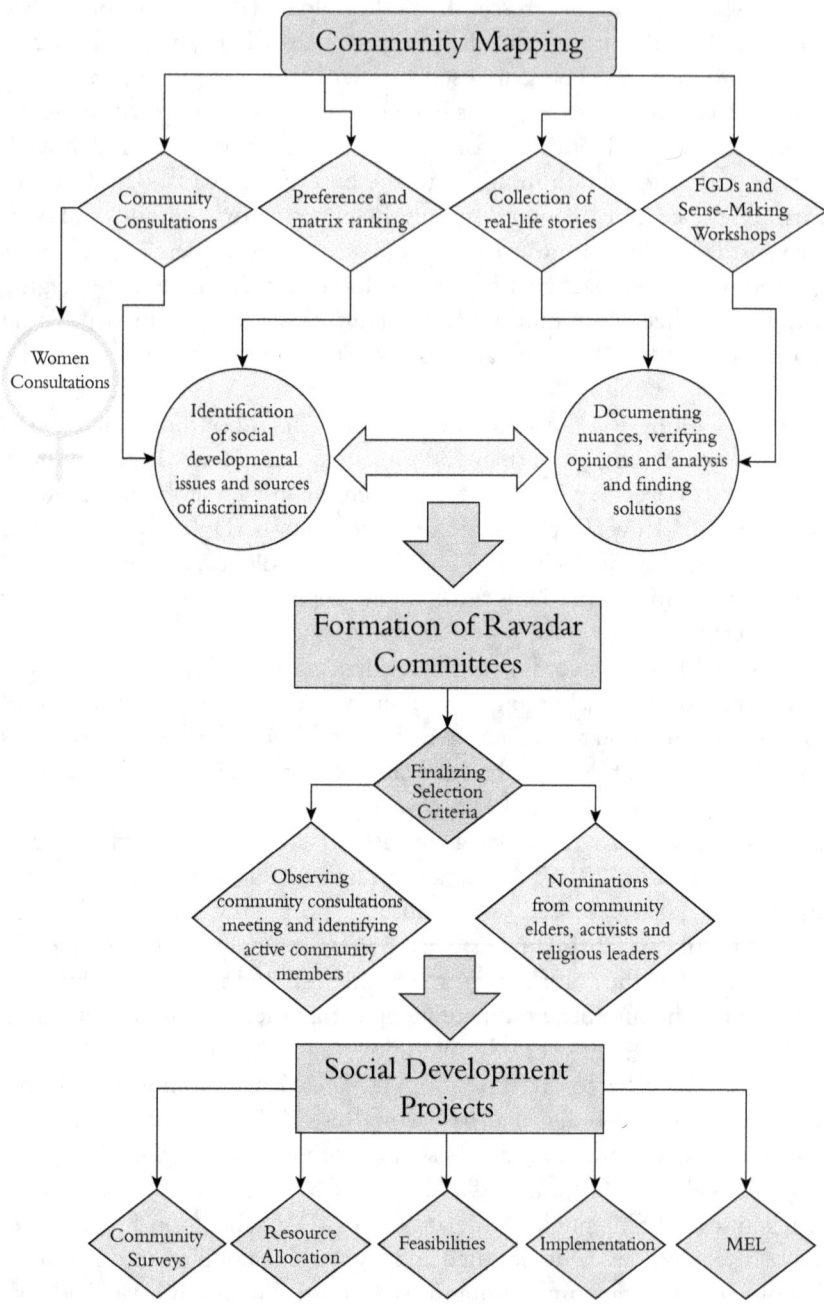

The selected neighbourhoods were unique in the sense that the communities in these neighbourhoods have been facing marginalization

as well as experiencing a history of violence due to their religious identity and beliefs.

Research methodology

Our participatory action research (PAR) approach included the following: initial consultations/community mapping exercise, storytelling, community consultations and matrix ranking. This process began with the community mapping exercise (see Figure 12.1), which helped us identify the resources within and outside the communities and gave us an initial picture of the living condition of these communities. The first step was to train the researchers, community interlocutors, researchers and activists.[4] These interlocutors from Shi'a and Christian communities mobilized community members, held consultations, developed working groups with the two communities and helped us to ensure sensitivities around the communities. For this purpose, the researchers were carefully selected from the same communities using the broad networks of our local partner, HIVE Pakistan, within these two religious communities. We have learned how crucial it is to have a researcher from the same religious background and community activists who are trusted by these communities. It is also essential to have female researchers and interlocutors to collect stories from the female members so the participants are at ease with each other and to collect insights and nuances in detail. Therefore, the idea of collaborating with the community interlocutors emerged. These interlocutors from Shi'a and Christian communities mobilized community members, held consultations, developed working groups with the two communities and helped us to ensure sensitivities around the communities.

Various community meetings were held with all the relevant stakeholders, interlocutors, social, political and religious leaders from these communities to identify potential respondents and the research focus areas. While all this helps build mutual trust between the respondents and the local partners, it also brings a sense of ownership and clarity of ideas among the community members.

Collection of stories through storytelling

Storytelling is an insightful way to get into the detail of someone's realities and experiences, and reveals the psychological impact of persecution when faced on a daily basis. We made sure that the religious identity, gender and language of the respondents matched those of the story collectors. Audio recordings helped us capture each detail. These were intense sessions using a technique that was relatively open and more 'respondent-driven' than 'researcher-driven'. In the three sites, it was through these stories that we learned in depth how the ghettoization these communities have faced for decades has impacted them hugely, how women in Joseph Colony are fearful of sending their children to school and that most of the children don't go to school due to the threat of violence.

Shazia, a housewife and resident of Joseph Colony,[5] shared the fact that she stopped sending her child to school because her daughter was facing discrimination. 'Many times my daughter came home and told me that she was called humiliating names because of her Christian identity. And I even couldn't complain in the school because I am really afraid.'

These stories brought out the nuances, everyday issues and struggle. The stories were more like listening to things that one will never hear or read unless one is from the community or lives there. Interviews are more structured (sometimes formal) and mostly restrict to questions, whereas the stories had touched small/minor everyday issues which contributed to or aggravated their persecution.

Community consultations

These sessions included in-depth multiple conversations with various members and the leaders of the community, analysing the vulnerabilities, social exclusion and marginalization, and economic insecurity in these three areas. These consultations were held in all three neighbourhoods with the Shia and Christian communities.

In Joseph Colony, we also conducted matrix ranking during the community consultation to understand how the community prioritized and highlighted the most prevalent issues faced by them. This exercise helped us understand the frequency of marginalization and identify the differences within the marginalized group better. They also helped inform the layers of marginalization and strategize and plan together with the community members for solutions.[6]

The participatory methods were extremely helpful in breaking the ice, developing trust and facilitating the process of sharing about the issues communities face in their daily lives. All the sessions were conducted by and with the help of the local interlocutors, community gatekeepers with the same religious background and in local languages. These consultations were very effective in the conceptualization of the social action projects/development projects. For example, in Rimsha Colony the women-specific community consultations led us to the installation of solar panels and renovation of a safe space. In Balti Basti the need for a community-based clinic was identified. In total, ten community consultations were conducted in Rimsha Colony, thirteen in Joseph Colony and four in Balti Bashti.

Women-only community consultations

Women from these communities face further challenges, and their experiences of marginalization are different from others within the communities, as well as from other groups outside. Due to patriarchal norms, the voices of the women are mostly missing or ignored or they are unable to participate in the community meetings; hence the issues specific to the women are not talked about. We ensured women's participation by organizing women-only community consultations. These sessions brought nuances and a completely different and enriching perspective. In Rimsha Colony, women were able to speak about the issues they face such as domestic violence, abuse and harassment. They recalled some of the incidents: for example, a single mother who was constantly being harassed at night and feared for her daughter's security and her own as she often found her door lock broken. These stories enabled these women to realize the need for a safe space to discuss their issues. One woman participant shared that 'we are divided and shunned in our houses. We are not allowed to work or to educate ourselves. Our social lives are limited to the kitchen and family. We need a place where we could spend some time and discuss our issues.'

In Balti Basti, it was only through the women-only session that the need for a 'female doctor' was identified as women face a lot of challenges while travelling outside the neighbourhood and it is not safe for them to travel alone. Women also don't feel comfortable or to discuss their issues with a male doctor, or don't get permission from their families to do so, and therefore prefer female doctors. During a post-project evaluation focus group discussion a resident of Balti Basti shared the following:

> Due to the presence of women in the clinic, women patients did not hesitate to come here. If we had a male doctor, women would not have come or very few women patients would have come. Some women feel hesitant to see men, but since we had women at the clinic such shy women also came and stated their illness clearly and got treatment.

Focus group discussions (FGDs)/sense-making workshops

This exercise aimed to understand the community's collective understanding of marginalization and to explore ways to find solutions together with the community members and leaders, including women and youth. This brought broader understanding and clarity and allowed us to probe into the data collected through the community consultations and storytelling sessions. We were able to corroborate the experiences and the accounts of the community gathered via storytelling and consultation through focus group discussion (FGDs).

Formation of Ravadar (local committees)

The final step is the formation of the local committees. These committees are formed in every selected neighbourhood by the community members. Ravadar committees are composed of women, youth, community leaders and activists and religious and active members of the community. These local committees ensured inclusion and representation of all the groups based on gender and age within the community, and focused on the development of the ideas and their successful implementation and sustainability. This step is key and unique as it gives the community a sense of ownership and control. In all three projects the local researchers and interlocutors facilitated the discussion around the problems the community faces. In Rimsha Colony, a preference ranking tool was used that helped focus the discussion and build consensus among the members. Once consensus was achieved, the facilitators (local interlocutors and HIVE staff) then discussed the resources and limitations of the community projects (to avoid building high expectations) and built consensus around the thematic area.[7] Various community consultations were held to develop and finalize ideas.

As a final step, the local Ravadar committees led the development work in their neighbourhoods, prioritizing those areas discussed during the consultation sessions which require an immediate and stronger focus/solution.

Reflections on the methodology

One of the interesting strands of PAR is its exploratory nature. None of the projects we implemented in Joseph Colony, Rimsha Colony and Balti Basti was either planned or anticipated; they emerged from consultations/community input. The distinctiveness of this approach is that it helps understand what is really required in the community and what serves the interest of the community rather than a donor. Also, as there is little or no existing literature focusing on the development of these communities, the participatory methods helped us to build our understanding of what would constitute 'development' from their perspective.

We had previously worked in different communities and conducted interviews and FGDs. The major difference we see in the participatory methodology is its community-driven approach, where a community or its members guide and explain issues faced by the community and propose solutions based on their urgent needs and suitability. This is where we understand – for example, through storytelling sessions – how the absence of necessities may aggravate the everyday life of an already marginalized community. These stories also establish an emotional/human connection between the community and researcher/practitioner which one may not witness in the quantitative and qualitative approaches which have disciplined structure and assumed/preconceived identification of (research) problems.

The participatory methods enabled us to see beyond the idea of 'a religious minority', a monolithic/singular concept of a group who share identical issues across the country. Based on the consultations and storytelling sessions, the lived experience of the Christian community in Lahore seems to be different from that of the Christian community in Islamabad as they face different levels of challenges and discrimination in these cities. For example, the testimonies of the participants from Joseph Colony and Youhanabad, who had witnessed violence and often come across the issue of blasphemy accusation, present a story of fear, discrimination and a lack of basic necessities such as clean drinking water, hospitals and schools. For example, Asma, a resident of Joseph Colony, shared that 'there is a problem of water over here and it gets worse in summer'. Almost all the respondents from Joseph Colony mentioned the non-availability of clean drinking water whenever they were asked about the discrimination they face.

Christians in 66 Quarters or Rimsha Colony in Islamabad, in contrast, complained more about discrimination in jobs and limited economic opportunities. Blasphemy violence, for example, is a country-wide issue for all Christians, but through the PAR we became aware of the everyday experiences and issues in majority Christian areas in different cities. Concepts such as discrimination or inequality need to be understood in context. For example, the absence of clean drinking water in Joseph Colony or waste in Youhanabad are two symbols of inequality because they are Christian neighbourhoods and they don't have great electoral appeal to Muslim lawmakers. Similarly, the consultative sessions with the community also helped us to understand conflicts within the communities and neighbourhoods, hierarchy and power and gender dynamics.

We observed that the storytelling sessions turned out to be cathartic for the members of the Shia and Christian communities. Some people became emotional while sharing the horrific cases of discrimination and violence. However, despite the intense nature of the conversation, the participants had developed this sense of possessing knowledge. As observed in testimonies and our discussion with the community interlocutors, the participants had the feeling of owning a space where, despite the presence of a facilitator (local researcher), they, the participants, could direct the conversation and define things as they are. One of the recurrent sentences we came across was 'Let me tell you' or 'Let me explain it to you'. We understand that self-confidence gives the participants a feeling that their lived experience is a form of knowledge and that, by sharing it, it could be even used to develop projects or action plans.

Limits and challenges for working with groups experiencing poverty and religious inequalities in unfolding their experiences of religious and socio-economic exclusion

There were some challenges we encountered using participatory methods in these settings where there is a history of systematic economic and religious marginalization, such as at Joseph Colony. A consultative approach may misguide or misdirect the needs of the community. For example, our interlocutors and HIVE Pakistan had noted various instances where people expected individual benefits over the community. For example, a person in one of the focus areas tried to have the roof of their house renovated by exaggerating the significance of the house in the community.[8] During community consultations in Joseph Colony a young person, who was very active in the community mobilization, tried to find or expected an employment opportunity. When he was told there were no vacancies, he stopped coming to the meetings.

The second issue is the element of fear and mistrust that prevents some of the core/structural issues from being addressed. For example, the issue of blasphemy violence and social exclusion is so sensitive and potentially risky that many respondents wanted to skip and jump to discuss basic issues such as water, unemployment and lack of opportunity, which, arguably, are common issues across all middle- and working-class localities. Due to fear of persecution, some find it difficult or uncomfortable to discuss the intersection of their religious identity and poverty in their marginalization and social exclusion. We addressed this challenge by collaborating with local interlocutors from the same community. They (the interlocutors) used to raise/share (in the local language) their own stories, for example, sharing their own story of being discriminated against because of their religion. This gave participants the impression that there is no need to hide the issues. The person who is facilitating the discussion (their interlocutor) had been through or understood the persecution they were facing and was 'one of us'.

During the women-focused consultation session in Rimsha Colony, our female interlocutors struggled to process the views shared by some women participants in which patriarchal violence and exploitation were not only internalized but normalized. In this scenario, any idea of discussing a women-focused or women 'empowerment' programme becomes challenging as some within the group of women may oppose the idea of women-led activities.

In the last three years we have used various adaptations prioritizing and considering community needs which worked well and produced results such as an increase in participation and people's interest in our project. For example, at the beginning, it was very challenging to include women in the community consultations due to patriarchal norms. To address this, we engaged influential men in the community and elderly women from their families who, by using their influence, really helped the inclusion of other women from the community to actively participate.[9]

We employed spontaneous strategies such as one of our interlocutors even interviewing the other interlocutor in front of the participants to make them relaxed and familiar with the proceedings. We changed our venue and took participants to a place where they would be comfortable. Our interlocutors and local partners even changed their working hours to accommodate and match the availability of the community members.

The Al-Khoei Foundation is a Shi'a faith-based organization, and it partnered with HIVE Pakistan, a secular and inclusive youth-led organization.[10] Our two focused communities were Shi'as and Christians. We hired specifically Christian interlocutors to mobilize and intervene in the Christian areas and the same for Shi'a areas. Awareness around positionality and reflexivity helped us to form trust and strong bonds with the communities. There is no hierarchy of suffering; every minority in Pakistan has its own experiences of discrimination and persecution. Shi'as face genocidal violence, yet they can identify themselves as Shi'as publicly unlike Ahmadi Muslims, who are constitutionally sanctioned as 'non-Muslims'.

We also found that existing networks within the community could complement the participatory methods, particularly in those settings where there is a history of violence and persecution which often results in mistrust and suspicion. The members of Balti Basti were sceptical of 'outsiders' (as the area is surrounded by anti-Shi'a militant organizations). Our local interlocutor was one of the caretakers of the only local *imambargah* (Shi'a religious and cultural space). The interlocutor helped us engage and mobilize the community members. It was very difficult to engage women, but later, with the help of the local networks, a local Ravadar committee was formed that also included women and youth. This particular example reflects the fact that a strong contact or network could influence or push certain things that were once perceived as difficult to achieve.

Conclusion

We suggest that adding or incorporating action-based plans into research or consultations would have potential to strengthen the participatory methods. We noticed particularly in areas that have attracted the attention of NGOs, such as Joseph Colony and Youhanabad, due to the history of violence, people in these localities are more critical of the modus operandi of the NGO–donor. There was the impression that NGOs come and fulfil donors' aspirations and leave. As a result, locals feel exploited and betrayed. A water filtration plant was one such example, which was identified, developed and implemented by the community itself during the process but had not been anticipated in our project proposal. As a result, a sense of ownership by the community, and the relationship the community has built with our interlocutors and the local partner, have outlived the life of the project. This relationship of mutual trust is evident in the invitations that our local partner (non-Christian) now often receives to different events being held in Christian areas. That knowledge is generated by the community itself is one of the key strengths of the participatory methodology; we can add that, when that specific knowledge can benefit the community, the participatory methods are more engaging and receive overwhelming responses. This action-based incentive will also address one of the challenges where some look for individual benefits. For example, those who initially asked for personal favours and benefits eventually became a part of the project as they see the Ravadar project as something that is being done by the community itself.

Notes

1. Ravadar, as an idea, was contemplated during the community scoping, when all the relevant stakeholders and key informants agreed that the programme should aim to build a community together in an inclusive manner with men, women and young people from marginalized groups to promote religious equality and freedom.
2. HIVE Pakistan is a secular non-governmental 'social-impact' organization that addresses 'issues of extremism and marginalization through community-led research ... and participatory collaborations'. More details about the organization can be accessed at https://hive.org.pk/.
3. Based in London, both of us are researchers and development practitioners and have worked in Pakistan with different religious and ethnic minorities. We are aware about own reflexivity and have ensured that our political and religious views do not affect or influence the interlocutors and research participants involved in the project.
4. These interlocutors are active community members in the trusted network of the local partner. They act as coordinators and liaisons between HIVE and the community members. They are essentially residents of the same community/neighbourhood. They come from the same religious background.
5. We have changed the name to protect the respondent's identity.
6. Such as limited mobility, gender-specific challenges (that is, women are restricted to home chores only) and the fear/threat of persecution which hinders, for example, education or economic opportunities.
7. Rapport building was the first step to building consensus during the community meetings. It included long-term engagement, multiple and regular community visits (sometimes without mentioning about the project) and various consultations. This proved to be an investment. Once we developed the rapport, as facilitators we ensured the inclusion of women and young people and encouraged them to speak and contribute by listening to them attentively, and at times since some of them were not articulate, our facilitators conveyed/interpreted their points to the committee members. This ensured that the committee members respected and listened to the young voices. One example is of a young woman in Joseph Colony who was initially not considered (by the men) for the local (Ravadar) committee, but who was later put in charge of the community funds because of her good management skills and educational background.
8. There was one person who said that his house was used by the members of the community as a base and for community affairs – he claimed that after the roof was broken, the

members had stopped coming. When HIVE discussed this with other members, they denied it. In fact, the person's house was used by members of one particular political party and the community hadn't benefited from the house.
9   These influential members allowed their own female family members to join the local committees, and this encouraged other members of the community to follow.
10 HIVE Pakistan ensures gender and religious diversity within its organizational structure. It currently employs people from Shi'a, Christian, Hindu, Sikh and atheist backgrounds.

References

Associated Press in Ottawa (2013) 'Rimsha Masih, Pakistani girl accused of blasphemy, finds refuge in Canada', *The Guardian*, 1 July. Available at: https://www.theguardian.com/world/2013/jul/01/pakistan-girl-accused-blasphemy-canada

DAWN (2013) 'Dozens of houses torched as mob attacks Lahore Christian locality', *DAWN.COM*, 9 March. Available at: https://www.dawn.com/news/791408/mob-attacks-christ%20ian-neighbourhood-in-lahore

Stanford University (2012) 'Mapping militant organisations: Sipah-e-Sahaba Pakistan'. Available at: https://web.stanford.edu/group/mappingmilitants/cgi-bin/groups/view/147?highlight=April%2B19

13

Using Participatory Methods with Ahmadis in Exile

M.K.

Introduction

This chapter explores the practitioner author's experiences of employing participatory methods to understand the lived reality of poor Ahmadi Muslim (AM) women in Pakistan, as part of research for the Coalition for Religious Equality and Inclusive Development (CREID) between January and November 2020. Due to the severe restrictions AMs face in Pakistan, subject to legislation which states that it is a criminal offence for Ahmadis to discuss their views and religious beliefs publicly, this research was carried out with Pakistani refugees registered with the United Nations High Commissioner for Refugees (UNHCR) in Bangkok, Thailand. Three focus group discussions (FGDs) were conducted with ten AM women aged 18–35, ten AM women aged 35+ and ten AM men. The aim was to reflect on the challenges facing poor AM women in Pakistan compared with the experiences of more affluent AM women, women from other Muslim sects (including Sunni and Shia) and AM men, and to provide tangible policy recommendations to redress the daily encroachments faced by the Ahmadiyya Muslim Community (AMC), and particularly poor AM women.

What were the purpose and objectives of the research?

I am a follower of the Ahmadiyya Muslim faith and a leader within the AMC in Thailand. I was forced to leave Pakistan due to the daily encroachments I faced due to my faith. The AMC is the most persecuted community in Pakistan, with the issues faced by AMs very different from those faced by other minorities in Pakistan.

The AMC believe that they are Muslims, but the constitution of Pakistan has declared them to be non-Muslims. Constitutionally they have denied a community the right to recognize themselves as Muslim. The constitution even says that if any AM 'poses' as a Muslim, it is a criminal offence. This is unbelievable.

If any non-Muslim – for example, a Christian or a Jew – says *as-salaam alaykum* ('Peace be upon you') as a greeting, any Muslim would be overjoyed. Yet, if an AM says *as-salaam alaykum*, according to the Pakistani constitution, they will be imprisoned for three years, and fined more than 100,000 rupees because they would be deemed as 'posing' as Muslims.

It is nearly unbearable for me stay in Pakistan, and I am hold a PhD and work for a large company. The situation for AM women is even more complex. In Pakistan, a normal AM cannot find a job, and even if they do find one, they face many challenges. Imagine this persecution compounded by poverty; financial issues increase the challenges faced by the AMC. The focus of this research was consequently to unpack this dynamic: to interrogate how poverty and religious marginalization intersect, and to understand the combined effects on women, who typically experience enhanced marginalization. This is due in part to the fact that many AM women are restricted to their homes due to fear for their safety and risk of harassment in public. AM women consequently have greater limitations on their ability to find work and pursue education. Many AM women are financially dependent on donations from the Ahmadiyya Muslim Jammat fund to meet their most basic needs under these constraints.

As far as I am aware, this is the first such study in the world to focus on the experiences of AM women, investigating the relationship between poverty and religious marginalization.

What was the methodology you employed, and why was it chosen?

I have used various research methods in the course of my work. For my PhD in construction management I primarily used a systems dynamics approach, which is a predominantly quantitative method utilizing mathematical modelling. When I commenced the research with CREID it took me three or four months to investigate what kind of methodology would be best suited to research the situation of the AMC. I found that participatory ranking methodology (PRM) was the best option, affording flexibility and opportunities not provided by other research methodologies.

The first reason is that PRM resembles an open-ended discussion, whereby issues can be explored and their drivers interrogated. Participants aren't bound by closed questions, or yes/no answers. PRM affords the freedom to discuss and interact more organically with people. Second, PRM implies both qualitative as well as quantitative data. Qualitative data is very rich, providing detail on perceptions not captured by quantitative data, while the quantitative ranking elements provide more information on the intensity of issues as experienced by participants. Triangulation of both quantitative and qualitative data therefore affords research rich in essence and content. Third, PRM is not a one-off exercise, but can be repeated as many times as necessary according to time constraints. For this research interviews were repeated twice, on different days and at different times. This is also significant as perceptions, assessments and rankings of risk will vary according to the time and context. The AM refugees interviewed were very concerned about their safety and security. In the first interview, they were tangibly scared, and some were not willing to participate. In these circumstances it is difficult to obtain honest results. During my first couple of visits and exercises, I spent a lot of time trying to assure and encourage people.

PRM gives you space to spend as much time as you want on an issue until both parties, the participant(s) and researcher(s), are satisfied, which is a real advantage in order to build trust. On the other hand, as mentioned, a key challenge for this research was finding people who were willing to respond, and to be open; this obstacle is particularly significant when interrogating issues such as religious inequalities, which are very sensitive – particularly in Pakistan. AMs can lose their lives if they speak about their religion publicly; it is a criminal offence. So when you ask people about their religion in an interview which is going to span many days, you can imagine that no one would be willing to participate.

At the same time, PRM solves many issues related to this challenge, with the word 'participatory' particularly capturing people's interest. Participatory research is relational: by participating you feel part of the participant's life, you are one of them. As part of the AMC, my position was significant in reassuring participants that the issues discussed would be used constructively, and that they themselves would not be able to be identified from the research.

My female research assistant and I spent many days with participants, almost four months in total; we felt like family by the end of the exercise. We convinced them that we are like them. I mean, I was not poor in Bangkok – I had a good job, money and my lifestyle was much better than those being interviewed. But they are Ahmadi, and I am Ahmadi. I feel very similar to them and share some of the same problems. Establishing this relationship of mutual trust is the beauty of participative research.

In research when we talk about ranking, it is supposed to be a very complex method. Quantitative studies use very complex ranking systems. In system dynamics, when I performed my research for my PhD, the ranking was so complex that my respondents were confused. But, using PRM, it was so interesting and so easy. The participants discussed and identified issues, then ranked them using toothpicks. Each participant was asked to assign a number of toothpicks to an issue (they had ten in total) according to its intensity.

When participants identified a particularly sensitive issue for them, PRM also afforded the flexibility to ask, why? Why is this issue particularly severe?

From the ranking exercise, I was surprised at the breadth of the issues identified: 25 in total. Many issues were also new to me, for example, AM women's difficulty finding a marriage partner, with many of them being too old according to AM tradition. In Islam, marriage is a very sacred act, and they are deprived of that. This finding was very interesting and unexpected, and arose only through the use of PRM.

Was there anything else that particularly surprised you, any other aspects that you weren't necessarily expecting?

The motivation of participants to engage in this research also surprised me. With PRM I found that, once participants were satisfied with me and with my assistant, and understood the purpose of the study, they were comfortable and interested in answering my questions. As a researcher, it can be very difficult to convince respondents to answer questions honestly, or to facilitate an open debate to understand the real essence of issues. However, the fact that this research was conducted in Thailand rather than Pakistan made it substantially easier; engagement of participants in Pakistan would be a completely different challenge.

Another interesting result was the kind of qualitative data produced. Usually, qualitative data is obtained through open-ended questions and discussions. But this kind of research is subject to boundaries; it is conducted and understood in accordance with pre-established categories.

Yet religion and religious identity are not fixed categories – they span the tangible and intangible realms. Religion is a boundary-less topic. Participants were very emotional speaking about their religion, and they became very upset. While the AMs living as refugees in Bangkok were safer than if they had been in Pakistan, participants reflected that they missed their country, and that they felt stuck. They wanted to go back home, but they could not.

When emotions and religious affiliation shape opinions, unpacking these becomes very complex. This complexity conveys advantages and disadvantages for researchers.

What were the ethical issues or challenges that you had to navigate? Were there any limitations of the participatory methods used?

If I had conducted this research in Pakistan there would be many risks; nobody would have been willing to speak about the subject, because it is forbidden to speak about your religion if you are an AM – it is a criminal offence, potentially leading to life imprisonment, or at least five years behind bars and a huge fine. You can even face the death penalty. Right now, around five Ahmadis are facing life sentences in jail just for talking about their religion and/or for carrying a Qur'an. In this context, the primary challenge was to convince people to take part in the research.

Even living as refugees in Thailand, AMs are not safe. Thailand does not recognize the status of refugees and is not a signatory to the refugee convention of the United Nations. AMs in Thailand consequently have no protection and are at risk of arrest by the Thai government. As illegal refugees, AM participants were very reluctant to sit with us for any length of time. It was very difficult to have long conversations with them for this reason. These security considerations, due to fear of police arrest, dictated that we held multiple sessions, which were short and held at different locations, on different days and at different times. We deliberately followed no fixed pattern and contacted participants inconsistently and in no particular order.

The second issue was that most of the refugees in Bangkok live in small communities in certain regions. People believed to be Pakistani and Muslim live in the same area. They are therefore more readily identified, and many refugees try to keep a low profile to avoid trouble with the police.

There was a palpable fear among participants of risking their third country resettlement; this presented an additional challenge when locating willing AM participants. We accordingly contacted the Ameer of the Jamaat (the Ameer is the religious leader of the AM community in a specific country, who is designated by the Ahmadiyya leader based in London) for his help to approach participants and to assure them of their safety and the confidentiality of the research. We promised participants that their names wouldn't be published – even my name is not published with the research for safety reasons.

A strategy we deployed to get people to participate in the research was through an initial pilot study. Five people who were in key positions in the executive council of the Ahmadiyya community in Thailand, were selected. We prepared a preliminary list of questions and issues through this pilot study discussion. The study was also useful in engaging key stakeholders as advocates for the research. Once they understood its purpose, they were motivated to assist in the identification of suitable participants.

How were the methods different from previous research you've conducted?

In my previous research I was working with professionals and experts in their fields. For this research I was engaging participants who were not very well educated, scared and marginalized, deprived of access to food or employment, who didn't even have enough food to eat. These basic issues they faced compounded their fear, and as AMs, they were also afraid of losing their lives. These factors change a person's opinion. When you ask a question of someone who is very satisfied and comfortable in their lives, their opinions and approach will be totally different from those of a person who is deprived of their basic needs.

For this research, the AMs interviewed were poor and religiously marginalized, and they were largely pessimistic. Many of them had been living in Thailand for ten years illegally, waiting to be resettled in a third country. They cannot go home to Pakistan due to religious persecution, and their resettlement had also been further delayed due to COVID-19 restrictions. You can imagine the psychological condition of these people, which was totally different from that of 'normal' people. They were very emotional. Sometimes emotional responses are not necessarily very rich in their essence, but it is important to explore them. Emotions can be revealing, helping to build a fuller picture – to reveal the inside story.

PRM is distinct from other research methods in affording this space for group reflection on situations participants have faced, and the qualitative data can be consequently very rich in helping to understand personal experiences and unpack emotional responses.

Would you be able to apply the participatory methodologies to your current work outside of the social sciences?

I later successfully applied the same methodology to conduct research on the issues faced by day-wage construction workers. The method was useful again for this research because of its simplicity, both of the ranking method and of the interactive discussions, which were accessible for all the participants to engage with despite low levels of education and/or literacy. I have therefore found PMs very helpful to understand issues of deprivation, and to research with poor marginalized groups. PMs places a greater onus on relationships and discussion, and the researcher can gain more valuable data through the space for follow up questioning.

Is there any key learning from your CREID research that you would like to share?

The research revealed the synergic effects of poverty and religious marginalization. There are many researchers who have worked on poverty and women – to understand their issues, why they are poor and how can their lives be improved – and researchers have also worked separately to understand religious marginalization. Yet interrogating these aspects together yields completely different results and new understandings.

I am an AM man, and I have a wife and two daughters who are also Ahmadis. I have a good lifestyle – I am not poor, my wife also works, and we have disposable income. My daughters have a very good lifestyle. Even so, as AMs, we face issues – we are not safe in Pakistan. We cannot tell our driver that we are Ahmadis; we cannot tell our maid that we are Ahmadis; we cannot hang our leader's photo in our home because we are afraid of the people who work for us. This is the situation of an AM who is well-off.

What about poor AMs? Poverty increases this fear and vulnerability. Close, congested communities in Pakistan are where many of the issues AMs face are exacerbated. Because I have money, I can afford to live with my family outside of the city, where it is safer for AMs. A poor AM cannot afford to do this; they are forced to live alongside majority Muslim communities, where they are more vulnerable to persecution.

If I wish, I can leave the country – I have money and a passport, I can run away from Pakistan. Poor AMs cannot do this. Ahmadis are being killed every other day in Pakistan. We are not even safe in our graves, which are regularly desecrated. It is often said that the only Ahmadis living in Pakistan right now are those who cannot afford to leave. Those who can afford to do so have already fled.

How would you suggest further research should be conducted on freedom of religion or belief (FoRB) in Pakistan and with the AMC more broadly?

The research focused on the experiences of poor AM women, and future research comparing these with the experiences of affluent AM women would be very interesting. While the AMC seems to be the most persecuted community in Pakistan, comparing AM experiences with other religious minorities in Pakistan may reveal some new insights and perspectives.[1]

Would you change anything if you did this research again?

Ideally I would have liked to have conducted the research in Pakistan. In Thailand, the participants were relatively safer, and this may have affected their ranking of the intensity of the issues they faced. The people who are living in Bangkok are poor and lead a very fearful and difficult life, but their lives are not necessarily at stake, as they would be in Pakistan.

In Pakistan, AMs are living in a very suffocating environment, and I am sure the ranking would have been different. Given the opportunity again, I would, if possible, conduct the research with AMs in Pakistan.

Do you think it would be possible to conduct the same research in Pakistan, given that the AMC cannot speak about their religion and issues outside of the home?

Right now, it is almost impossible because of the threats AMs face. But, if you want to get to the real essence of the issues the AMC faces in Pakistan, then of course it is necessary to conduct the study in Pakistan.

Conclusions

Participatory methodologies are not really my field, and they were not well known to me before this research. I have since applied this methodology to my work in construction management, which has never been employed before, and my friends and colleagues were very shocked. They are accustomed to collecting large amounts of data via questionnaires, and then interpreting this information through statistical tools, such as the Statistical Package for the Social Sciences. However, with this approach, unless respondents are familiar with the topic of the questionnaire, it can be difficult to get responses or to understand the underlying reasons for them. PMs provide robust data through their ability to reveal these underlying understandings without necessitating causal extrapolation arising from complex mathematical modelling.

PMs also allow for the engagement of participants not necessarily familiar with the topic of research, through providing the space to explain the ranking and to allow for discussion, and this reveals new and interesting data.

This methodology is consequently very important to apply to other fields of research, not just the social sciences. It should be taught in different universities, including for courses on engineering, technology and the sciences. I have never seen these methods being taught in these areas, but they could be very powerful in transforming our understandings.

Note

[1] To read more on the complexity of the intersections of gender, class and religious marginality in shaping the realities for women from religious minorities in Pakistan see Tadros (2020).

References

Tadros, M. (ed.) (2020) Violence and Discrimination against Women of Religious Minority Backgrounds in Pakistan, CREID Intersections Series, Coalition for Religious Equality and Inclusive Development, Brighton: Institute of Development Studies

14

Addressing the Intersection of Religious and Other Inequalities through Participatory Methodologies

Mariz Tadros and Jo Howard

Introduction

In this book we set out to reflect on and share our learning around two areas. First, what have we learned about using participatory methodologies to research freedom of religion or belief (FoRB)? What are their strengths for researching this topic, and in these contexts? How have they been applied and adapted in context? What have been their limitations, and where have they not worked? What have been the ethical issues? Second, we have sought to understand what the use of PMs has revealed about the nature of FoRB, that other methods do not capture. What have we learned that is important for the FoRB research community? We reflect on these two areas of inquiry in this closing chapter. We do so in dialogic form, as we did in the introduction. Jo speaks from the perspective of PMs, and Mariz takes an FoRB lens. Each perspective offers its own insights for scholarship and practice; and in the intersections between these perspectives there is a richness and nuance – finding these has been the particular satisfaction of developing and editing this book together. Bringing our different perspectives, expertise and positionalities to this task and into dialogue has enabled us to learn together and generate new knowledge. We then jointly discuss the challenges and limitations of participatory methods and conclude with some reflections on how such methods have enhanced our understanding of religious equality and freedom of religion or belief.

Part I: The benefits of using participatory methods to explore FoRB

Whichever methods are chosen to capture and understand the state of FoRB, none will be perfect in every way. Choices will necessarily involve trade-offs, entailing a privileging of certain factors over others, such as between capturing the global scale of FoRB versus a nuanced understanding of the particularities of the phenomenon within any given context. For example, methodologies that establish global rankings of freedom of religion or belief violations such as the Pew Survey (see Baronavski et al, 2022) are necessarily ones that involve focusing on country-level data. Even when they rely on multiple sources of data, they necessarily entail an aggregation of data at a country level which may not make it possible to capture the divergences between and across groups and regions domestically.

One of the most rigorous methodologies for measuring the situation of FoRB across different countries is that developed by academic Jonathan Fox via the Religion and State Project (Fox, 2018). Marshall (2021) notes that the strength of the methodology is its granular variables, which allow for systematic analysis, but that, as with other approaches that rely on large datasets, there is a trade-off between the quantitative data that allows for the identification of global patterns and inferences regarding the nature of freedom of religion or belief violations and the qualitative data that would uncover the drivers behind the phenomenon in a differentiated manner. Sometimes the research methods and their applications are informed by a focus on one particular religious group. Examples include the publication by Open Doors, a Christian non-profit organization of the widely known annual World Watch List (WWL), a report that ranks the status of Christians in 73 countries around the world (Open Doors, 2022). Another example is the UK-based Muslim Council of Britain, which publishes reports on the state of media reporting on Islam and Muslims by analysing media content online and in broadcasting. An example of their methodology and output is their report British Media Coverage of Muslims and Islam (2018–20, launched in 2021). However, the trade-off in relation to methodologies that focus on one group is that they do not enable a situational analysis of how other religiously marginalized groups in the same context and time period are faring.

In other cases, methodologies may combine qualitative and quantitative data and rely on a wide array of sources; however, they are necessarily all among the elites. For example, one of the most authoritative sources of information on freedom of religion or belief is the annual report published by the US State Department, the Report on International Religious Freedom. Their primary sources of information are US embassies, where staff collate the initial information, which is then corroborated with key members of civil society and the media in-country; the Office of International Religious Freedom, based in Washington, DC, then undertakes additional consultation with foreign governments and international actors (Office of International Religious Freedom, unpaginated). Access to the preliminary information is partly contingent on the degree of access to information of embassy officials as outsiders in a given country, as well as the degree to which an embassy prioritizes the collation of such information (Marshall, 2021). However, here the methodology is also constrained by the fact that in many parts of the world it would be dangerous for local actors to be seen to be collecting grassroots data on religious freedom for a foreign government. They might be accused of treason or espionage. The methodology is necessarily constrained in capturing granular experiences of religious inequality.

Some methodologies are focusing on one particular form of FoRB violation across time and space. For example, the Organization for Security and Co-Operation in Europe (OSCE) via its Office for Democratic Institutions and Human Rights (ODIHR) releases regular reports on hate crime and hate speech. Its 2020 data, for example, covers 37 countries informed by state and civil society inputs (OSCE, 2020). The strength of such a methodology is that it enables a methodical documentation of patterns across time and countries; however, the trade-off here is that hate speech is only one of many dimensions of FoRB and well-being more broadly. Another set of methods deployed to identify and analyse FoRB are those that monitor incidence of violence. Marshall's (2021) scoping of observatories that monitor incidents as they happen through online media include, for example, the European Parliament intergroup on FoRB and religious tolerance (RT) and the Al-Azhar Observatory for Combating Extremism. The strength of such methods is in contexts where it is very difficult for security reasons to collect empirical data, such as Myanmar or Syria. However, as noted by Marshall (2021), the trade-off here is that reliance on AI-generated data still bears bias and inaccuracy in how the evidence is weighed.

Participatory methods, like all other methods, involve a number of trade-offs in scope, depth and generalizability. Moreover, the objective of data collection as well as consideration of how it will be deployed will influence every aspect of the methods chosen, with ensuing trade-offs. In promoting participatory methods for understanding FoRB, we are deliberately making certain choices which reflect our agenda of putting the realities of groups on the margins at the heart of our approach to the generation of knowledge on FoRB. These groups, although by no means homogeneous, are comprised of individuals and communities at the intersection of religious discrimination, socio-economic and political exclusion. Below we reflect on how our use of participatory methodologies has informed the choices we make about understanding and measuring freedom of religion or belief and religious inequalities.

Participatory methodologies necessarily involve empirical research

While recognizing that the analysis of secondary resources may allow for the extrapolation of large-n data sets (surveys involving large numbers of individuals, households or contexts) on freedom of religion or belief, our use of participatory methodologies is informed by the belief that subnational and local-level empirical studies are central to acquiring a nuanced understanding of religious inequalities. First, the situation of religious minorities is not the same throughout any given country. It varies along several lines, including the extent to which they are perceived as a threat by state and non-state actors, their numbers and the group's own repertoires of strength. For example, how the Indian state may engage with Christian Dalits would be different from the Muslim counterparts and also distinct from the treatment of the Adhivasis, as is evident from the chapters on India in this volume and also in Mader (2022). Hence, methods that aggregate an overall assessment of the level of FoRB in a country from secondary sources fail to capture the differentiated realities of different religious groups in that country. Participatory methods that deliberately seek to engage with various groups and contexts within a country allow for an understanding of the myriad ways in which groups are targeted and are differently positioned in relation to state and non-state actors.

The strength of empirical studies that allow for a situated analysis of the multiple realities on the ground is their generation of data that challenges how we talk about freedom of religion or belief. For example, any research inquiry that focuses on the non-Muslim minorities in Pakistan would necessarily exclude one of the most persecuted religious minorities in the country: the Ahmadiyya, who consider themselves part of the Muslim majority even if they are not recognized as such by government or society (see M.K., Chapter 13). Similarly, research methods that focus on 'religious freedom' will necessarily overlook the realities of indigenous people who may not practice a religion per se, but who they have their own worldview, rites and rituals which constitute sacred beliefs. If an aggregation of country data on freedom of religion or belief did not encompass empirical studies, their realities might easily be missed (see, for example, Tifloen et al, 2022, Muhumuza, Vanwing and Kaahwa, 2022, and Mader, 2022).

Seeing FoRB through the experiences of the marginalized

Several approaches to understanding and capturing FoRB rely on questionnaires with elites from within the same community. The strengths of such an approach is that elites are often familiar with the macro-level dynamics of the situation of FoRB (for example, parliamentary representation of minorities, level of freedom of worship, understood broadly, and so on). While this is important, when elites come from privileged classes and are urban-based they may have a limited understanding of how religiously marginalized and socio-economically excluded individuals experience the full spectrum of discrimination. A recurring theme in this volume is when those from the same community who occupy a position of privilege on account of education, class or profession are trained to use participatory methods, they report that they 'discover' new layers of reality that they had not been aware of. This is not to suggest that elites are not themselves targets of discrimination. Indeed, many activists and dissidents who hail from the classes of the privileged become the targets of violence, incarceration and terror precisely because of their role in speaking out against the injustices of their community. However, in some cases, because they are recognized in the public arena (for example, religious leaders or renowned public figures), their targeting attracts the attention of the media and on occasion the international community.

In CREID, our agenda was to make visible the invisible intersecting inequalities that are experienced by individuals and groups when they are religiously 'otherized' but are also discriminated against on the basis of class, gender, geography, ethnicity and so on. The idea here is not to suggest that some voices count more than others by creating an artificial binary of the elites vs the poor, but rather to engage in methodologies that complement elite understandings of power dynamics with the experiences of the silent majority among the ranks of the religiously marginalized. One of the greatest contributions of participatory research methodologies to understanding and measuring religious inequalities is the evidence they have generated on the intersections of religious marginality with a wide array of identifiers including class, caste, ethnicity, gender, geography, profession and political orientation, to name but a few. Participatory methodologies reveal the highly dynamic ways in which people's experiences of power and powerlessness are influenced by the interplay of these identities. For example, from India, we see how caste (being Dalit) intersects with religious marginality in highly differentiated ways. The experience of abandonment is shaped by the fact that a poor Hindu Dalit is far removed from the centres of Hindutva power, even if s/he is considered as having the same religious affiliation. The experience of being a Dalit Muslim is again shaped not only by caste and class but also by belonging to the most despised of religious minorities in India. In Nigeria, participatory methodologies shed light on the complexity of intersectionality in shaping experiences of religious marginality by showing the interplay with both ethnicity and geographic location. The concentration of groups of different ethnic and religious backgrounds in the country means that being a minority is very much contingent upon which part of the country one is in – which highlights the importance of a differentiated geographic approach to the study of FoRB in Nigeria.

The participatory methods applied in Pakistan confirmed some common grievances across all religious minorities (such as the application of blasphemy law, unequal access to political representation, social stigmatization and social vilification, hate speech). These would have been identified in many country-level studies drawn through conventional methodologies. However, what the participatory methodologies applied brought to the fore is the vastly different *sites* and experiences of inequality brought about by the different intertwining of ethnicity, caste, religious affiliation and class, among many other elements. For example, in Baluchistan the Hazara Shias' experience of religious marginality is shaped not only by belonging to the Sunni majority but also by the racial/ethnic identity of being from the Hazara community and by being perceived as a security threat by the Pakistani government on account of their geographical proximity to neighbouring Iran, a Shia majority country. On the other hand, among the Christians and Hindus who are perceived to be from among the ranks of the Scheduled Castes (or Dalits), the intersection of caste and class inform the experiences of extreme socio-economic exclusion, stigmatization and psychological and physical harassment. Unlike the Christians and Hindus, whose quest for recognition is as non-Muslim religious minorities, the Ahmediyyas' struggle is for recognition as Muslims; thereby, the dynamics of intersecting drivers become further complicated by the role of ideology. In the case of Iraq, an intersectional approach has revealed that marginality is complicated by the role of linguistic distinctness, which cannot be extricated from religious marginality. Participatory methodologies applied in Iraq showed that the Assyrians perceive their existential struggle as a religious minority as necessitating the freedom not only to practise their faith but also its expression in the Assyrian language of their ancestors, which is distinct from the Arabic or Kurdish languages spoken in Iraq.

These intersections deeply enrich understandings of religious equality in ways distinct from other methodologies of FoRB capture in several respects. First, they illuminate ways in which religious affiliation to the mainstream religion does not make individuals immune from religious marginality, as is clear for the Dalit Hindus in India. Second, they show that the power dynamics shaping the realities of different marginalized groups are highly varied in how different factors work together. Disentangling different drivers of inequality becomes possible through participatory methods because they encourage participants to analyse their own realities, not only describe them. Third, it shows that, while religious marginalization may be driving religious discrimination, its content may not only be religious. The example of the Assyrian or Yazidi populations is a case in point where the language is a constituent dimension of religious identity, and not a distinct one.

The evidence generated through such methodologies is particularly robust and powerful because of its granular nature: capturing everything from individuals' experiences of COVID-19 lockdowns on their livelihoods and safety (see Chapters 2–4 from India, and Chapters 5–7 from Nigeria) to experiences of religious exclusion in access to water and education (see Chapters 8–10 from Iraq and Chapters 11–13 from Pakistan). The capture of everyday forms of encroachment through participatory methodologies provides findings that are distinct from those enabled through methodologies that capture incidence of targeted violence or capture particular variables of discrimination in specific areas of FoRB, such as freedom of worship or freedom from violence. Capturing everyday forms of encroachment can reveal new sites of discrimination not previously identified through pre-set variables: for example, in Pakistan, Christian domestic servants were expelled from homes and the Hazara Shias had their mobility severely circumscribed, in both cases because of prejudice assuming they were carriers of COVID-19. Methodologies informed by pre-set variables may not have grappled with these new forms of discrimination that became part of minorities' everyday life specifically after COVID-19.

Participatory methodologies recognize that the robustness of data on FoRB is directly tied to the legitimacy of those who preside over the process of data-gathering and analysis

Participatory methods, more than other methods, require the facilitator to be mindful that power is exercised before, during and after the participatory exercise, and that their own biases and blind spots may undermine the legitimacy and usefulness of the engagement (see, for example, Chambers, 2012). A distinct contribution that the CREID programme has introduced to engaging FoRB and which has informed all the cases in this book is the absolute necessity of addressing the power dynamic of religious affiliation in the selection of the facilitators. In all the cases presented in this book, the facilitators of the research belong to the religiously marginalized group with whom they are engaging. A person's personal faith practices was not taken into consideration when selecting them; however, the group perception of their legitimacy and capacity to trust them was key. A critique may be that this entrenches a sectarian caveat to the research process.

However, research on FoRB often takes place where there are deep sectarian fault lines and where communities have harboured mistrust of the intentions of researchers from the mainstream religious majority. Shared religious affiliation alone is insufficient to secure trust if it is not accompanied by other qualifying factors (see the section below on participatory methods by Jo). Conversely, even if the facilitator exhibits other important factors such as empathy, strong research competencies and deep understanding of FoRB but does not belong to the same community, participants may suspect them of being an agent of the state and mistrust their agenda or how they will use the data. We therefore sought to recruit facilitators who are not only members of the same religious affiliation but who also have substantial credibility in their communities (such information about how they are perceived emanated from our knowledge of the context). Our research has shown that the positive contribution of choosing the right person from within the community (and not just a token leader) impacts the findings in at least two ways. The first positive dynamic associated with the researcher being from the same community is related to being privy to the community's 'hidden scripts', a concept we borrow from James Scott. In communities that have experienced systemic oppression for a long time, people develop hidden narratives to discuss their experiences and perceptions of those in positions of power – for example, those belonging to the dominant religion in their area. Scott's (2008) study of class relations between the landowning class and the peasants of Sedaka in Malaysia suggested that faced with the wealthy landowning class's exercise of power, both ideological and material, over the peasants, the latter develop their own 'hidden scripts' – ways of countering hegemonic discourses through their interrogation of the claims made by the powerful, as well as developing their own oral narratives making sense of the world. These hidden narratives are expressions of internal resistance to and dissent from attempts at penetration and co-option by the powerful. This is highly relevant to the study of religiously marginalized people where the survival of the community, existentially, is reliant upon the ability to counter the vilifying stereotypes, rumours and narratives about how they are as a group. The ability to share among a group a counter narrative, however, needs first and foremost to happen through hidden scripts so as to minimize risk of targeting and assault. In that sense, being a member of the same religious minority affords the researcher access to the hidden script, with all the inferences and indirect references to power dynamics that they are well equipped to understand and relate.

The second positive dimension of researchers being drawn from within the community is legitimacy of voice in representing the findings. For example, in our research on the intersections of gender and religious marginality in Iraq, we were cognizant of a rich and prominent scholarship in feminist studies that was highly critical of research critical of Islam, Muslims and masculinities in Muslim majority contexts. Western scholarship that focused on the plight of Yazidi women at the hands of ISIS, for example, was often accused of being Islamophobic, orientalist and sensationalist. By having Iraqi women researchers from within the communities, such as Zeri (Yazidi) and all the other minority backgrounds (Sabean-Mandean, Kakai, Assyrian, Chaldean, Shabak), it was possible to counter claims of Western appropriation of secondary data for the West's own ends. The women and men from within these communities developed their own policy recommendations informed by the participatory encounters they had undertaken (Tadros, Shahab and Quinn-Graham 2022).

The premise of participatory methodologies is that capacity can be built in how to use the tools and methods even if prior expertise in research is lacking or a full mastery of the laws and policies of freedom of religion or belief is missing. This is critical for the area of FoRB research, where rarely has explicit attention been paid to who is facilitating the collection of the data and the extent to which they have legitimacy among the subjects of the research. For example, Shahab (Chapter 8) shows how peer researchers undertaking research with women of different religious minority backgrounds in Iraq were able to draw upon their own knowledge and experiences. This enabled them to help identify core themes in relation to FoRB for inclusion within the FGDs that were particularly pertinent to their community and which an external researcher may be unaware of.

The significance of participatory methodologies for uncovering the immaterial dimensions of agency in contexts of religious inequality

The concept of agency is intrinsically connected to the ability of individuals to act on their aspirations or to exercise their agency or 'power to'. Individuals and groups who experience religious-based targeting are undeniably denied FoRB as well as a gamut of other rights. However, they still have agency, the power to see themselves and their realities in ways other than as victims. The problem with many methodologies that focus exclusively on the material dimensions of religious inequalities is that they may fail to engage with the immaterial dimensions which people value and consider as key dimensions of their well-being. This is poignantly articulated in Shah and Shah (Chapter 2):

> To that extent, we deliberately employed available participatory methods to enlarge both our ethical imagination and our epistemic understanding concerning what it means to be human. This required asking what it means to be a human being who is socially, politically and economically disrespected and diminished, especially amid the upheaval and distress brought about by COVID-19, and yet *simultaneously* deeply religious and drawn to the transcendent and to ultimate sources of dignity, freedom and flourishing.

Despite the conspicuous violations on material dimensions of well-being such as economic resources, bodily safety and so forth, there was an 'invisible' dimension to their personhood or humanness which is intrinsically associated with their spiritual repertoires. As Ramstedt (2021: 234) notes, for indigenous peoples, for example, the religious and social are not two distinct spheres but deeply interwoven in people's perceptions of the everyday. Methodologies that do not capture immaterial repertoires of power and strength may miss key features of how and why people respond to FoRB violations the way they do. In many cases, drawing on spiritual repertoires is extremely important and can be understood not as a protective response to religious inequalities but through their interpretive lens, as direct action (see for example Chapter 5). We consider this as significantly enhancing methodologies of FoRB in broadening what we understand as of worth and value to an individual, even if it is outside the realm of the conventional criteria of what accounts as FoRB. For example, one of the key findings from India was the way in which individuals mix and match elements of different faiths and heritages in their personal lives. Maintaining the ability to transcend demarcations across different popular heritages and religious expression is crucial for their sense of agency and coping with life's ebbs and flows. Methodologies that focus on specific violations for example, may benefit from participatory approaches that capture how homogenizing political projects undermine these more syncretic expressions of agency (Tadros, 2020).

The majority of methodologies highlighted at the beginning of the chapter (those that use quantitative ranking, those that test out variables, observatories of incidence of violence in communities and online or those that collate country-level data on the status of a group) focus on the phenomenon of discrimination. Participatory methodologies enable a capture of the interface between discrimination and agential responses in their dynamic interaction.

The process of generating data needs to be directly useful for participants and not only to be used by researchers, advocates and policy makers on their behalf

A key question underpinning any methodology seeking to understand freedom of religion or belief is: what will the data generated be used for, and by whom? All, or almost all, of the methods generally deployed are used by actors commissioning the research for agendas that they primarily set, even if on occasion they consult with elite members of a religiously marginalized group. Many FoRB-capturing methodologies (see Marshall, 2021) tend to rely on secondary sources in the form, for example, of embassy officials' reports. The power dynamics informing how public perceptions of these foreign actors influence the nature of information they have access to, how the agendas of their own governments influence their interpretive lens or whose perspectives they captured are rarely discussed. This can lead to a narrow lens being applied to understanding complex realities on the ground at best, and a distortion and misrepresentation at worst.

However, the logic of participatory methodologies enables the subjects of inquiry to directly name the phenomenon for themselves and sometimes challenge the fundamental notions of how we talk about FoRB, from its very conceptualization to its operationalization. For example, in Iraq, both Yazidis and Christians spoke of FoRB as 'racial persecution'. They saw their experiences of discrimination and targeting as being associated with an indistinguishable ethno-religious identity. Participatory methodologies allow participants to shape the agenda of what is important to discuss regarding how freedom of religion or belief features in their lives, which aspects count most and why. In doing so, subjects wield power over articulating what aspects of freedom of religion or belief matter most and what role they play in their lives. Collectively identifying and then ranking what affects their daily lives most through the group inquiry and participatory ranking paves the way for a process of naming what is most important for the community itself. As Dayil notes in Chapter 5 (p 92), the findings are owned by the community:

> This is due to the fact that they have been given time to reflect, and what is conveyed is the lived reality of these oppressed groups. In the sense that problems and solutions are self-identified, the PM provides a sense of self-fulfilment.

The effect on the subjects of inquiry participating in these group sessions is often directly felt. For example, in some groups, the collective articulation of experiences of suffering was therapeutic, and it is not uncommon for participants to become deeply emotional and on occasion shed tears (see the section on 'Emotion' below). While the handling of such situations requires exceptional convening skills on the part of the facilitator, often the empathy shown by others in the group is also deeply affirming. The implications are that the process of engaging with FoRB does not only involve understanding realities, as with conventional methods, but also enables a process of making sense of how to cope with these sensitive issues.

Another way in which positioning subjects as agenda-setters is crucial for engaging with freedom of religion or belief is that it encourages a process of collective realization and analysis of issues that they may wish to organize to tackle and challenge. For example, the data from India shared in Shah's chapter, revealed that while police violence was high in the participatory ranking of grievances by Dalit Hindu and Dalit Muslim men in Bangalore, this was not cited as a concern in Chennai. Therefore this may translate into different policy intervention areas in discussions with government officials from one region to another, so that the greatest impact is achieved in the day-to-day lives of the marginalized.

Another significant dimension of participatory methods relates to how the findings are interpreted and presented, which are key aspects of local ownership of data generation. The central importance given to subjects being actively involved in the synthesis and interpretation of the data means that there is great care that an issue as sensitive and potentially incendiary as

FoRB is tackled cautiously. This is particularly important for individuals and groups who tend to have very few opportunities and spaces for engaging with research in any capacity. In our own experience on the CREID programme, accessing groups and communities on the margins such as the Ahmadiyya in Pakistan or the Kakais in Iraq (see Abdulkhaliq, 2023) is very challenging, because their small numbers and lives lived on the margins make them particularly vulnerable. However, building the capacity of members of the community to engage through participatory methods is met with less hesitancy because it maintains local ownership of the process. In other words, had we suggested some external, more intrusive methods of data collection that involve outsiders setting the agenda, interpreting and presenting the facts (as FoRB methods conventionally entail), we might have met with a great deal more reluctance or rejection altogether.

The fact that participatory methods involve a collective mediation of the meaning of experiences of religious inequalities paves the way not only for intra-group reflection but also for inter-group encounters around different community experiences. Where appropriate, this is critically important for making sense of the patterns of inequality experienced by different groups but also their distinctness. Most FoRB methodologies undertake the research process in a compartmentalized manner, with processes of data collection happening separately with different religious groups. While such parallel processes of data-gathering are beneficial in creating a safe environment for sharing and avoiding divisive politics, there are nonetheless times when the opportunities of sharing across groups are beneficial. If the convenor has the trust and legitimacy of groups across different religious fault lines, and the participants feel safe and are keen on listening to others, these sessions can help us understand inter-group dynamics of freedom of religion or belief in deeply meaningful ways. These processes can help individuals experiencing religious inequalities to discover some common actors or drivers responsible for their oppression, or enable empathy with members of groups other than one's own (see Suleiman, Chapter 7). In such cases, participatory methods are incredibly useful for the subjects who take part in them in helping them uncover for themselves the sources of oppression. Participatory methods can also be beneficial for their cathartic impact among individuals who have expressed deep religious conflict (see Tadros, 2015 for Muslim–Christian encounters after the ousting of the divisive rule of the Muslim Brotherhood in Egypt).

Jo

A participatory research activity or process must always be sensitive to power relations – in the room between participants, between participants and facilitators and, outside the room, between the group and the wider context. Working with CREID, I have noticed that this is heightened in the context of discrimination on the basis of faith, or where religious, ethnic and economic inequalities intersect in the contexts where the authors are working, and discrimination can quickly escalate to violence. People are profoundly fearful. Moreover, intra-group inequalities such as gender-based norms intensify people's (and especially women's) sense of insecurity and powerlessness. The participatory research process is therefore an opportunity to address some of these power inequalities, but also a risk for participants. Extreme care and sensitivity are required, starting with careful reflection by research teams about their identities and positionalities, building greater understanding of how their identities shape relations of power between them and others, and how these can be assets or barriers to the research.

While reflexivity is important in all kinds of research, in a participatory workshop the researcher must be a facilitator, who is sensitive to the emotions and concerns of participants, and agile in helping them to talk openly about their experiences, guiding the wider group to listen, reflect and analyse. In a group setting, this requires carefully creating and sustaining a space of trust, confidence and support within the group. The researcher's facilitation skills are critical, as the facilitator is required to probe sensitively, hold the group, enable the less confident to speak and draw out reflections and analysis by the group, without judgement or criticism. Researcher reflexivity therefore becomes not just a good idea but fundamentally important and necessary if participatory methods are to be used appropriately. Some key considerations are outlined below.

Reflexivity

Working with people unaccustomed to participatory research methods requires training in how to use the method but also (more importantly) preparation for developing a participatory mindset. This means reflecting on the relationships within the research process, and requires researchers to reflect on their own beliefs and attitudes around the topic and the group they will work with (that is, their subjectivity) and their own power and privilege or lack thereof (that is, their positionality). Often, when researchers are already thinking about inequalities, and care about the issues, when we give them participatory tools to practise, we are pushing at an open door. In this case, the majority of the researchers had not used PMs before, and describe how they embarked on the research with both excitement and suspicion (see Dayil, Chapter 5, Mang, Chapter 6). As Mang acknowledges with refreshing honesty and insight,

> I had come with some bias and, although not uncommon, it is important to appreciate its impact on research and how much it should

be avoided. Just because they were from rural backgrounds, I had assumed they wouldn't grasp the concepts. (Mang, Chapter 6, p 111)

As discussed further below, Mang found his biases to be misplaced, and was humbled by the experience of enabling participants to discuss and analyse the issues themselves.

In this research, the teams generally decided not to leave sensitivity to the specific religious minority to chance and therefore ensured that the researcher share the same religious identity. In many cases, this was essential for trust to be built because of the high levels of fear of reprisal (as discussed in Chapters 7, 10 and 13 on researching with Izala women, Yazidis and Ahmadiyaa Muslims). This trust or rapport-building often took time and creativity to establish relationships with the research participants, as described in Chapter 11:

Rapport-building is an organic and dynamic process which leads to the in-depth exploration of intersectional marginalization. Researchers tried to establish rapport with the community by making recurrent visits and multiple conversational methods such as the use of vignettes as prompts. (Shoaib and Mirza, Chapter 11 above)

The authors describe how their own movement and access to participants were restricted, and in some instances, the insecurity and fear experienced by some groups meant that they were asked to leave, or for the audio recording to be deleted (Shoaib and Mirza, Chapter 11). In all settings, in addition to being of the same religious background, it was judged necessary for the researcher/ facilitator to be of the same gender to allow free discussion – this was especially important in settings where women are expected to defer to men and are 'shy' when men ask questions (Zeri, Chapter 10).

Good facilitation requires the researcher to go beyond a focus on data collection and connect with people in order for them to trust the process, and to open up with each other. Most participants had not openly discussed their experiences before, and even within a group where all share the same religion and gender, there are other identities which create insecurities: for example, ethnic identity in Nigeria or caste in India, where there is a deeply entrenched hierarchy, but also age in contexts where youth or older people are marginalized, disability and mental illness, and degrees of economic hardship. Enabling participants to recognize what they have in common can help to overcome these insecurities, as Zeri notes in the context of Yazidi women:

As they shared their experiences in these intimate, warm sessions, I observed that the participants felt they belonged to each other; there was a strong camaraderie born from suffering from the same problems.

> All participants had been exposed to discrimination, marginalization and racism, despite their different ages. I no longer felt that age played a significant role. Older women were discussing with younger girls the same types of problems and feelings. (Zeri, Chapter 10 above)

It is therefore essential for researchers to be not only knowledgeable about the topic (that is, how we understand 'expert' in academia), but also able to create and hold a safe space for people unaccustomed to being heard, to share their stories. As Sofya (Chapter 8) notes on the process in Iraq:

> In this way it is not so much the experience of the researcher in matters relating to FoRB and women's rights as their ability to connect with people and to make them feel confident in sharing personal details about their lives and experiences that allows a greater insight into the everyday lived experiences of those from religious minorities and how these experiences impact their right to freely identify with and practise their beliefs.

Emotion

An important contribution of participatory methods is that they enable surfacing and acknowledging emotions and feelings in research. An inquiry into people's lived experience requires not only cognitive reflexivity about how we produce knowledge (Allan and Arber, 2018), but also emotional reflexivity – how our identities and experiences interact and the emotions that we experience which shape our perceptions (Aabye, Gioacchino and Wegner, 2021). Capturing the knowledge that is generated through our emotions is made possible particularly through creative arts-based and performative methods. In this collection, drawing and storytelling are part of this repertoire. Mang (Chapter 6) describes the creative process thus:

> The activity of drawing the events of their 'Road of Life' was quite unique; the respondents' sense of creativity and their emotions as they described their life experiences during the period made me realize how powerful the inquiry group instrument is as a qualitative research tool. Indulging the respondents in not just discussion but in a creative activity that they could further elaborate on provided a much deeper and wider picture than conventional focus group methods.

Mang identifies the value of the creative method, which enables the participant to articulate emotion and provides space for them to elaborate based on their drawing, to deepen and enrich their story. This is important in research that wishes to understand how religious inequalities intersect with other inequalities. The intersections become apparent as the storyteller is given the space to reflect on and analyse their experiences.

Moreover, Watkins and Shulman (2008: 268) argue that participatory research can be valued as therapeutic 'in the original sense of the care or attending of the soul'. In circumstances where discrimination and marginalization are wearing people down, participatory research (and especially participatory action research) which enables people to articulate their experience, learn from others' testimonials and identify and take actions to support each other and address injustices is an act of 'psychological restoration' (Watkins and Shulman, 2008: 268). In the field of FoRB, allowing emotions to be accessed and expressed, and attending the soul, seem particularly appropriate. As M.K. puts it, with reference to research with Ahmadiyya Muslims,

> religion and religious identity are not fixed categories – they span the tangible and intangible realms. Religion is a boundary-less topic. Participants were very emotional speaking about their religion, and they became very upset. While the AMs living as refugees in Bangkok were safer than if they had been in Pakistan, participants reflected that they missed their country, and that they felt stuck. They wanted to go back home, but they could not. (M.K., Chapter 13 above)

Participatory research offers tools for engaging with emotions, and also the responsibility to hold these safely and responsibly in the group. While the value of therapy in the research process is contested (some feel that it is not the realm of research but should be in the domain of professional counselling), in contexts where people experience multiple and intersecting forms of exclusion being heard can be transformative because it gives credence and value to the lived experience of the person.

> ... as they shared their feelings and problems with each other, I saw how this seemed to have a therapeutic effect: it reduced their feelings of loneliness and isolation through the opportunity to explore and discuss shared experiences of pain and exclusion. When each woman heard the problems of the other women in the group, including those of her peers, friends or even neighbours, she then felt empowered to disclose her own experiences. Each woman therefore gained strength from the group. (Zeri, Chapter 10 above)

Dialogue

The participatory research process engages the individual within a supportive group so that their experience and perspective can be brought into dialogue with others.

> This group space provided an enabling environment for the women to connect and to feel encouraged to share their experiences, to tell their story and thereby to identify and rank key issues facing the community. (Suleiman, Chapter 7)

In this way critical subjectivity (Heron and Reason, 1997) can be enabled, as common issues are identified and the group reflects together about the underlying causes of their shared experiences, and potential sources of support and actions for change. As Suleiman puts it,

> ... we were sharing experiences to form a story, to construct a narrative which could, hopefully, be used for change, so that their daughters and future generations of Izala women would not have to share in their experiences of discrimination. To raise awareness of the fact that they do have rights and they can have rights, and access to education. (Suleiman, Chapter 7)

This critical subjectivity is facilitated by the use of multiple methods which include creative and visual to access different ways of knowing that is tacit/ experiential, expressive/ presentational, conceptual and practical (Heron, 1992; Howard, Ospina and Yorks, 2021). The methods are embedded in a process which often begins with the individual telling their story through the vehicle of a picture – the River or Road of Life. This story is then shared with the wider group, who listen carefully and may offer encouragement or ask the storyteller to deepen their account. In so doing, they bear witness to the storyteller's unique, personal experience, and acknowledge their reality. The co-participants in the group then engage in dialogue together, speaking up where they see resonances and similarities with their own stories, and reflecting on why these similarities exist. They also acknowledge difference: for example, where one person has experienced difficulties due to the particular convergence of factors or drivers of inequalities in their life, their narrated experiences can challenge their co-participants' assumptions rooted in norms around age, gender and other identities (see Howard et al, 2021). Dialogue can therefore build solidarities in situations when people have felt very isolated. It can also enable the group to identify sources of support or prompt ideas for collective care and action.

Part II: Challenges and limitations

We have outlined above the methodological strengths of participatory research: we have highlighted, for instance, the importance of promoting reflexivity, allowing emotion, enabling dialogue, articulating granular experiences of FoRB and generating analysis and ownership of this analysis.

However, we are also alert to the challenges and limitations of participatory methods in these contexts, and when working within restricted timescales. In this section, we consider the risks of using PR in challenging contexts, and reflect on what we did to mitigate these risks. We also reflect on how challenges and opportunities can be interlinked, and the affordances of participatory methodologies for strengthening peer researcher skills, for building in researcher reflexivity and promoting iterative approaches to knowledge generation.

Like all methods used to understand and measure freedom of religion or belief, participatory methods have their limitations. We highlight five key limitations here: (1) avoiding political capture; (2) avoiding conflating perception with factual evidence; (3) personal safety and security; (4) level of intensity and time; (5) generalizability and scaling up.

Avoiding political capture

Freedom of religion or belief is a deeply political issue. Caution is therefore needed in not conflating local ownership of data generation with the instrumentalization of research in ways that undermine its integrity and rigour. There is no magic wand to prevent the hijacking of participatory methodologies for partisan agendas; however, there are a number of measures to mitigate against capture of the research process. Deep knowledge of the power dynamics of the context as well as careful selection of those who will be facilitating the sessions are key to avoiding capture. Moreover, clear criteria on how participants will be selected and a review of the transcripts as well as collaboration of sources and triangulation of methods (see below) allow for monitoring of the participatory research processes.

Perception vs evidence

People's own accounts of their realities are important to capture because they provide insights on a people-centred lens into FoRB. These perceptions may or may not reflect a reality which is complicated and multifaceted. For example, some of the participants whose voices are documented may speak very positively of the religious institutions to which they are affiliated, including places of worship and faith-based organizations. This is not to suggest that these institutions consistently exercise power in the most enabling or inclusive way; however, it is important to remember that the objective of the inquiry was not to evaluate these actors' performance but rather to understand experiences of religious inequality from the perspective of individuals living on the margins.

We recognize the need to disentangle a person's interpretation of a certain situation and the actual evidence on the ground. The two are sometimes congruent, and at other times they diverge greatly. In one context, a member of a religiously marginalized group insisted that their community suffered more than all the other religious minorities. This is partly because they were not familiar with the realities of the other groups and particularly because they were convinced that certain determinants of their reality (especially in the legal domain) meant that no other group could be as equally oppressed. However, CREID's work with a multitude of religious groups in that context did not support this particular group's perspective. In another context, members of a group were claiming that another religious minority group was discriminatory towards them, yet the stories they shared and examples they gave suggested a lack of trust between the two communities rather than categorical evidence of targeting.

The importance of disentangling perception from factual evidence is also important in order not to inadvertently spread what would potentially be considered hate speech. The process of synthesizing the data therefore becomes particularly important to ensure that participatory methodologies do not momentarily empower individuals to share their thoughts while putting them at risk of a backlash thereafter. As discussed in the introduction to this volume, the credibility and validity of the data ensuring from the use of participatory methods can be secured via corroboration of evidence (for example, does it run against all the contextually nuanced evidence?) and triangulation of methods (does the application of other research methods both qualitative and quantitative challenge the strength of the evidence?).

Personal/group safety and security

The strength of participatory methodologies in creating a safe environment for participants to share is that, if the right facilitator is involved, all necessary measures can be taken to create a safe and enabling environment. However, in many authoritarian contexts where sectarian fault lines run deep, there may be genuine security risks in bringing people together to discuss issues of religious inequalities. Informants may be planted in such meetings; neighbours may overhear and report with accusations of fomenting sectarian strife or even of gathering people to engage in blasphemous talk. It is important to note, however, that if security encroachments are severe, it is highly unlikely that any method that involves empirical research will be safe to implement on the ground, whether participatory or not. Where experts who do not live among the religiously and socio-economically marginalized poor, they may craft interview or survey questions to be as specific and focused as possible on capturing the particularities of FoRB violations, yet in contexts where there are extreme risks to talking openly about FoRB issues people may not be forthcoming, or may even deny the occurrence of violations. The possible strength of participatory methods is that by co-creating the parameters of the research inquiry with the subjects themselves, this creates opportunities for the group to agree on a number of euphemisms and indirect ways of talking about sensitive FoRB issues as a way to minimize security risks.

Level of intensity, resources and time

Some methods deployed to gather data on freedom of religion or belief can be rapid: for example, a questionnaire circulated among experts on a particular religious group or community can be returned in a fairly short period of time. Methods that involve an analysis of secondary sources may require thorough and systematic analysis but ultimately may not be exceptional in the intensity of its undertaking. On the other hand, participatory methods, even if they do not extend into action research, can be time-consuming, intense and may require considerable resources if demands on people's time are substantive. The deep contextual knowledge required for the identification of the right partners, facilitators, site for group gatherings, selection of persons and so forth means that so much planning needs to precede any initiation of the process of engaging with subjects. Such a planning process may take months in order to ensure that all ethical, security issues are taken into consideration as well as the integrity of the process itself. Moreover, it is not only the undertaking of the participatory interactions with the subjects but also the processes that follow that involve recurring meetings to ensure validation of data. The iterative nature of engaging with participatory methodologies in terms of co-creation of agenda, data production, analysis, validation, synthesis and narration can take several months, and may be particularly time- and human-effort-intensive in the light of the political sensitivities associated with FoRB.

For some of the research teams (India, Nigeria), the time frame required to deliver the research and provide feedback on the situation of FoRB during the pandemic meant that the participatory sessions had to be a one-off event rather than a series of meetings over months, as was the case in the Pakistan research, for example. Moreover, operating during the pandemic and in conflict contexts meant that security was a constant concern, resulting in one context where the venue for the meeting was arranged by a vigilante group, who also offered to guard the place throughout the research exercise. This group, as Dayil explains in Chapter 5, 'had to be deployed because the crisis was still ongoing in several sections of the state and Bassa LGA in particular. The presence of the vigilante group reassured the respondents about the researchers' safety and sincerity.'

Undertaking group-based research with people from very marginalized communities can also raise expectations of benefits, and this was the case in Nigeria, with far more people than anticipated (over 100) arriving for the meetings, in the hope of receiving food or credits (see Howard et al, 2021).

These fledgling attempts at participatory research are not always satisfactory. However, we believe that small steps towards a more participatory approach to research into FoRB are important and provide learning and pointers for new ways of researching and accompanying people experiencing religious inequalities. The group-based process was recognized as useful by all researchers, contributing to increased confidence among participants, a sense of togetherness when many had felt extremely isolated and, in some cases, a shift in critical subjectivity, towards recognition of rights and identification of shared goals and potential actions. Where the process allowed for a series of meetings (Pakistan, Iraq), groups were able to progress from ranking issues to identifying actions for change.

Generalizability and scaling up

While participatory ranking exercises generate quantifiable data that can be aggregated, it is highly unlikely that the number of group inquiries using such a method will be repeated in sufficiently diverse parts of the country and with sufficiently representative cohorts to enable the generation of generalizable data for a whole country. The challenges of scaling up such methods also poses challenges for the creation of datasets that allow for comparisons across countries. Since participants play a central role in the agenda-setting around the inquiry on FoRB at very local levels, this may make the comparability of data across countries challenging. For some policy makers and activists, the underlying goal behind collecting data on FoRB is to generate rankings and scales of intensity of FoRB violations across countries (Marshall, 2021). Global data on FoRB is in high demand (see Introduction). Participatory methods may not allow the production of such data, however, because, as discussed in the introduction, global data on FoRB is necessarily problematic on grounds of reliability and rigour of methodology. Hence, it may be that we need to live with a trade-off between an accurate but localized pulse of the situation of the religiously marginalized on the ground through participatory methods, with global datasets premised on the aggregation of datasets collected through problematic methods.

Navigating risk and identifying opportunities through reflexive, adaptive research processes

In some cases, local facilitators reflected on the participatory methods and found limitations in their context. The facilitator of a Dalit Christian group in India critiqued the storytelling and matrix ranking because for her it focused too much on an individualized experience and did not provide the process to link this to the community:

> While the participants were encouraged to provide a visual depiction of the impact of the pandemic on their lives, the tool restricted each participant to framing their own perceptions and their own lived realities as isolated individuals. ... At least within the parameters of this particular visual method, she could not readily depict what happened to her community, or how her community shaped her, for better and for worse, in the course of the pandemic. (Lata John, Chapter 3)

This shortcoming could have been addressed there and then, had there been more time available, and with greater facilitator experience and confidence to adapt the method, by inviting participants to return to their 'rivers' and reflect on the role that their community had played in the different moments portrayed in the pictures. This highlights how, ideally, participatory research should unfold over several sessions, allowing for reflection and learning to inform adaptations to the methods and activities. It also highlights the importance of building the skills and capacities of participatory research facilitators, supporting them to navigate their roles as insider/outsiders (Eyben, 2009). Engaged and committed participatory researchers are not neutral or dispassionate but still need to be able to step back, reflect and adapt where required to enable participants' agency and manage risk in the emergent participatory process (see Shah and Shah, Chapter 2).

On the other hand, for Dayil in Nigeria, despite the short time frame and the challenges of the conflict and COVID-19 context, using PMs was valuable to the participants since 'The PM goes beyond data collection by allowing respondents to reflect on some of the challenges that have negatively impacted them, as well as what helps them build resilience' (Chapter 5). This suggests that not doing fully fledged Participatory Action Research does not mean nothing can be attempted – although the limitations and risks of shorter-term participatory research which can stray into extractivism need to be weighed against the risks and benefits of multiple encounters which can make people more visible and vulnerable but can build greater agency and generate action among the group.

In Part I of this chapter we identified the importance for researchers to have deep knowledge of the conflict settings, to share important identities such as religion/faith and gender, and to develop relationships with the participants to build trust for them to participate. This is not always possible – Shoaib and Mirza (Chapter 11) encountered challenges in the Pakistani context to find female researchers, since women in these marginalized settings are often denied education. However, they found a solution which involved strengthening the skills and capacities of individuals from the community to be peer researchers, working in pairs alongside trained researchers.

The research team also identified the importance of working with the peer researcher (members of the religious minority community from the same locality with the lived experience of the issues under discussion) to improve the level of trust between the researchers and the community. The researchers who worked in pairs retrieved more rich stories than the individual, 'outsider' researchers. It is highly recommended to work with the peer researchers, accompanied by a highly trained researcher to bring out the nuanced experiences (Shoaib and Mirza, Chapter 11).

This approach was also adopted in Iraq, where participatory methods were embedded in a methodological approach which emphasized relationship-building, modelling and accompaniment to enable 'two-way open and honest dialogue and feedback' between lead researchers and peer researchers (see Chapter 8). This shifts the research relationship into one of mutual learning, as Shahab describes it: 'we positioned the research process and partnership as a form of accompaniment whereby working alongside the peer researchers was a collaborative learning process.'

Another way to build trust and capacity is through long-term engagement with the groups and communities, as in the case of activists like Suleiman, who explains:

> it would not have been possible to conduct this research with the Izala women without the use of participatory methods, or without the trust that I have built with the community through over 14 years of engagement with religious minorities in rural Wase; this, for an isolated and reclusive minority group, was a crucial enabling factor for the research. (Suleiman, Chapter 7)

In sum, while there are risks inherent in bringing people experiencing religious inequalities together in participatory research meetings, these can be mitigated to some extent through working closely with local organizations, through careful planning, providing training in participatory research principles and ethics, ensuring contextual adaptation of methods and building the capacities of local researchers including community peer researchers, allowing them space to reflect and adapt.

Part III: Final reflections

Bringing participatory principles, processes and methods to FoRB researchers has significance for the field. Bradbury and Reason (2006) propose 'enduring consequence' as an indicator of the quality of a participatory research process. There are indications of the enduring consequence of the research in this collection. In Nigeria, Suleiman's work with Izala and non-Izala women has generated intercultural dialogue, which has changed non-Izala women's perceptions of Izala women. A Christian woman who participated in the research commented:

> 'I have never been part of this type of research. It's It has been almost one year, and the way I see Izala women has changed considerably. (Christian woman, cited in Suleiman, Chapter 7).

In Iraq, the research process generated understanding among the women of the importance of education, and of the value of mutual help – of women mentoring other women. Zeri (Chapter 10) explains the challenges of engaging Yazidi women in the research but also the transformation that their participation afforded, as the women came together and supported each other:

> ... the participants have become accustomed to fear, and reticent to express themselves as an oppressed minority. This fear has become ingrained and is now being passed on to the next generation. ...
>
> I noticed how the women gained self-confidence in these vulnerable moments – they identified with each other, and together formed new networks and friendships. friendships. [...] This research has led to a strengthening of the relationships amongst the women who participated.

Where people have come together to support each other, in a number of chapters there was also a recognition that they have rights – this awareness is galvanized though listening to each other's stories, and through their dialogue and analysis (see for example Suleiman, Chapter 7, and Shahab, Chapter 8). The learning cycle (Kolb, 1984) of reflection and dialogue that are embedded in participatory research enable participants to reflect on their experience and formulate concepts that can be applied to new action, and to make decisions about that new action. This must then be tried out in new situations. This can, according to Mahdi (Chapter 9), contribute to challenging the 'otherization' of religious minorities, helping to break the cycle of discrimination and marginalization.

It is on this point that my own thinking around power relations and participatory methods has been enhanced through this collaboration. As per the Introduction, religious otherization means 'more than having a different religion: we mean where this difference in religious affiliation (real or perceived) becomes the basis of identifying someone as "the other", as not "one of us". With reference to the use of the term "religious otherization" in our context, it is reflective of a relationship of power, rather than a numerical status.' Participatory methodologies are rooted in traditions of challenging unequal power relations that perpetuate inequalities, uncovering how they operate, building confidence and strengthening capacities of those who are marginalized to analyse their realities and take actions. Participatory researchers and practitioners are also keenly aware that for change to happen we need to see the system beyond the marginalized group, and develop strategies to engage and involve those who hold more power. Thinking about this in the context of FoRB has generated ideas and questions. Participatory research enables dialogue, which builds connections within the group. How can this dialogue be extended to other groups within the 'system' of religious otherization, so that humanity and mutual care can be restored? How can participatory researchers pay more attention to the power relations around religious identities and otherization and understand better how they intersect with other more familiar categories such as class, race and gender, to ensure that we are not complicit in marginalizing people on the basis of their religion or faith or non-faith?

The theme of freedom of religion or belief will always be contentious not only because one ideal approach for measuring its scale or intensity does not exist but also because the nature of data collection and how it is used on this topic will always be deeply political. In this book we have shown how our experimentation with the adaptation of participatory methods for understanding FoRB in India, Iraq, Pakistan and Nigeria has been highly beneficial on a number of grounds. First and foremost, the ontological premises for a participatory approach are critically important for recasting freedom of religion or belief conceptually. Rather than engage with participants with preconceived notions of what FoRB constitutes and signifies, subjects experiencing religious inequalities define what it means to be religiously marginalized in their own words.

Furthermore, rather than engaging in methodologies that seek to extract data to measure, compare and contrast FoRB, participatory methodologies generate opportunities for the subjects of the research to directly benefit from, and feel ownership of the processes of, identifying, measuring, analysing and validating this data. Moreover, the opportunities to gather both qualitative and quantitative data via participatory methods enable the generation of very rich data that sheds light on the day-to-day experiences of encroachment and targeting in their complexity and their dynamism. We believe that the possibilities of adapting participatory methodologies for understanding religious inequalities and FoRB are endless: they can be used by community development practitioners, academics of all disciplines and human rights activists in sensitive contexts. Undoubtedly, the nature of FoRB or religious equalities requires certain sensitivities be taken into account that may not be as critical in the study of other social phenomena. The chapters in this book have shown conceptually and practically what makes the adoption of participatory methodologies in contexts of religious inequalities both so challenging but also so rewarding. We hope these chapters challenge, inspire and encourage readers to invest in thinking about whose realities count when we seek to understand FoRB, and to frame our inquiries and methodologies around what would be most meaningful to them.

References

Aabye, L.K., Gioacchino, G. and Wegner, F. (2021) 'Holding space for emotions in participatory action research: reflections from the experiences of a youth organisation exploring PAR through creative practices', in D. Burns, J. Howard and S. Ospina (eds), *The SAGE Handbook of Participatory Research and Inquiry*, London: SAGE, pp 263–75.

Allan, H.T., and Arber, A. (eds) (2018) *Emotions and Reflexivity in Health and Social Care Field Research*, London: Palgrave Macmillan.

Baronavski, S., Majumdar, V., Webster, B. and Crawford, S. (2022) Religious Restrictions around the World, Pew Research Center. Available at: https://www.pewresearch.org/religion/interactives/religious-restrictions-around-the-world/

Bradbury, H., and Reason, P. (2006) 'Conclusion: broadening the bandwidth of validity: issues and choice-points for improving the quality of action research', in P. Reason and H. Bradbury (eds), *The Handbook of Action Research: Concise Paperback Edition*, London: SAGE, pp 343–51.

Center for Media Monitoring (2021) British Media's Coverage of Muslims and Islam (2018–2020). Available at: https://cfmm.org.uk/resources/publication/cfmm-report-british-medias-coverage-of-muslims-and-islam-2018-2020-launched/

Chambers, R. (2012) Sharing and Co-generating Knowledges: Reflections on Experiences with PRA and CLTS. IDS Bulletin 43(3): 71–87.

Eyben, R. (2009) 'Hovering on the threshold: challenges and opportunities for critical and reflexive ethnographic research in support of international aid practice', in C. Widmark and S. Hagberg, (eds) *Ethnographic Practice and Public Aid: Methods and Meanings in Development Cooperation* (Studies in Cultural Anthropology 45), Uppsala: University of Uppsala, pp 71–98.

Fox, J. (2018) *A World Survey of Religion and the State*, New York: Cambridge University Press.

Heron, J. (1992) *Feeling and Personhood: Psychology in Another Key*, London: Sage.

Heron, J., and Reason, P. (1997) 'A participative inquiry paradigm', *Qualitative Inquiry*, 3(3): 274–94.

Howard, J., Ospina, S.M. and Yorks, L. (2021) 'Cooperative Inquiry as Dialogic Process', in D. Burns, J. Howard and S. Ospina (eds) *The SAGE Handbook of Participatory Research and Inquiry*, London: SAGE, pp 427–43.

Howard, J., et al (2021) Understanding Intersecting Vulnerabilities Experienced by Religious Minorities Living in Poverty in the Shadows of COVID-19, CREID Intersections Series; Religious Inequalities and COVID-19, Coalition for Religious Equality and Inclusive Development, Brighton: Institute of Development Studies, DOI: 10.19088/CREID.2021.012

Kolb, D.A. (1984) *Experiential Learning: Experience as the Source of Learning and Development*, vol. 1, Englewood Cliffs, NJ: Prentice-Hall.

Mader, P. (2022) 'We put God and drums in the front': spirituality as strategy in an Adivasi self-empowerment movement', in M. Tadros (ed.), *What About Us? Global Perspectives on Redressing Religious Inequalities*, Brighton: Institute of Development Studies, pp 115–44. Available at: https://opendocs.ids.ac.uk/opendocs/handle/20.500.12413/17660

Marshall, K. (2021) Towards Enriching Understandings and Assessments of Freedom of Religion or Belief: Politics, Debates, Methodologies, and Practices, CREID Working Paper 6, Coalition for Religious Equality and Inclusive Development, Brighton: Institute of Development Studies, 10.19088/CREID.2021.001

Muhumza, M., Vanwing, T. and Kaahwa, M. (2022) 'The integration of traditional religious beliefs in the conservation of the Rwentzori Mountains National Park, Uganda: processes, and lessons learnt', in M. Tadros (ed.), *'What about Us': Global Perspectives on Redressing Religious Inequalities*, Brighton: Institute of Development Studies, pp 177–218.

Office of International Religious Freedom (2021) Report on International Religious Freedom. Available at: https://www.state.gov/reports/2021-report-on-international-religious-freedom/

Open Doors (2022) World Watch List 2022: Trends. Available at: https://www.opendoorsuk.org/persecution/persecution-trends/

OSCE (2020) 2020 Hate Crime Data. Available at: https://hatecrime.osce.org/infocus/2020-hate-crime-data-now-available

Ramstedt, M. (2021) 'The right to freedom of religion and from religion in non-state legal orders: the case of indigenous peoples', in S. Ferrari, M. Hill, A.A. Jamal and R. Bottoni, *Routledge Handbook of Freedom of Religion or Belief*, London: Routledge, pp 232–46.

Scott, James (2008) *Weapons of the Weak: Everyday Forms of Peasant Resistance*, New Haven, CT, and London: Yale University Press.

Tadros, M. (2015) Decrypting Copts' Perspectives on Communal Relations in Contemporary Egypt through Vernacular Politics (2013–2014), IDS Working Paper 456. Available at: http://www.ids.ac.uk/publication/decrypting-copts-perspectives-on-communal-relations-in-contemporary-egypt-through-vernacular-politics-2013-2014

Tadros, M. (2022) *What About Us? Global Perspectives on Redressing Religious Inequalities*, Brighton: Institute of Development Studies. Available at: https://opendocs.ids.ac.uk/opendocs/handle/20.500.12413/17660

Tadros, M., Shahab, S. and Quinn-Graham, A. (2022) Women of Religious Minority Background in Iraq: Redressing Injustices, Past and Present, Intersections, CREID, Institute of Development Studies. Available at: https://opendocs.ids.ac.uk/opendocs/bitstream/handle/20.500.12413/17780/CREID_Intersections_Iraq_Introduction.pdf?sequence=11&isAllowed=y

Tifloen, R., and Makgoba, M. (2022) 'Sustainable faith and livelihoods: promoting freedom of religion or belief in development' in M. Tadros (ed.), *'What about Us': Global Perspectives on Redressing Religious Inequalities*, Brighton: Institute of Development Studies, pp 145–76.

Watkins, M., and Shulman, H. (2008) 'Liberation arts: amnesia, counter-memory, counter-memorial', in *Toward Psychologies of Liberation*, Basingstoke: Palgrave, pp 232–64.

Widmark, C., and Hagberg, S. (2009) 'Ethnographic practice and public aid: methods and meanings in development cooperation', *Studies in Cultural Anthropology* [University of Uppsala] 45: 73–100.

Index

Note: References to figures appear in *italic* type;
those in **bold** type refer to tables. References to endnotes show
both the page number and the note number (161n1).

66 Quarters, Islamabad 184–5, 197

A

action-oriented approach, definition 17–18
affordable housing 39
agency 40, 141, 218–19, 231
 of Dalit Hindu men 49
 of religion 100
 through storytelling and matrix ranking 182
Ahmadi Muslims (AM) 27, 199, 213, 215
 women 202–3, 204–9
Ahmadiyya Muslim Jammat fund 203
Ameer Mauvia Sector 191
Ancha 25
anti-Ahmadiyya riots 174
anti-minority politics 174
Arthur, B. 3
Asad, Talal 48
Assyrians 26, 163, 215

B

Baghdad 26
Bahai 25
Bahar Colony 184
Bahzani 163
Balochistan 27, 215
Balti Basti 191, *192*, 194, 195, 199
Bangalore 23–4, 38, 39–40, 45, 66–71
Bashiqa 163, 164–5, 167, 168
Bassa Local Government Area (LGA) 25, 79, 82–3, 101–3
Beaman, L. 10, 13, 14
Behzane 26
Bergold, J. 130, 132
bias 16, 103, 111, 174, 216, 222–3
 and AI-generated data 212
 and positionality 179
 and triangulation 20
Bielefeldt, Heiner 11

Birdsall, J. 10, 13, 14
blasphemy violence 197, 198
Bloom, B.S. 161n2
Boal, Agosto 3
Boko Haram 24, 82
Bradbury, H. 232
British Media Coverage of Muslims and Islam report 211
Buhari, President Muhammadu 24

C

castes 23, 55, 56, 59, 214, 215
 in Pakistan 26, 27
Chambers, Robert 3
Chennai 23, 38–9, 45, 48, 55
Christian Dalits 27
Christians
 Dalit 38, 45, 54, 55, 56–63, 215
 in India 23
 in Iraq 26, 126, 127
 in Nigeria 25, 80, 81, 82, 101–12, 233
 and racial persecution 220
 see also Pakistani Christians
Citizenship Amendment Act (CAA)/India 23
climate change 24
Coalition for Religious Equality and Inclusive Development (CREID), description 7–8
'communicative space' 6
community consultations 194–5, 196, 198–9
community mapping exercise *192*, 193
conflict 3, 126, 221
 managing 156
 in Nigeria 24, 80–1, 82, 100, 101, 103, 120
conversions, forced 174, 181
Cornwall, A. 129–30
corroboration of research 20–1
COVID-19 pandemic
 in Dalit communities 48, 49–51, 57–8, 60, 62–3, 66–71

238

INDEX

in India 55–6
in Iraq 145
in Nigeria 79, 88, 91–2, 93–4, 103, 107–10, 112
in Pakistan 216
criminal offence, and religion 204, 205–6
critical subjectivity 226, 230
curriculum, pro-pluralism religious education 144–5, 147, 151–6

D

Daesh 126–7, 128
Dalit Christians 38, 45, 54, 55, 56–63
Dalit Hindus 22, 41, 45, 214, 215
  on religion 49–51
  in Sindh 27
Dalit Muslims
  in Bangalore 45, 65–75
  in Chennai 23, 38–9, 44, 45, 46–7, 48, **49**
  in DJ Halli 64
  most despised of religious minorities in India 214
Danjuma, Mr Mathew 82–3
Denning et al 5
dialogue 225–6, 232–3
  see also storytelling
discrimination
  faced by Christians 155, 191, 194, 197, 216
  gender-based 114
  institutional 158
  of Yazidis **117**, 128, *146*, 166, 168
diversity 151, 157, 158
DJ Halli 64
domestic violence **105**, 109, 195
drawing, as liberation 68–9

E

Easter, celebration of, banned during lockdowns 107
economic marginalization 198
education 144–61, 181, 233
Egypt 9, 15, 19
Electronic City 39
elites 213–14
emotion 220, 224–5
empowerment 60–1, 141, 150, 157, 158, 166
equality, religious 8, 9, 145, 156, 157
Erbil 26
ethnic identity 215, 223
ethnic violence **105**, 109
ethno-religious identity 220
European Asylum Support Office 81
evidence vs perception 227–8
exclusion
  in Iraq *146*, 157, 158
  in Nigeria 94

in Pakistan 173, 181–2, 183, 185–6, 194, 198
experiential learning cycle, Kolb's *149*, 156, 233

F

facilitator, role of 72–4
Fals Borda, Orlando 3
Farr, T. 11
fear of reprisal 15, 67, 223
FIDA (International Federation of Women Lawyers) 116, 120
focus group discussions (FGDs)
  in Iraq 127, 133–5, 136, 137, 140, 167–8
  in Nigeria 110–11, 116
  in Pakistan 176, 195, 202
formal labour sector 26
Fox, Jonathan 13, 211
Franck, M. 11
Freire, Paolo 3
Fulani 24, 25, 80, 81, 82, 101

G

Gatti et al 15
Gaved, M. 131
gender-based discrimination 114
gender-based violence (GBV) 114, 116, 138, 140
gender marginalization 125, 128, 129, 130, 137, 140, 141
genocidal violence 199
Global South 40, 46, 73
Gonan Rogo 25
'goondaism' 45
grounded theory approach 12, 28
Guy, B. 3

H

Hall, J. 131
hate crime 212
hate speech 212
Hausa-Fulani 80, 81, 82, 101
Hazara Shias 27, 215, 216
health 39, 103, **105**, 109
hidden narratives 217
higher education 181
Hindus
  and fights with Muslims 64–5
  in Pakistan 26, 181
  see also Dalit Hindus
Hindu temples, closed during the pandemic 50–1
HIVE 175, 180, 187, 193, 198, 199
Horton, Myles 3
housing 38–40
Hukke 25
Humanitarian Aid Relief Trust 25
human rights 11, 12

Hurra village 82–3
Hussainiyat 183

I

identity
  ethnic 215, 223
  ethno-religious 220
  religious 55, 59–60, 163, 178, 198
income, lack of 109
India 22–3, 38–40, 41, 43–52, 64–74, 219
  and caste 214
  Korukkupet 54, 55–63
inequalities, power 9, 12, 222
informal labour sector 26
Ingold, Tim 45
Inquiry Groups (IGs) 39
'insider' 73–4
institutional discrimination 158
intensity, level of, participatory methods 229–30
intercultural dialogue 232–3
International Federation of Women Lawyers (FIDA) 116, 120
International Religious Freedom, Office of 212
intersectionality 178, 214
intersectional marginalization 173, 174, 181–6
Iraq 9, 25–6, 125–37, 139–41, 163–9, 215
  and education 144–61, 233
  and racial persecution 220
Iraqi Kurdistan *see* Kurdistan Region of Iraq (KRI)
Islam
  in Iraq 145
  and marriage 204
Islamabad 173, 182, 184–5, 191, 197
Islamabad Capital Territory (ICT) 174–5
Islamic education 151
Izalas 115, 116–21, 232–3
Izala Society 115

J

Al Jamaat 23
Jama'at Izalatul Bid a Wa Iqamatis Sunnah (Society for the Removal of Innovation and Re-Establishment of the Sunnah), also called JIBWIS *see* Izala Society
Jewkes, R. 129–30
Jos 79, 81, 82
Joseph Colony 180–1, 184, *192*, 194, 198
  and non-availability of clean drinking water 191, 197
Jos North 87–90, 91, 92, 101

K

Kaduna 25, 82, 100
Kaka'i 25, 126, 127, 128

Kano 82
Karachi 27, 191
Karnataka 23–4, 65, 67
Kerala 23
Al-Khoei Foundation 199
Kolb's experiential learning cycle *149*, 156, 233
Korukkupet 38, 55–63
Krause, J. 82
Kurdistan Region of Iraq (KRI) 26, 125, 126, 127

L

Lahore 173, 182, 185, 191, 197
Lashkar e Jhangvi 191
learning cycle, Kolb's experiential *149*, 156, 233
legitimacy 18, 19, 216–17
Lingarajapuram 39
lockdowns
  in India 54–5, 70–1
  in Nigeria 79, 82, 88, 93–4, 107–10

M

Mader, P. 213
majority–minority relations 9, 10
marginalization
  of Ahmadi Muslim women 203
  economic 198
  intersectional 173, 174, 181–6
  in Iraq 135, 137, 140, 141
  of Izalas 115, 119
  in Nigeria 94
  in Pakistan 181–2, 183–4
  and poverty 207, 208
  of Yazidis 163, 166
  see also religious marginalization
marriage 126, 185, 205
Marshall, K. 11, 212
Masih, Rimsha 191
matrix ranking
  criticisms of 230–1
  Nigeria 88–90
  Pakistan 179–80, 182, 185–6, 187, 194
Miango 82–3, 87–90, 91, 92, 107–8
microteaching 149, 151–6, 157
Middle Belt region, Nigeria 80
minority persecution 174
mistrust 6, 18, 19, 198, 199, 216
mobility, lack of **105**, 109, 163, 167, 191, 216
Mochi Gate 181, 185
Model Town 184
Modi, Narendra 54, 67
Mosse, David 12
multidimensionally poor 55
Murphy, E. 20
Muslim Council of Britain 211

INDEX

Muslims 22–3, 25, 26, 27, 64–5, 199
   Ahmadi 202–3, 204–9
   in Iraq 126
   in Nigeria 80, 101, 107–8, 115
   see also Dalit Muslims
Myanmar 9, 18, 19, 212

N

New Lingarajapuram 39
NGOs 62, 94, 139, 199
Nicholl, J. 20
Nigeria 9, 24–5, 79, 84–95, 99–112, 114–22
   and intercultural dialogue 232–3
   and intersectionality 214
   religious minorities, situation for 80–3
Ninevah valleh 26
Northern Minority Groups (NMGs) 81

O

O'Cathain, A. 20
Office for Democratic Institutions and Human Rights (ODIHR) 212
Open Doors 211
Organization for Security and Co-operation in Europe (OSCE) 212
otherization, religious 8, 233, 234
'outsider' 73–4

P

Pakistan 9, 26–7, 173–87, 190–200, 202–9, 216
   and common grievances across all religious minorities 214–15
Pakistani Christians 26, 175, *192*, 193, 199
   in 66 Quarters 184–5
   and higher education 181
   in Islamabad 182, 191, 197
   in Lahore 182, 191, 197
   on social exclusion and fear of persecution 183, 186, 194
pandemic, COVID-19 *see* COVID-19 pandemic
participative/participatory ranking methodology (PRM)
   in Iraq 127, 135
   in Nigeria 117–18, 121–2
   in Pakistan 191, 203–5, 207
participative rapid appraisal (PRA) 121
participatory action research (PAR) 175–81, 193–6
participatory learning and action (PLA) 147, 148, 158
Participatory Rural Appraisal (PRA) matrix ranking 99, **105–6**, 109–10, 111, 112
patriarchy 6, 118, 119, 195, 198
peer research 127, 128–9
peer researchers 19–20, 130, 131–40, 231–2
perception vs evidence 227–8

persecution
   fear of 174, 181, 183, 194, 198
   minority 174
   in Pakistan 186
   racial 220
   religious 175, 207
Petersen, P. 11
Pew Survey 2, 13–14, 211
'Plateau Crisis' 101
Plateau State 24–5, 79, 80, 81, 92–5
   attack in Hurra village 82–3
   and COVID-19 87–90, 91, 99–112
pluralism *see* pro-pluralism religious education curriculum
police violence 45, 220
political capture, avoiding 227
poor, multidimensionally 55
positionality 18–19, 72–4, 138, 167, 179
poverty
   and religious identity 198
   and religious marginalization 203, 207, 208
power dynamics 9–10, 94, 227
power hierarchies 1, 4, 9
power holders 9
power inequalities 9, 12, 222
power relations 18, 221–2, 233–4
pro-pluralism religious education curriculum 144–5, 147, 151–6
Punjab 26, 174–5
Purdah 119

Q

Quetta 27

R

racial persecution 220
Rajesh Tandon 3
Ramstedt, M. 218
Rana, Noushan Ali 183
rapport-building 180–1, 223
Ravadar 190, 196, 199, 200
Reason, P. 232
reflective practice 150, 156–7, 158
reflexivity 222–4
relationship-building 131–3
religion
   and criminal offence 204, 205–6
   during the pandemic 108, 112
Religion and State Project 211
religious diversity 151, 157
religious education (RE) 144, 156, 157, 161n1
religious equality 8, 9, 145, 156, 157
religious gatherings, prohibition on 93–4
religious identity
   of Dalit Christian women 55, 59–60
   in Pakistan 178
   and poverty 198
   of Yazidis 163

religious marginalization 207, 215
　in Iraq 125, 128, 129, 130, 137, 141
　in Pakistan 178, 198, 203
religious minorities
　in Iraq 146, 157, 158, 163, 166
　in Nigeria 80–3, 91–2, 95, 100
　not the same throughout any given
　　country 213
　in Pakistan 174, 178, 182–8
religious otherization 8, 233, 234
religious persecution 175, 207
religious pluralism 1, 151
Report on International Religious Freedom
　(Office of International Religious
　Freedom) 211–12
Rimsha Colony 191, *192*, 194, 196, 197
　and patriarchal violence and
　　exploitation 195, 198
risk, managing 231, 232
River of Life
　in India 43–4, 56–8, 60, 69, 70–1
　in Iraq 133
　in Nigeria 80, 87–90, 92–3, 101–3,
　　111, 112
Road of Life 85–6, 87–90, 101–3, 104,
　108, 110

S

Sabean-Mandaeans 25, 26, 125, 126, 127, 217
safe spaces 129, 132, 133, 140, 195, 224
safety 109, 228–9
Sait Palya 39, 65
Sargent, J. 131
scaling up, participatory methods 230
Scheduled Castes (SCs) 23, 27, 55, 215
Scheduled Tribes 23
Schirrmacher, T. 11
Scott, James 217
security 228–9
semi-structured interviews (SSIs) 21, 86, 99,
　101, 110
Shabaks 126, 133
Shah, T. 11
Sharia 24, 82
Shias
　Hazara 27, 215, 216
　in Iraq 25, 126
　in Pakistan 27, 182–3, 185, 191, *192*,
　　193, 199
Shulman, H. 225
Simpson, Audra 37
Sindh 26, 27
Sipahe-Sahaba Pakistan (SSP) 191
situated minoritiness 9
slums 38–40, 54, 55, 64, 65
social exclusion 173, 181–2, 183, 185–6,
　194, 198
STAR (situation, task, action and
　result) 150, 156

Stewart, Frances 12
storytelling 176–9, 187, 193–4, 195,
　196–7, 226
　created sense of belonging 173
　criticisms of 230–1
　focused on 'bottom up' knowledge
　　creation 182
　and marginalization 183–4
　was cathartic 197
subjectivity, critical 226, 230
Sunni Muslims 25, 27, 126, 185
Sustainable Development Goals 12

T

Tablighi Jamaat 67
Tamil Nadu 23, 55, 65
Tamil Nadu Slum Clearance Board
　(TNSCB) 38
Tanko, A. 81
Teachers Training programme 145, 147–61
Thailand, and Ahmadiyya community 206–
　7, 208
Thomas, S. 130, 132
time frame, of participatory methods 229–30
trauma 19–20, 93, 120, 128
triangulation 20, 204, 227, 228
trust 131–3, 140, 180, 204, 216, 223, 232
　with communities 199, 200
　and time 187
Turkmen 126

U

Universal Declaration of Human Rights 11
Unlawful Activities Prevention Act
　(India) 23, 64

V

vaccine, COVID-19 88
violence
　blasphemy 197, 198
　domestic **105**, 109, 195
　gender-based 114, 116, 138, 140
　genocidal 199
　in Nigeria 103–4
　in Pakistan 183, 184, 194
　patriarchal 195, 198
Vyasarpadi 38–9

W

Wase 116, 118–19
water, non-availability of clean
　drinking 191, 197
Watkins, M. 225
women
　Ahmadi Muslim 202–3, 204–9
　and community consultations 195,
　　198–9
　Dalit Christians 54, 55
　Dalit Muslims 65–75

education discouraged 181
face multiple forms of marginalization 94
Izala 116–21, 232–3
not allowed to vote or to be voted for 114
Yazidi 26, **117**, 127, 128, 163–9, 233
World Watch List (WWL) 211

Y

Yazidis 25, 126, 220
   women 26, **117**, 127, 128, 163–9, 233
Yazidi Survivors Law 168
Yazidiyat 183
Youhanabad 27, 184, 197

www.ingramcontent.com/pod-product-compliance
Lightning Source LLC
Chambersburg PA
CBHW071156070526
44584CB00019B/2807